BIRKENHEAD REFLECTIONS

Ian Collard

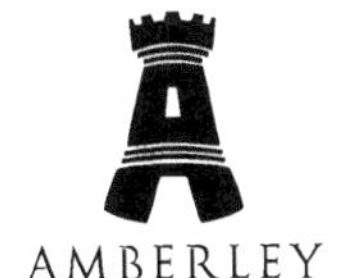

AMBERLEY

First published 2021

Amberley Publishing
The Hill, Stroud, Gloucestershire, GL5 4EP
www.amberley-books.com

ISBN 978 1 3981 0518 8 (print)
ISBN 978 1 3981 0519 5 (ebook)

British Library Cataloguing in Publication Data.
A catalogue record for this book is available from the
British Library.

Typesetting by SJmagic DESIGN SERVICES, India.
Printed in Great Britain.

Introduction

Benedictine monks who established a priory at Birkenhead in 1150 were renowned for their hospitality to travellers and the Priory was built next to a landing stage at the river near Woodside. These and the Black monks who moved from Chester were the first inhabitants of Birkenhead, which was described as the little headland of the birches. King Edward I was entertained at the Priory in 1275 and in 1277 when he came to Cheshire to prepare a campaign against the Welsh.

It is claimed that the origin of the name Birkenhead came from the old Norse word 'heafod' of the Birken or Birket, a river of Wirral which rises near Grange Hill, West Kirby, and flows to Wallasey Pool. However, others feel that it is derived from the Anglo-Saxon where 'head' is a promontory of the birches. It is known that this part of the Wirral was densely wooded and a couplet states, 'From Birchen Haven to Hilbree. A squirrel might skip from tree to tree'.

In 1817 a new half-hourly ferry service from Tranmere to Queens Dock in south Liverpool was inaugurated and a steam ferry was later introduced on the Woodside service and the population continued to increase. The new services from Liverpool to the Wirral encouraged people and merchants to move to Birkenhead and the population of 200 in 1821 was doubled in the following two years. William Laird moved to Liverpool in 1810 to help attract orders for his father's rope works in Greenock and soon became a director of two shipping companies. He was initially interested in a scheme to sail ships up the River Dee and cross the peninsular by canal to Birkenhead.

Laird then decided to buy some land near Wallasey Pool at Vittoria Wharf and he built a boiler house which later became the Birkenhead Iron Works. The Great Western Railway and the London & North Western Railway were interested in gaining access to the Mersey docks. When Sir John Tobin and John Askew purchased land they asked Thomas Telford to look at the possibility of building a port on the Wirral side of the river. The Improvement Commissioners were established to raise £8,000 in rates and tolls. At their first meeting on 25 June 1833 they discussed plans to appoint police and firemen, purchase fire engines and to build a market. The first police force consisted of one constable and three nightwatchmen, who in 1834 were responsible for attending the lime-washing of the houses in Back Chester Street following an epidemic of cholera. The town was developed with streets and houses built from Hamilton Square on a plan devised by John Laird.

Joseph Paxton designed Birkenhead Park and it was also opened on 5 April 1847. Birkenhead was the first town to ask Parliament for the powers to build a park and the opening was attended by over 10,000 people. In 1850 the Birkenhead Street Tramway was established and operated from Woodside Ferry to Birkenhead Park, and was the first street tramway in Europe. The Birkenhead Gas and Water Company was purchased by the Improvement Commissioners in 1859 and Birkenhead, Oxton, Tranmere and Higher Bebington became a parliamentary borough in 1861.

A petition requesting a Charter of Incorporation was granted on 13 August 1877. The Great Seal was affixed to the charter, which was granted to the mayor, aldermen and the burgesses of the borough. The parliamentary constituency covered an area of 3,850 acres and the first election for the new council took place on 14 November 1877 creating fourteen aldermen and forty-two councillors. By 1878 the population of the borough was 77,260 and under the Local Government Act of 1888 the town was created a county borough and the population had increased to 99,000. The borough included the parish of Birkenhead St Mary and the townships of Bidston, Claughton with Grange, Oxton, Tranmere and part of Bebington, later known as Rock Ferry. Landican, Prenton and Thingwall were included in 1928, followed by Noctorum, Upton and Woodchurch in 1933.

The Local Government Act 1972 created the Metropolitan Borough of Wirral, in the metropolitan county of Merseyside by merging Birkenhead with Wallasey, the municipal borough of Bebington and the urban district of Hoylake. It contains the parliamentary constituencies of Birkenhead, Wallasey, Wirral South and Wirral West.

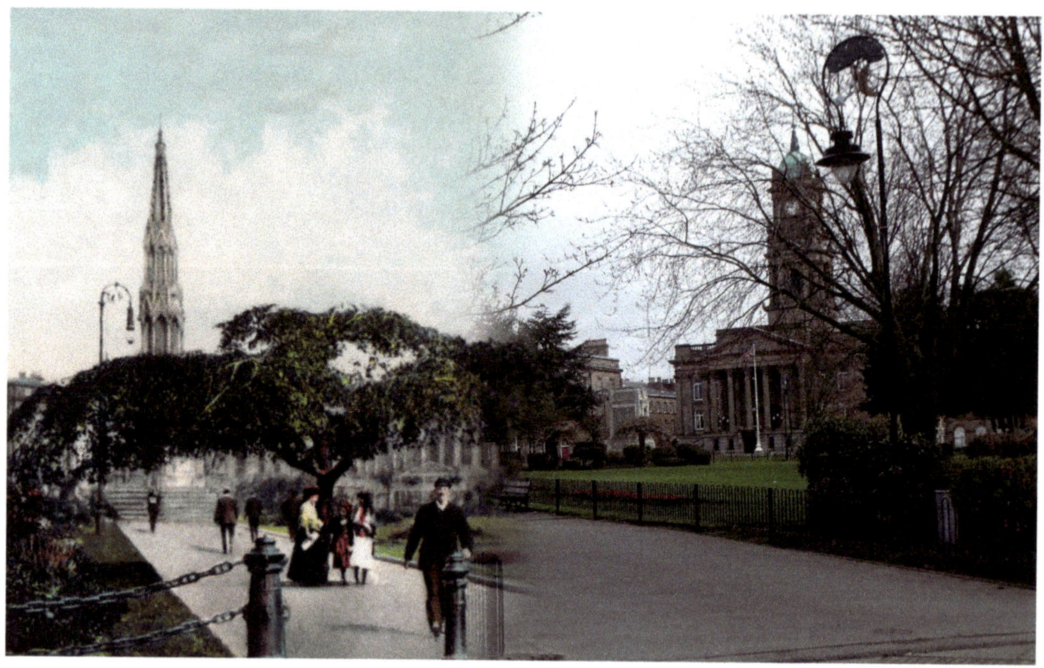

Hamilton Square

Hamilton Square was designed by the Edinburgh architect James Gillespie Graham and was named after the family of the wife of William Laird. Gillespie's design involved long and straight avenues with elegant town houses, and work commenced in 1825. However, lack of finance meant that Hamilton Square was the only part of the plan to survive and a plot was left empty for a town hall. In 1835 this area was used to establish the town's first market and ten years later a much larger market was opened nearby.

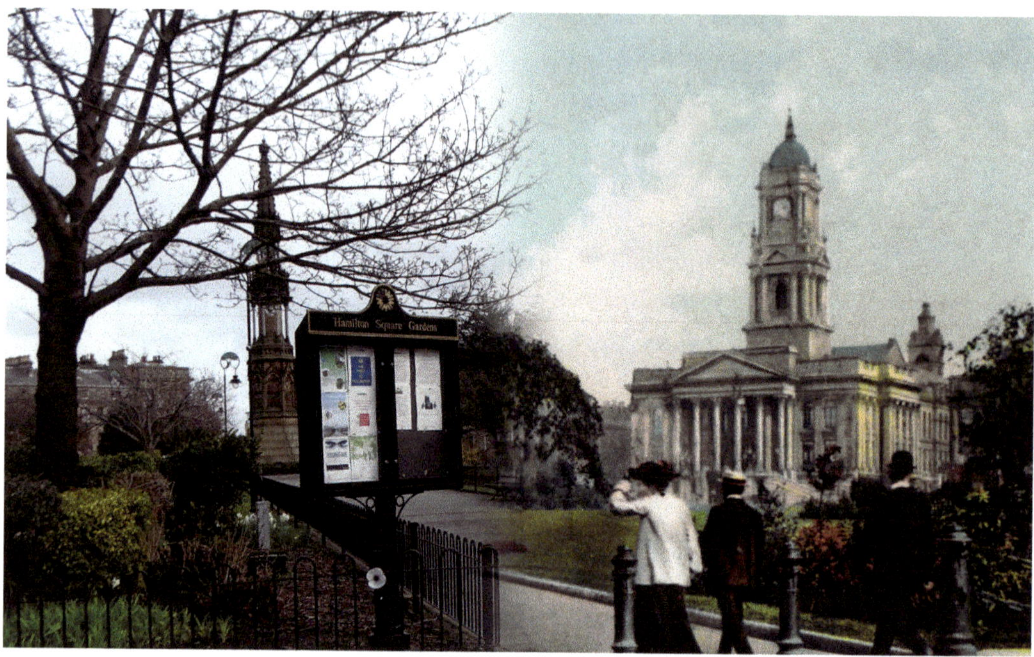

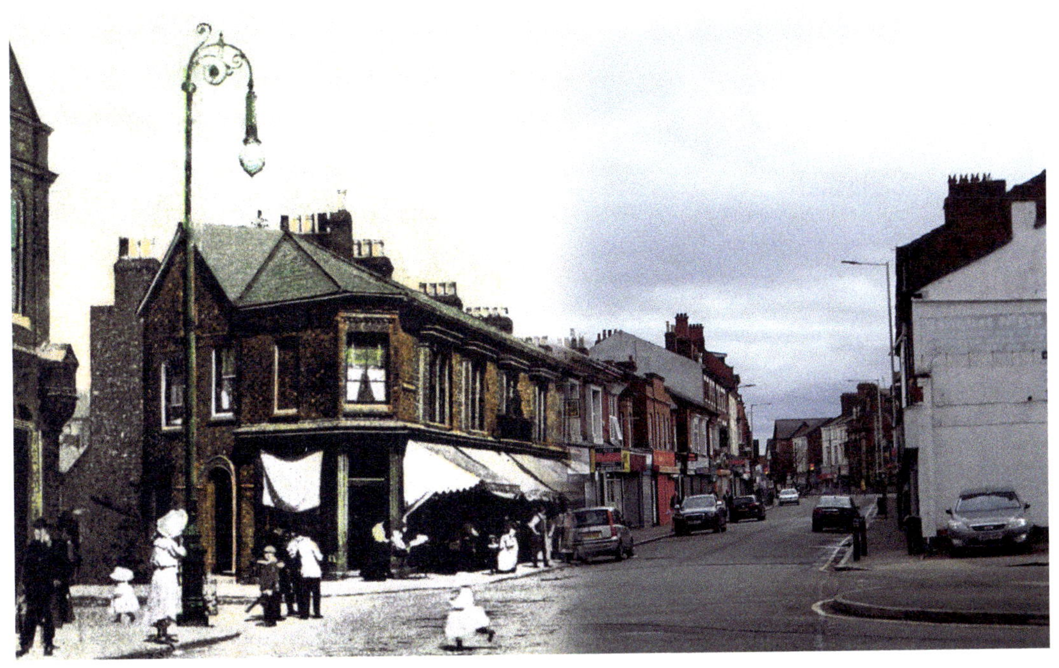

Grange Road West

Grange Road West looking towards Charing Cross and Grange Road. The monks at Birkenhead Priory farmed the land and their nearest farm was at The Grange at Claughton. Grange Road, Grange Mount and Grange Road West led to the farm.

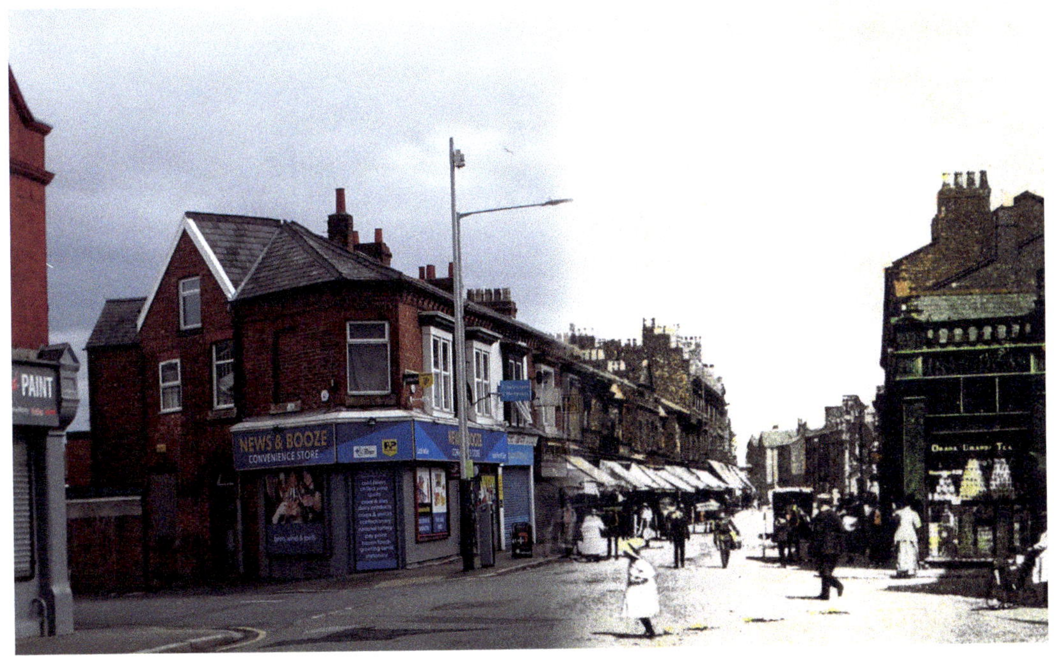

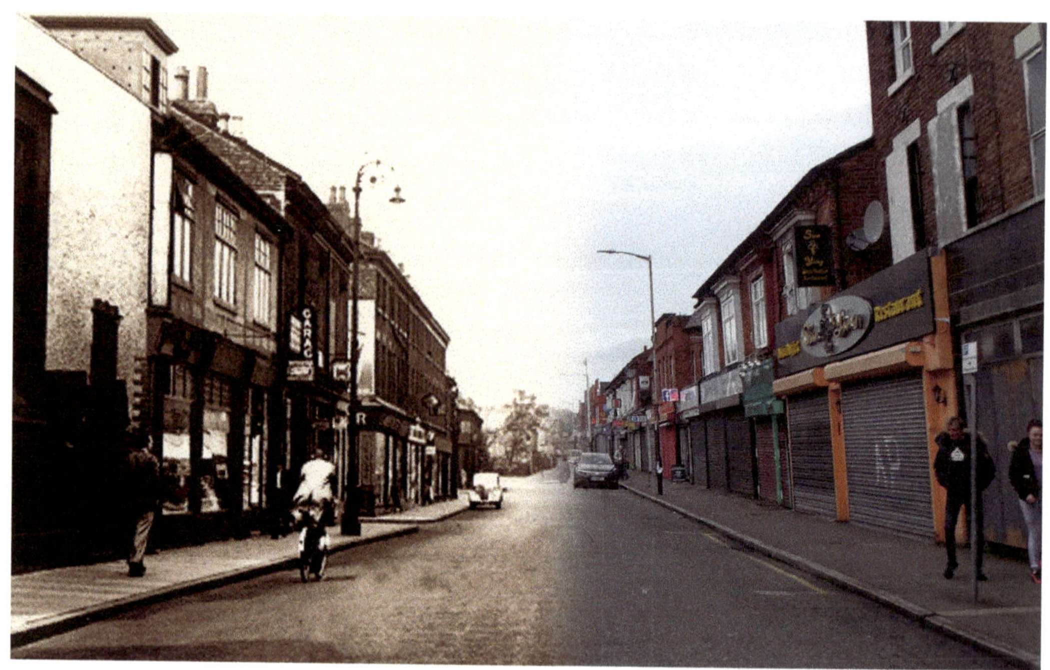

Little Theatre, Grange Road West

The Little Theatre in Grange Road West was built as the Grange Road Presbyterian Church of England in 1848 and served as a place of worship for exactly 100 years. The last service took place on 14 July 1948 and the congregation helped to finance a new church at Bebington. The church in Grange Road West was later purchased by the Birkenhead Repertory Theatre Ltd. The theatre is home to the Carlton Players, and is regularly hired out to other community drama, musical and dance groups.

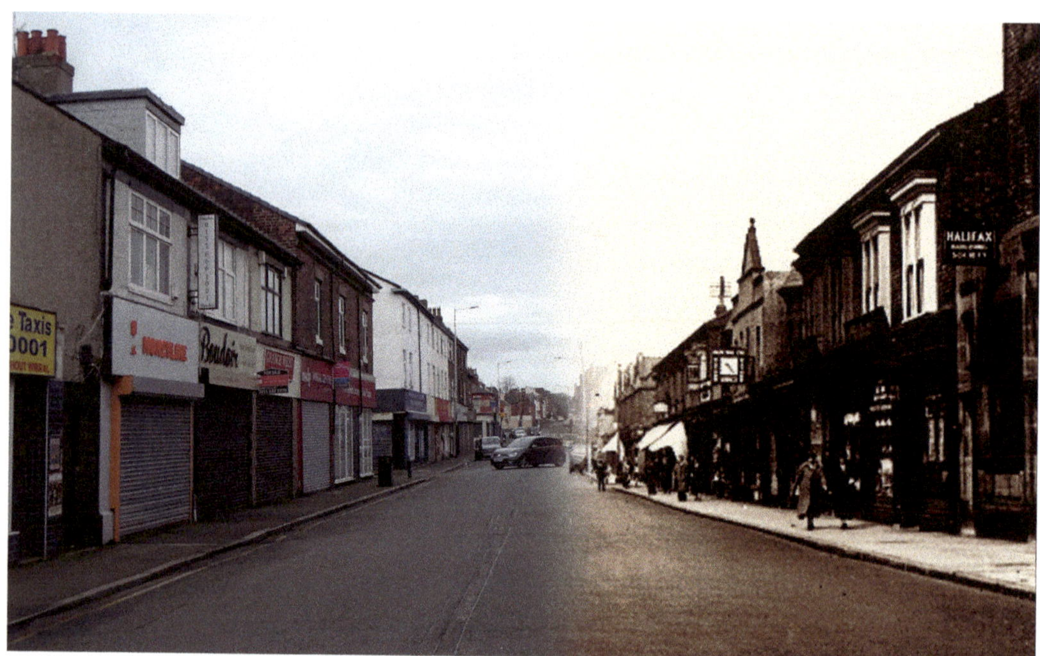

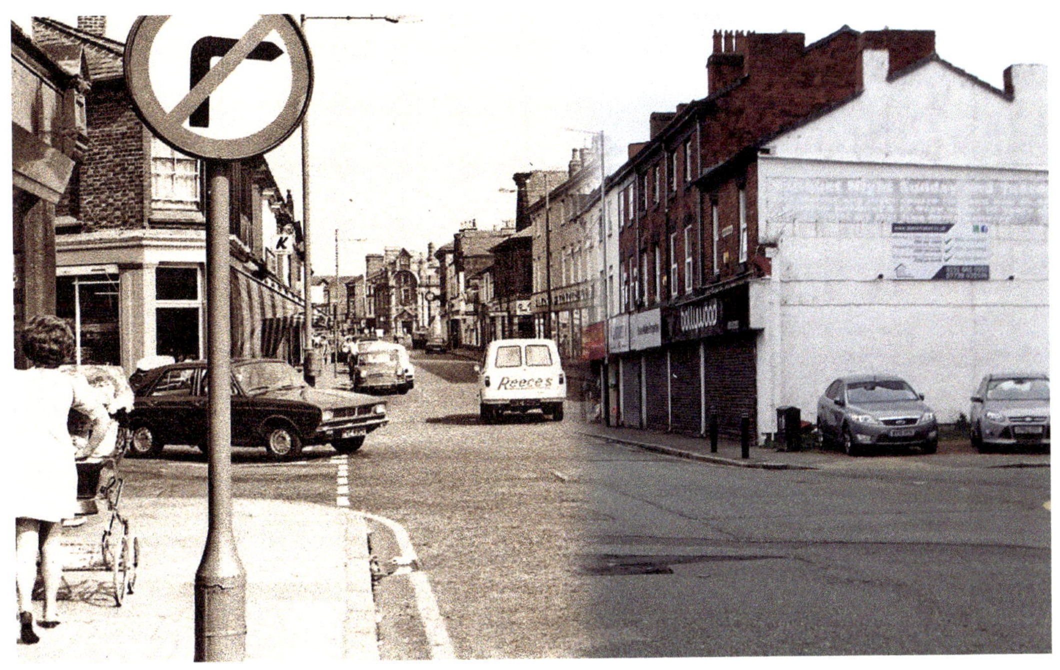

Reece's Delivery Van

A Reece's delivery van passes a police car parked outside Scott's food store. Other businesses in Grange Road West were Roberts & Jobson, James McKenzie, MANWEB, Rediffusion and R Byrne.

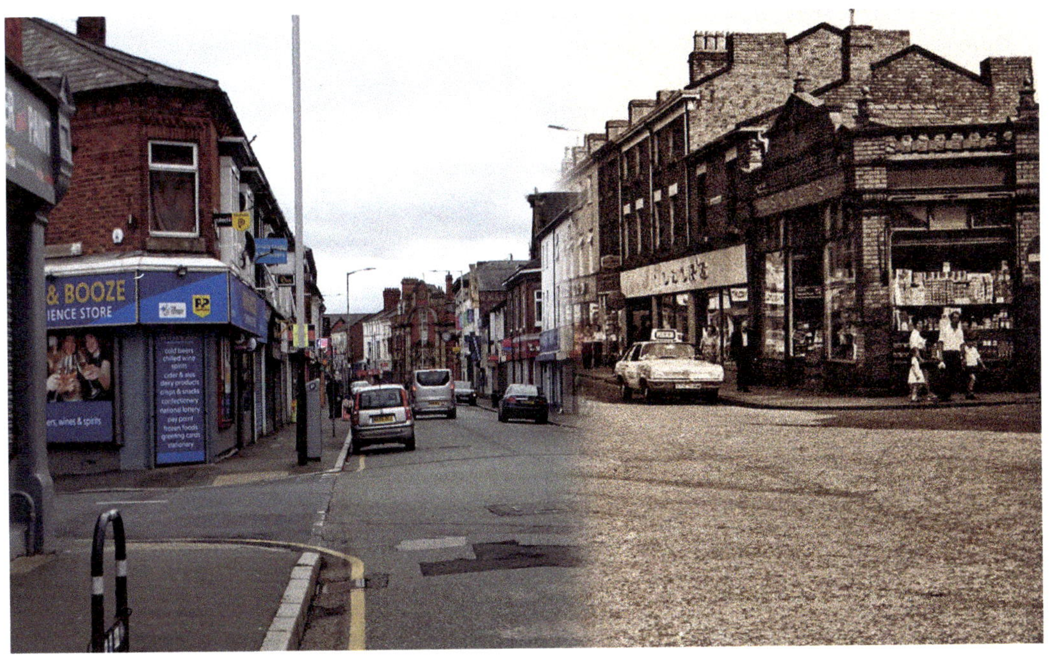

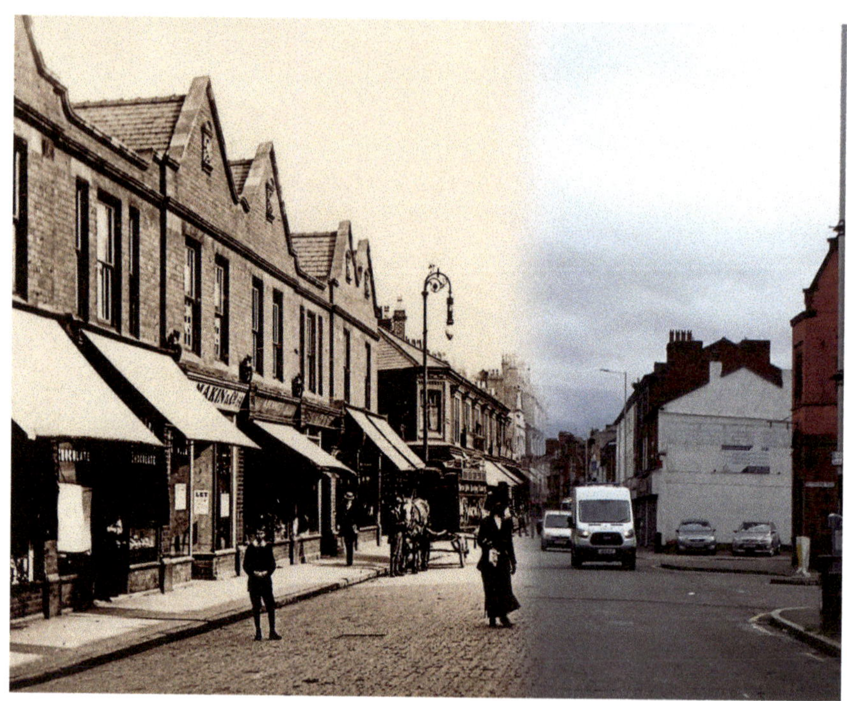

Grange Road West

Beno Dorn was a Polish-English master tailor who was known for providing the Beatles with their first suits out of his shop at No. 19a Grange Road West in Birkenhead. The Beatles' manager, Brian Epstein, was a personal friend of Dorn and was responsible for changing the group's image with modern, collarless Beno Dorn suits made in Grange Road West.

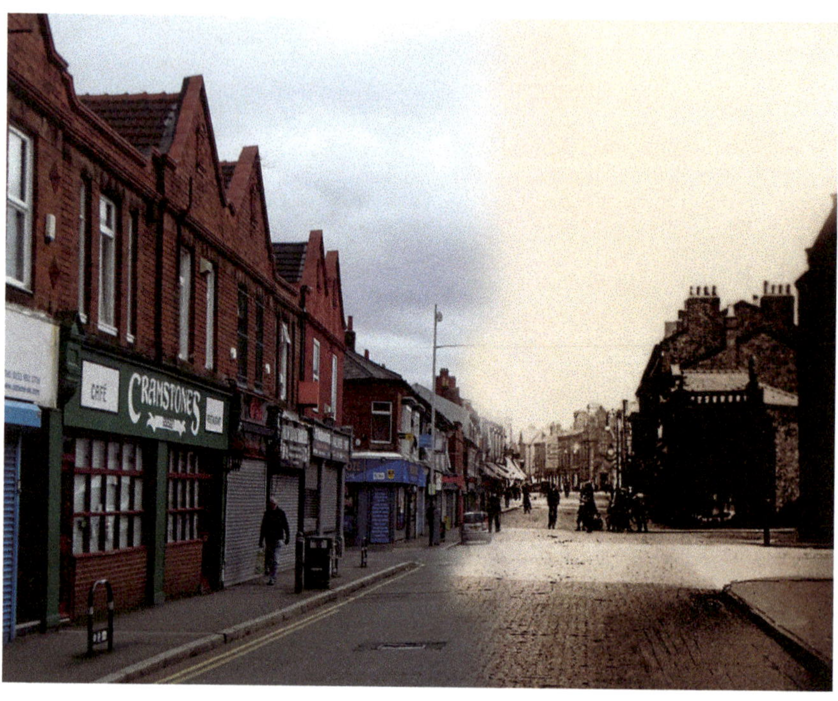

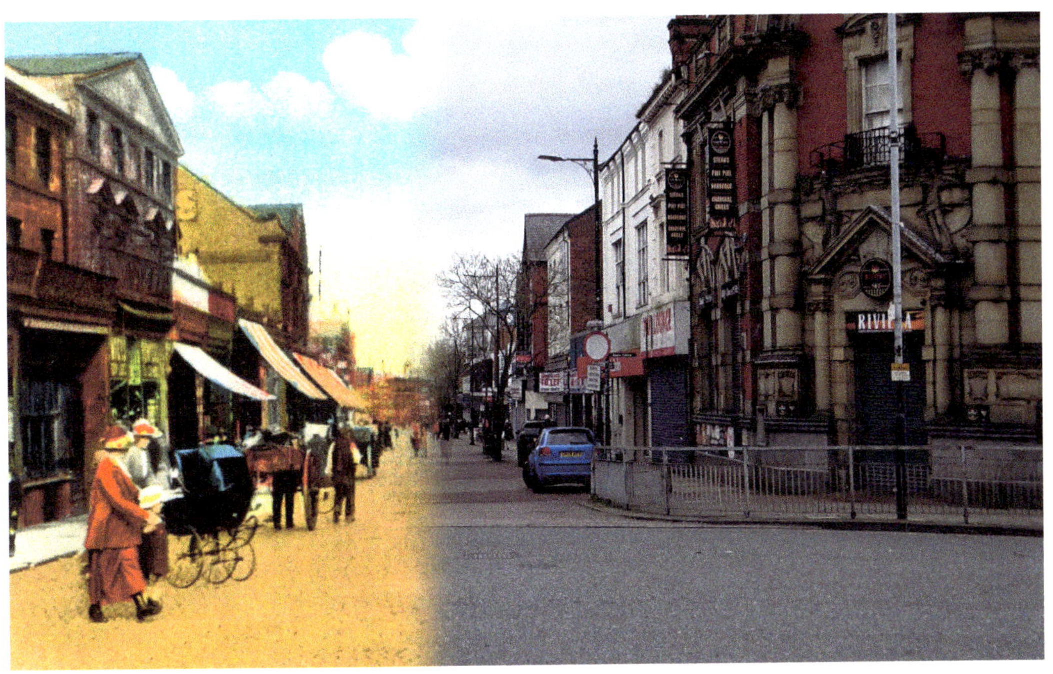

Grange Road from Charing Cross

Grange Road is the main shopping centre in the Wirral. There are others at Liscard, Wallasey, Moreton, Upton, West Kirby, Hoylake and Bromborough. The Birkenhead Brewery public house, Grange Hotel, was built in 1840. The pub was closed in 1982 and demolished, and is now the site of a fast-food restaurant. Martins Bank, later Midland Bank, was built in 1901 and has now been converted into a bar. The roundabout has now vanished, being replaced by traffic lights.

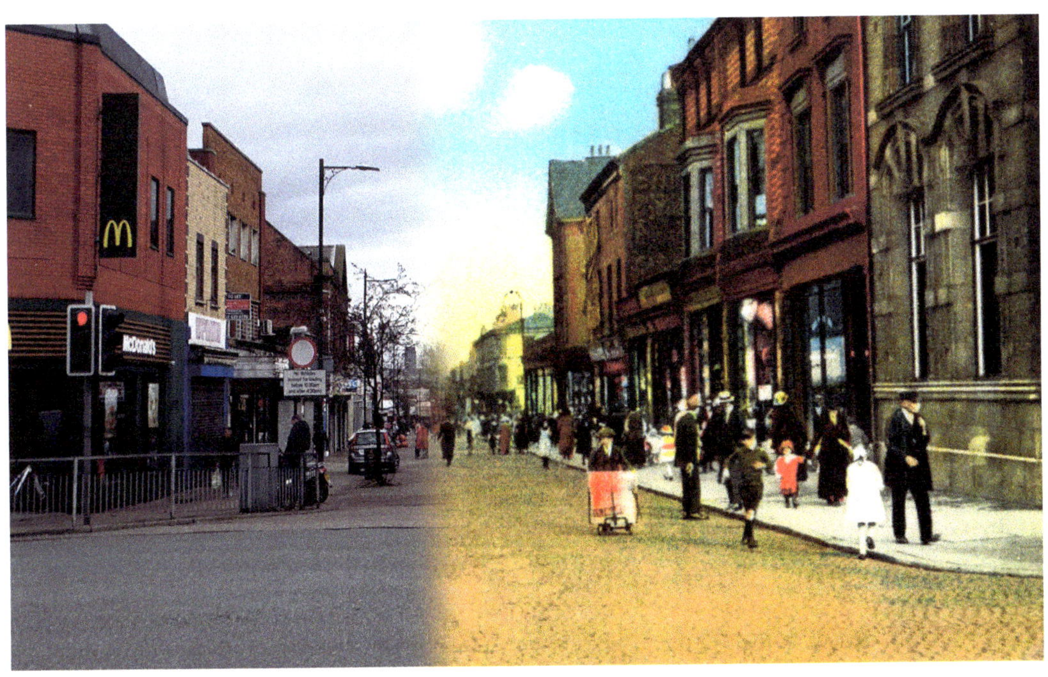

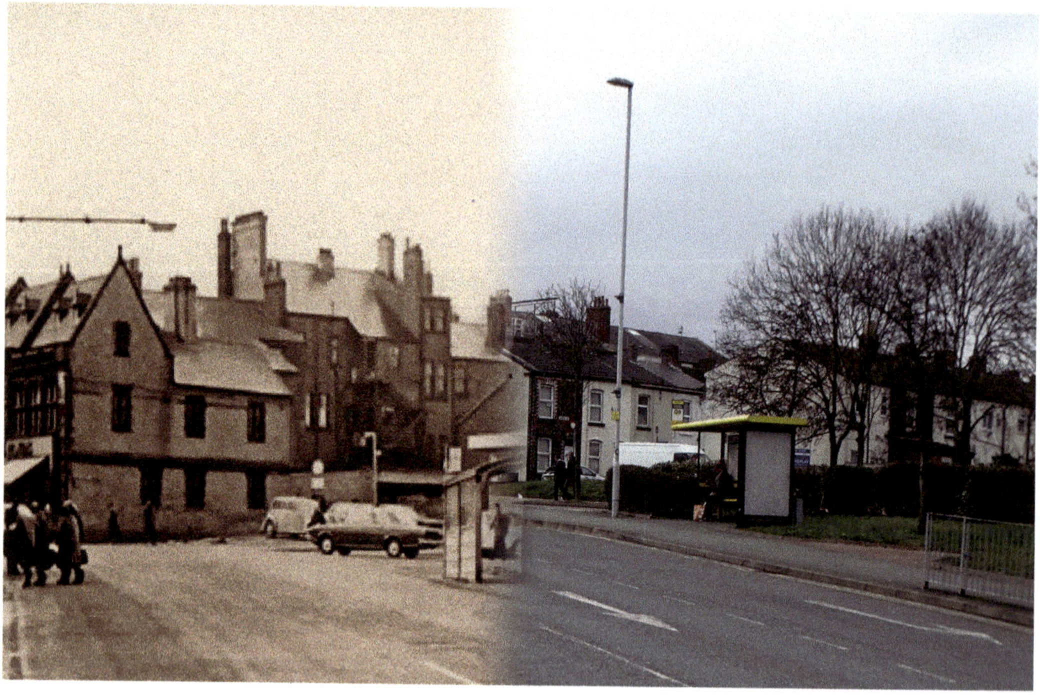

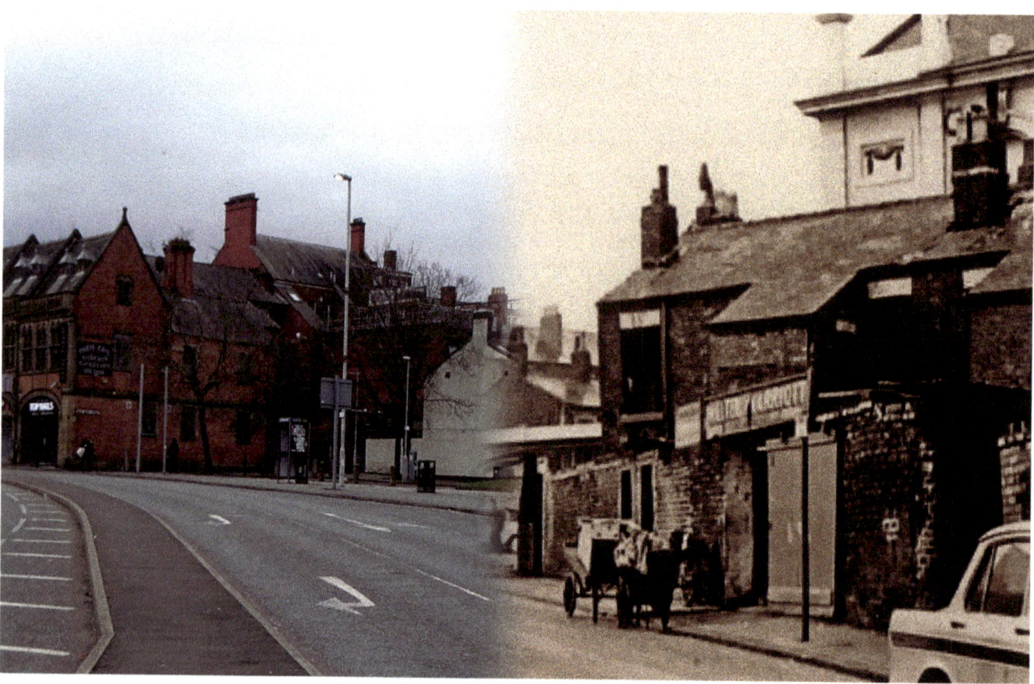

Exmouth Street

At the top of Exmouth Street there is a row of four shops, stepped downhill, that are similar to each other. They have two storeys: the lower storey is in brick with stone dressings, and the upper storey is in stone. Along the top of the front is a balustraded parapet on corbels. The roof is steeply pitched and has two small dormers.

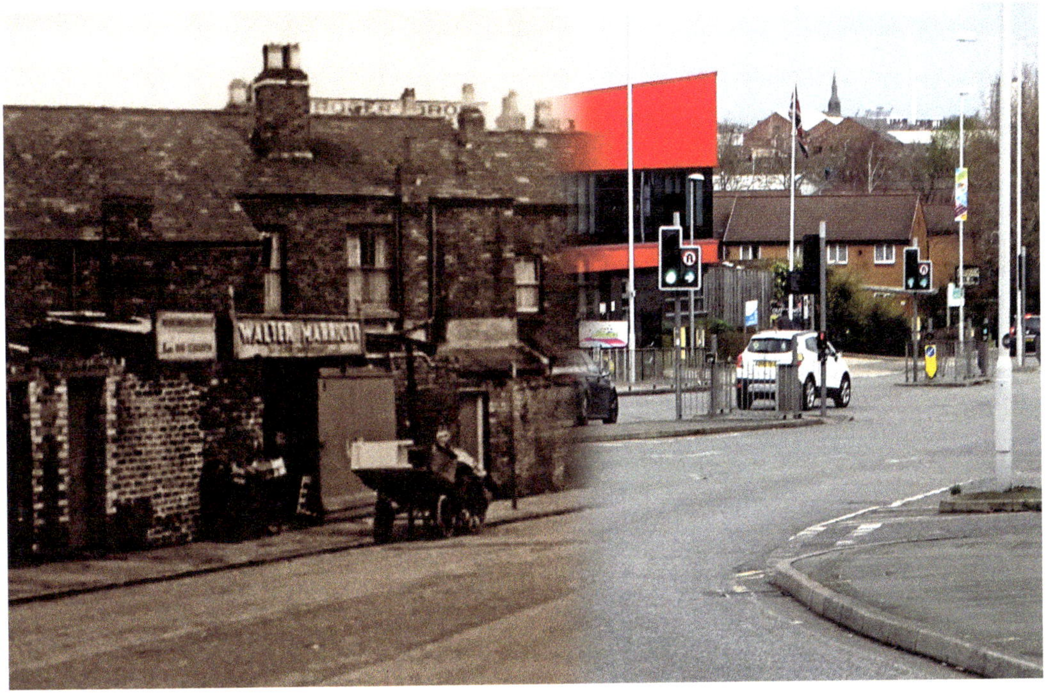

Exmouth Street

The premises of the scrap merchant Walter Marriott were further down Exmouth Street, and at the other side of the traffic lights were a number of shops. These have since been demolished and are the site of Birkenhead Fire Station.

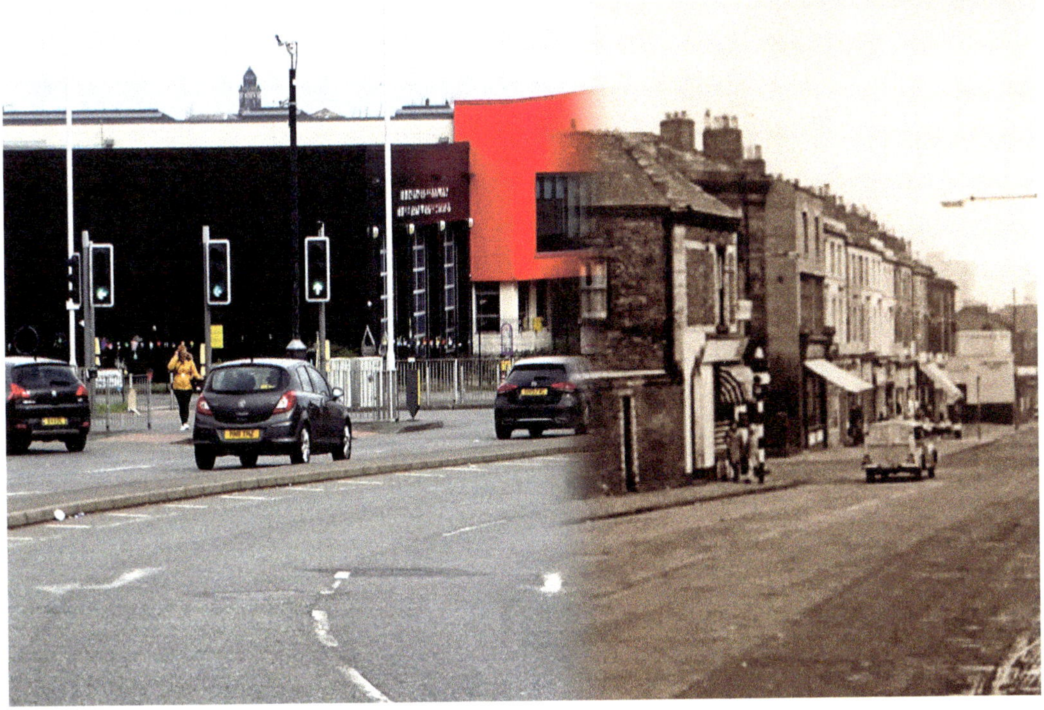

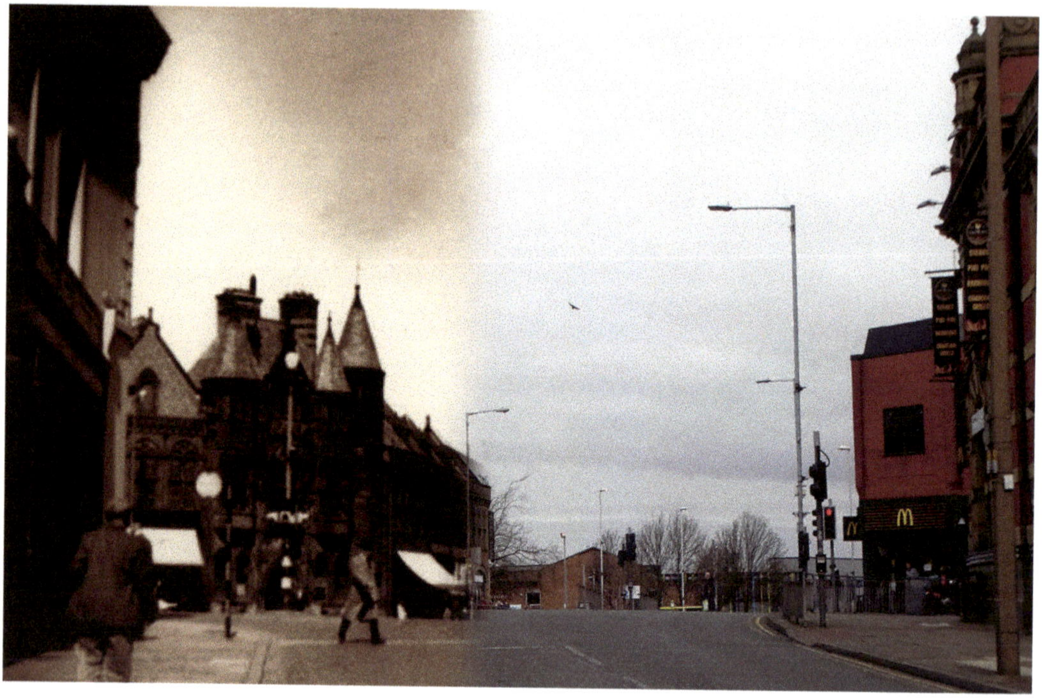

Charing Cross

A mother guides her children across the road at Charing Cross. The road is one of the busiest junctions in Birkenhead. At one time there was a roundabout at the junction but it is now controlled by a series of phased traffic lights.

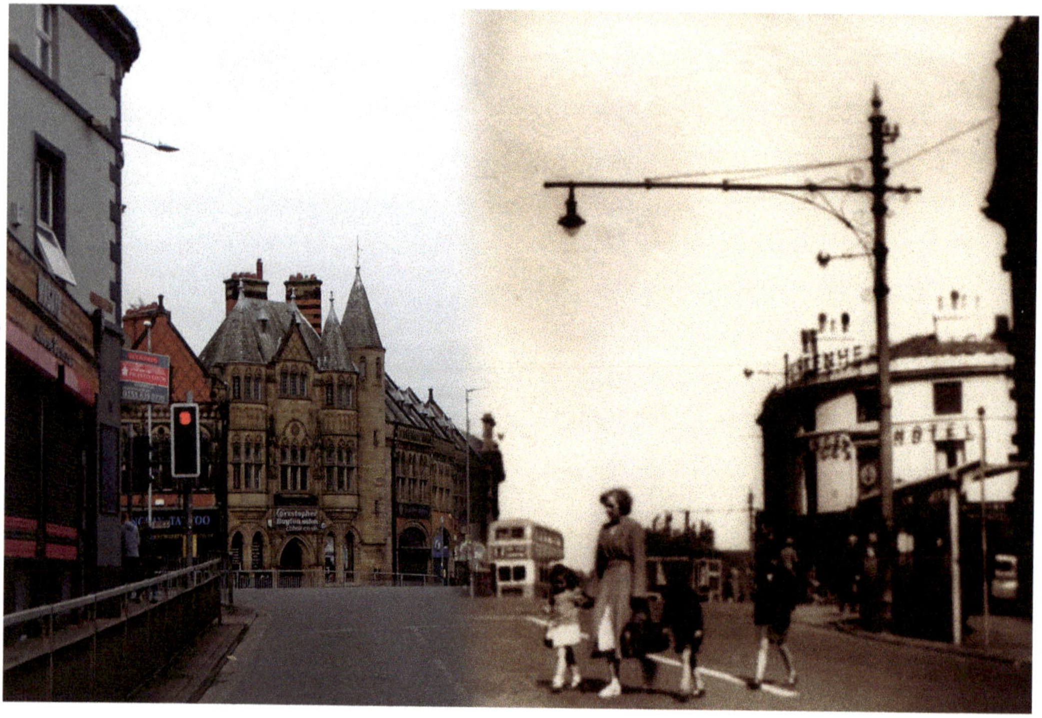

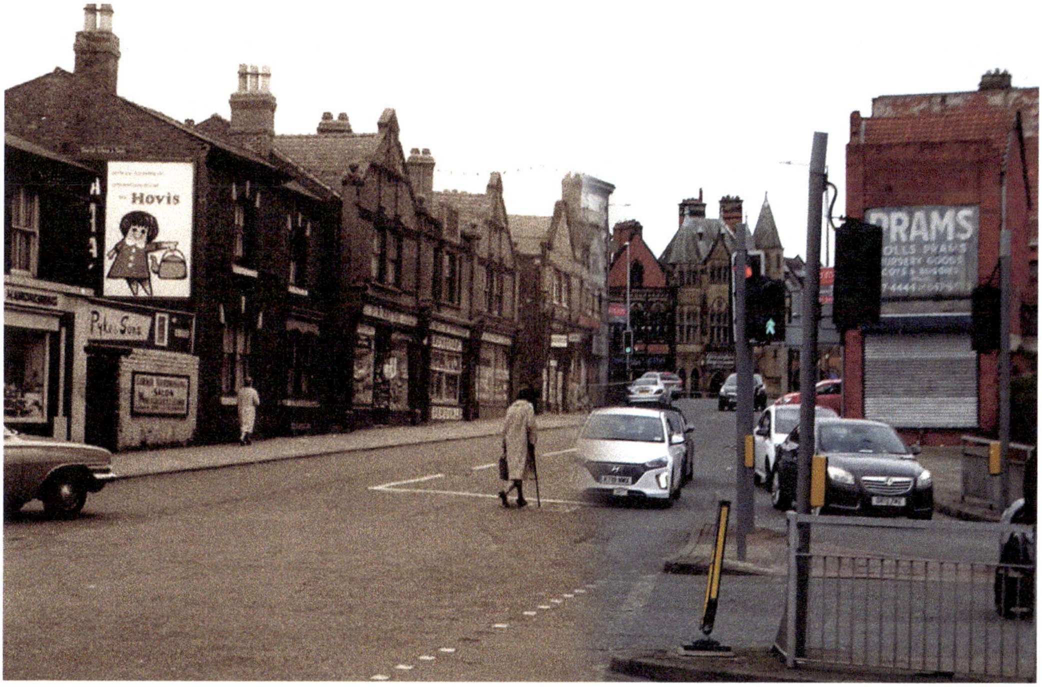

Charing Cross from Borough Road

The road has been redesigned several times due to changes in road traffic demands in the town centre. The fire station to the right of the photograph has been relocated to a new purpose-built facility in Exmouth Street.

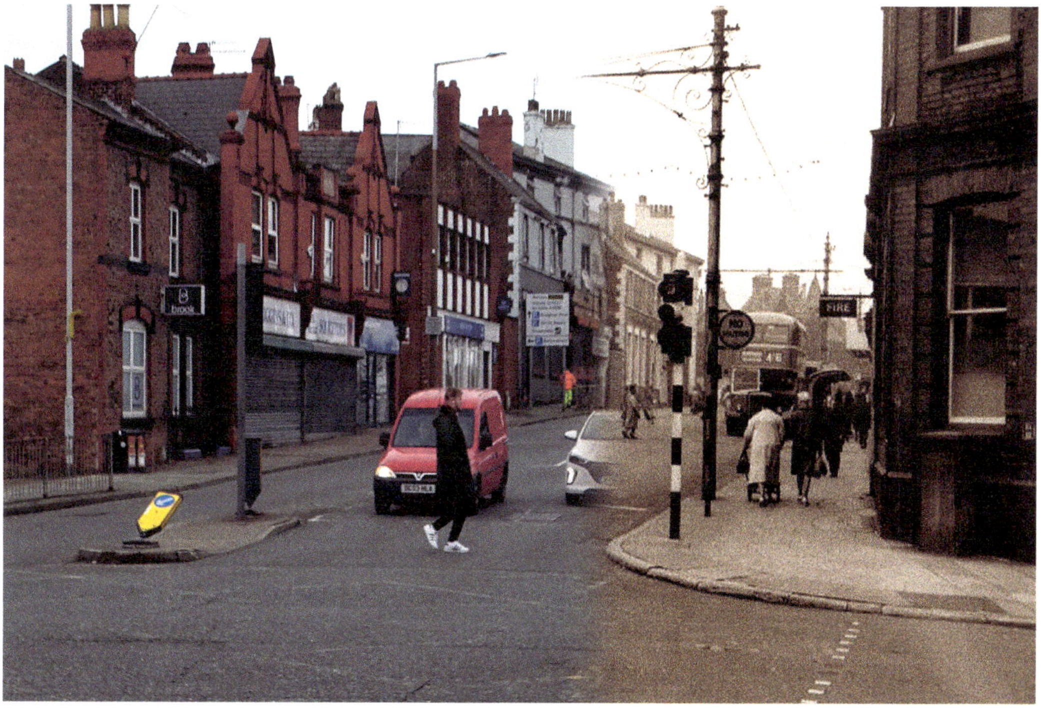

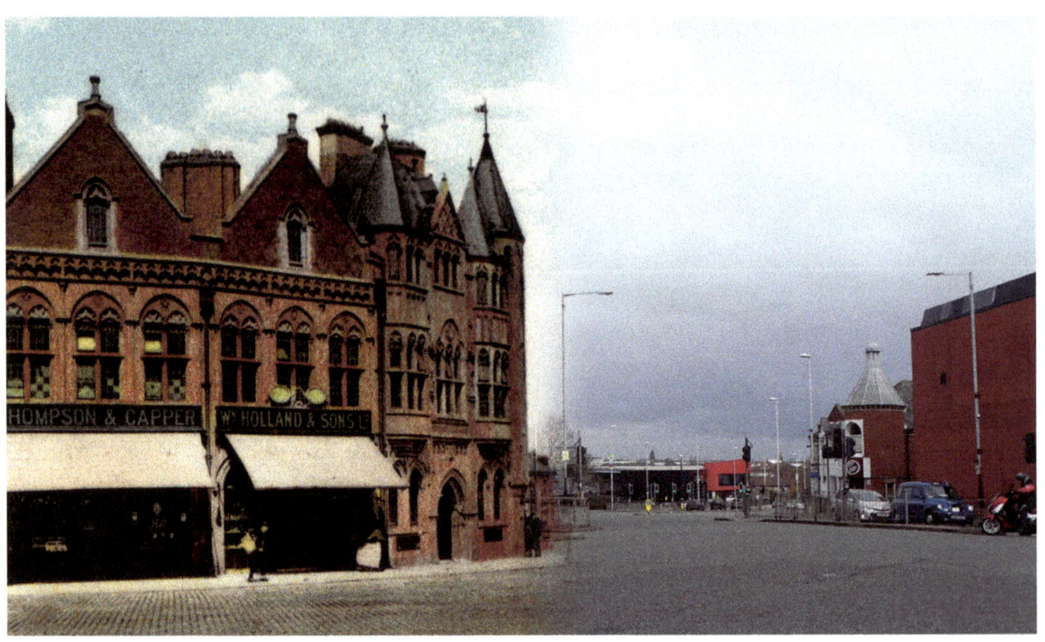

Bank Building, Charing Cross

The Bank Building at Charing Cross was constructed in 1901 for the Bank of Liverpool and consists of offices and shops which extend towards the north along Exmouth Street and the west along Grange Road West. It is recorded in the National Heritage List for England as a designated Grade II listed building. It is built in Gothic style and is constructed mainly in ashlar stone with some brickwork, and with roofs in Westmorland green slate. It is believed that there was a cylindrical lantern on top of the lamp post which used to flash a red light whenever there was a fatal accident on the roads in Birkenhead.

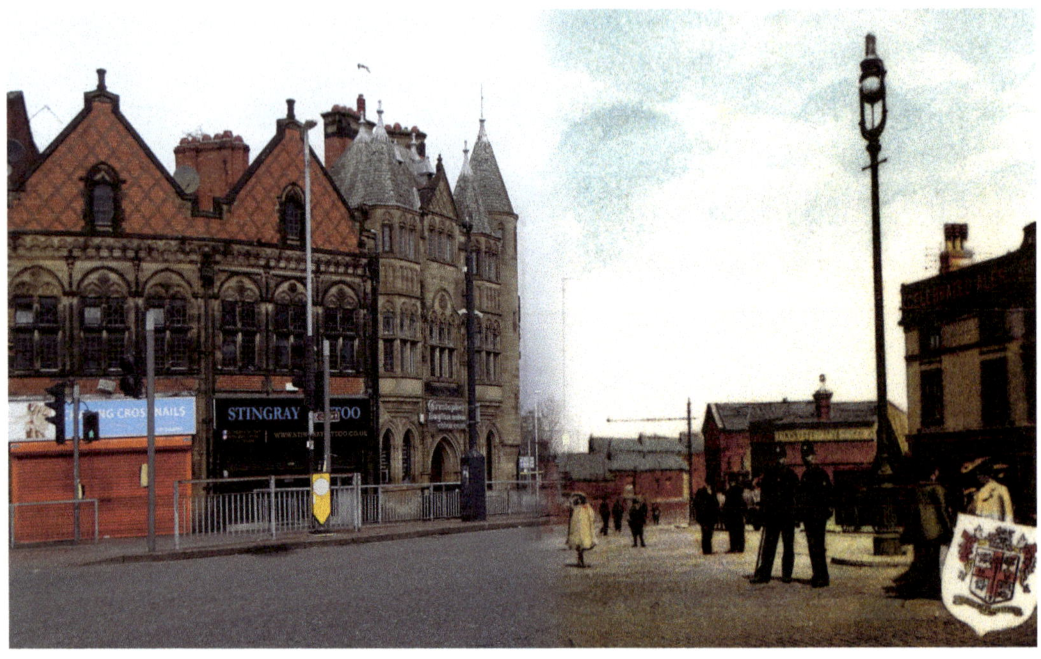

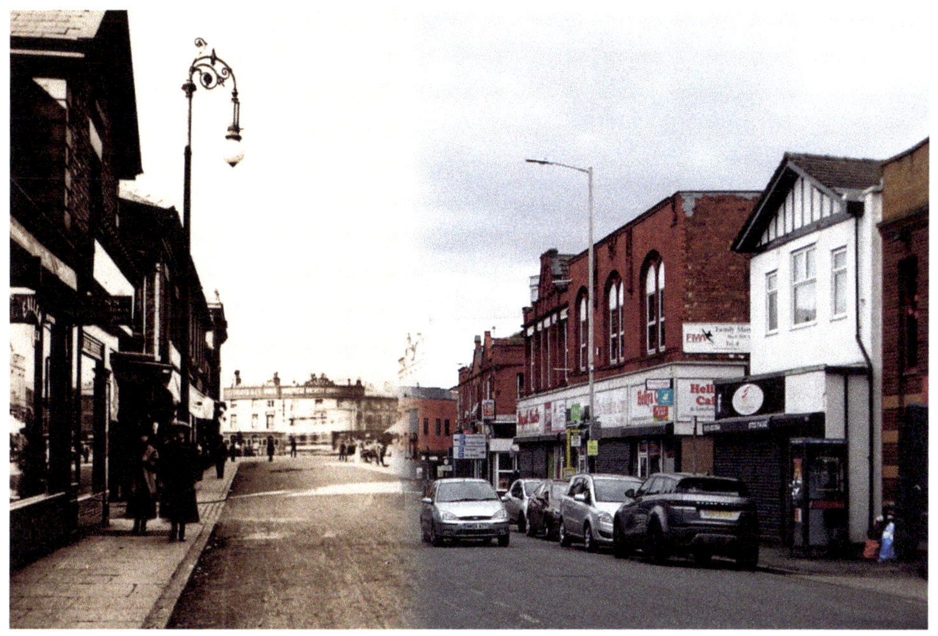

Looking Down Oxton Road towards Charing Cross

Tutty's store operated in Oxton Road from 1904 to 1937, when they were taken over by Rostances, who survived on the site until 1977. Tutty's shop at No. 17 Oxton Road was opened in 1904 and the following year he purchased Nos 19 and 21 Oxton Road, and was trading as an ironmonger. He also had a chandlery, ironmongery, glass and china shops at No. 9 Rose Mount, 102a Woodchurch Lane, 176a Bedford Road, 44 Upton Road and 18 Bebington Road. The shop in Oxton Road remained there until 1937 when it was moved to Grange Road West.

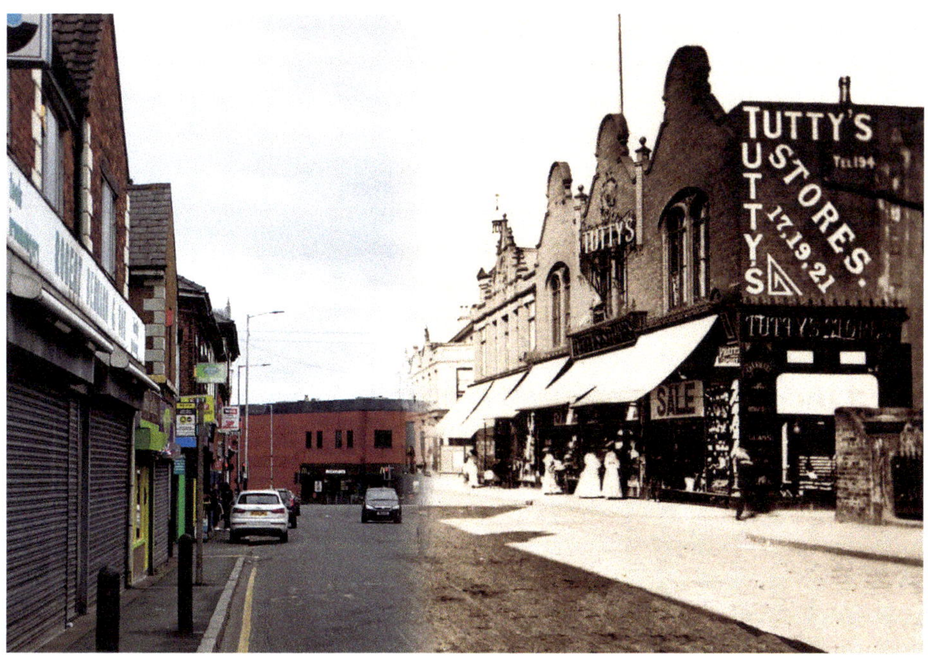

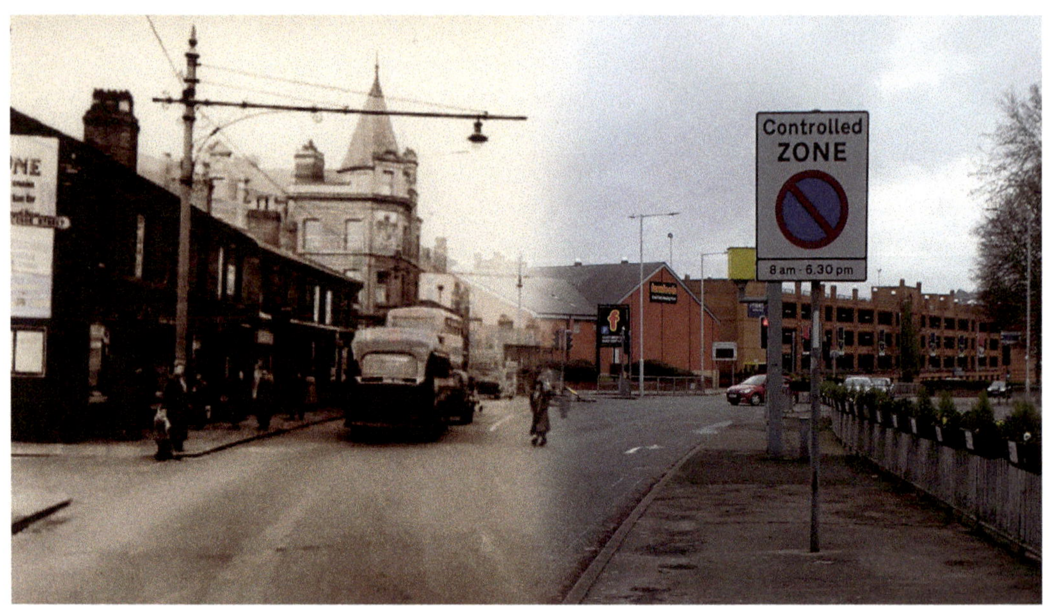

Fire Station, Borough Road/Whetstone Lane

The fire station in the centre of the photograph was opened on 9 December 1895, replacing those at Hamilton Street and Dale Street. A telephone line was installed linking Whetstone Lane with the exchange, and two stations on Birkenhead docks were also connected to the exchange. The fire service received ninety-five calls that year. In 1938 flats and two additional appliance bays were built on the site of the former stables fronting onto Borough Road at the side of the main station. Two additional bays were also added on Whetstone Lane. A second block of three-storey flats were also built facing onto the yard with their back to Dale Street. The new Exmouth Street fire station was opened on 28 March 1973, replacing the seventy-eight-year-old Whetstone Lane station.

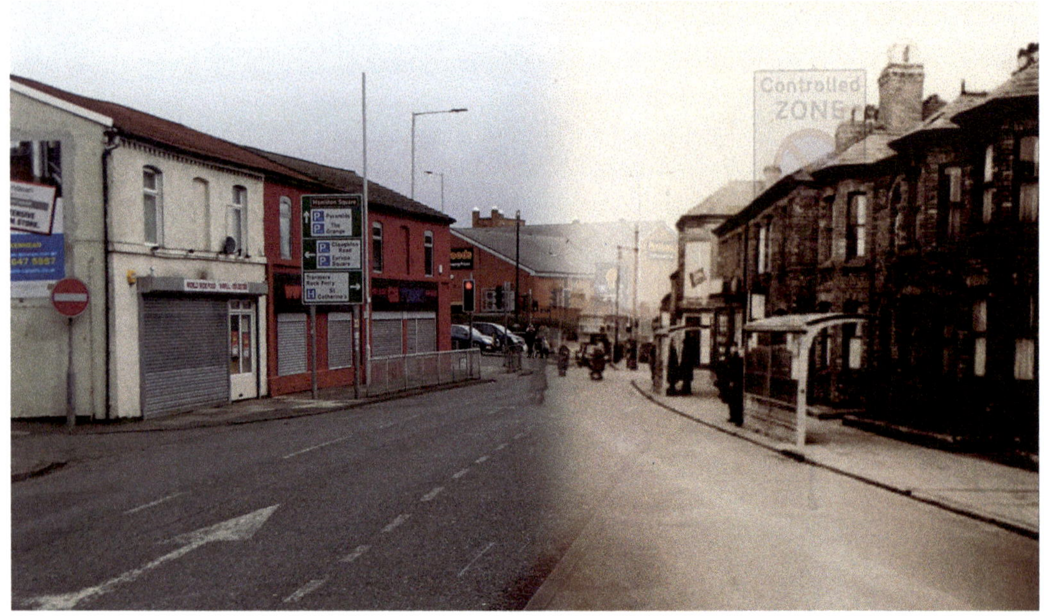

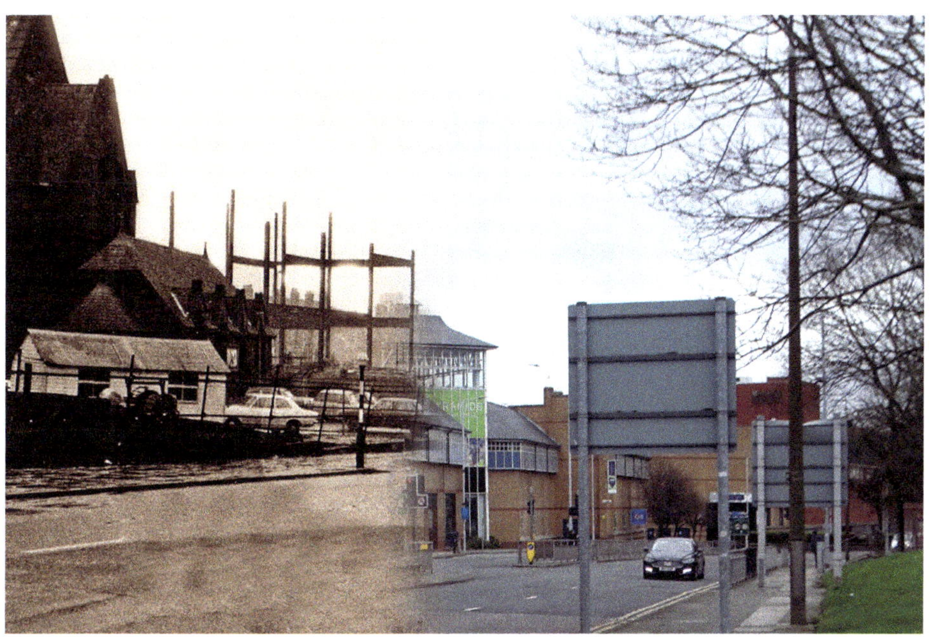

Borough Road

This image shows the Pyramids Shopping Centre under construction. One of the courses of the ward and old township boundary follows the old stream, which was more or less on the line of the present Borough Road. In the 1870s Birkenhead became a borough and the new status was marked with the naming of one of the main roads in the town as Borough Road. Houses were demolished for the construction of the Pyramids Shopping Centre, which is open seven days a week, hosting over fifty retailers and a food court, The Conservatory. The centre offers a parent and child room, free wheelchair hire and toilets. There is also a multi-storey car park with 750 spaces and direct access to the shops via a walkway.

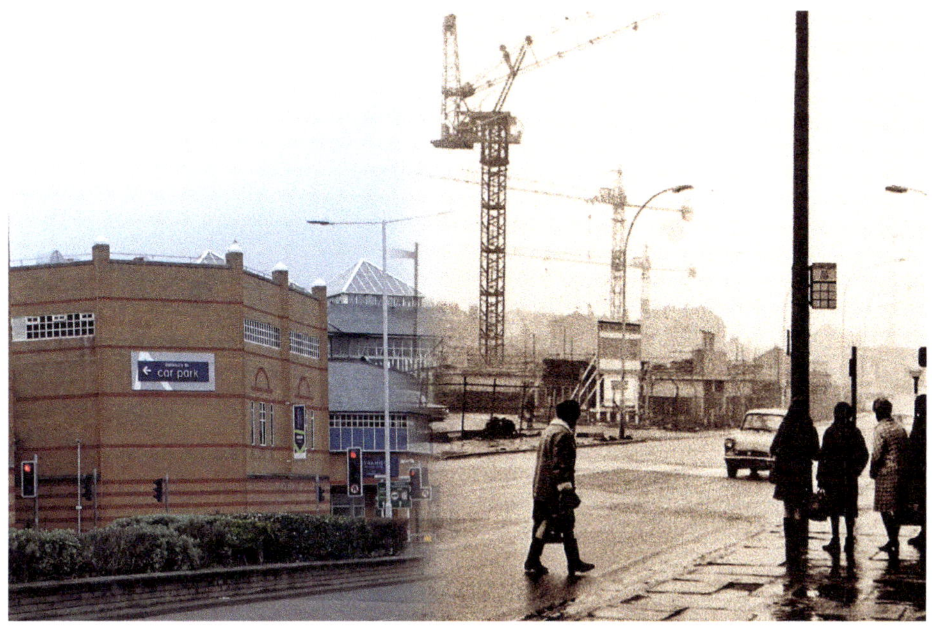

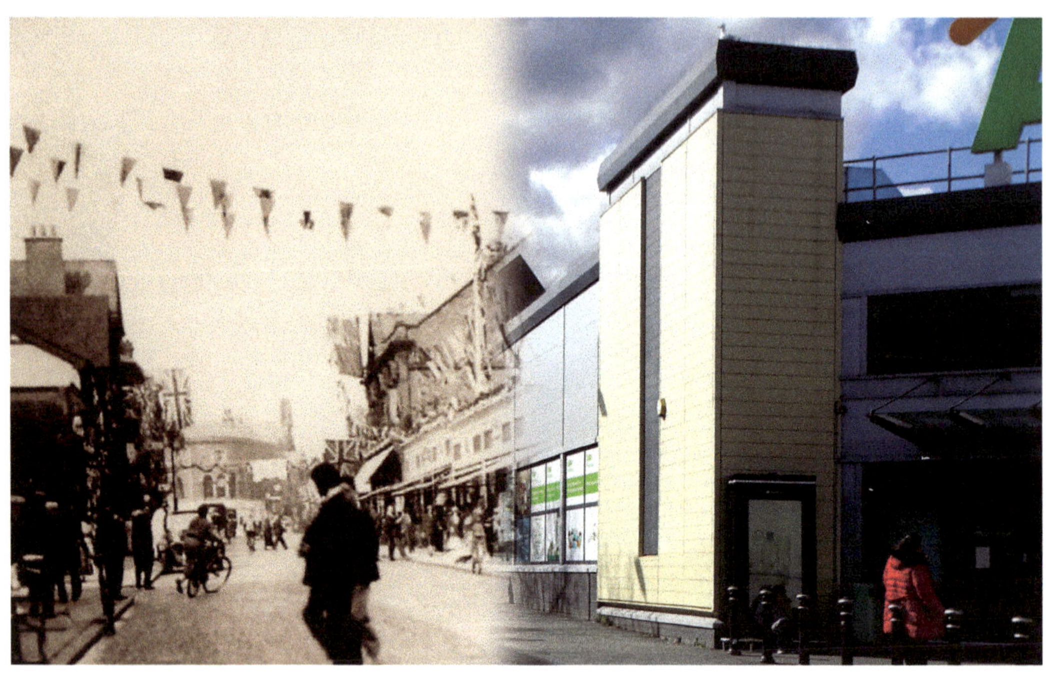

Grange Road looking towards Charing Cross

In the early 1960s Birkenhead Borough Council agreed to the redevelopment of the existing shopping centre based at Grange Road. A plan was approved in conjunction with the Borough Engineer and Surveyor, Planning Officer, Borough Valuer, Estates Manager and consultants. It was to make Grange Road pedestrianised, with modern shopping units and car parking on the perimeter. The relocation of Birkenhead Market to the site was also included in the project.

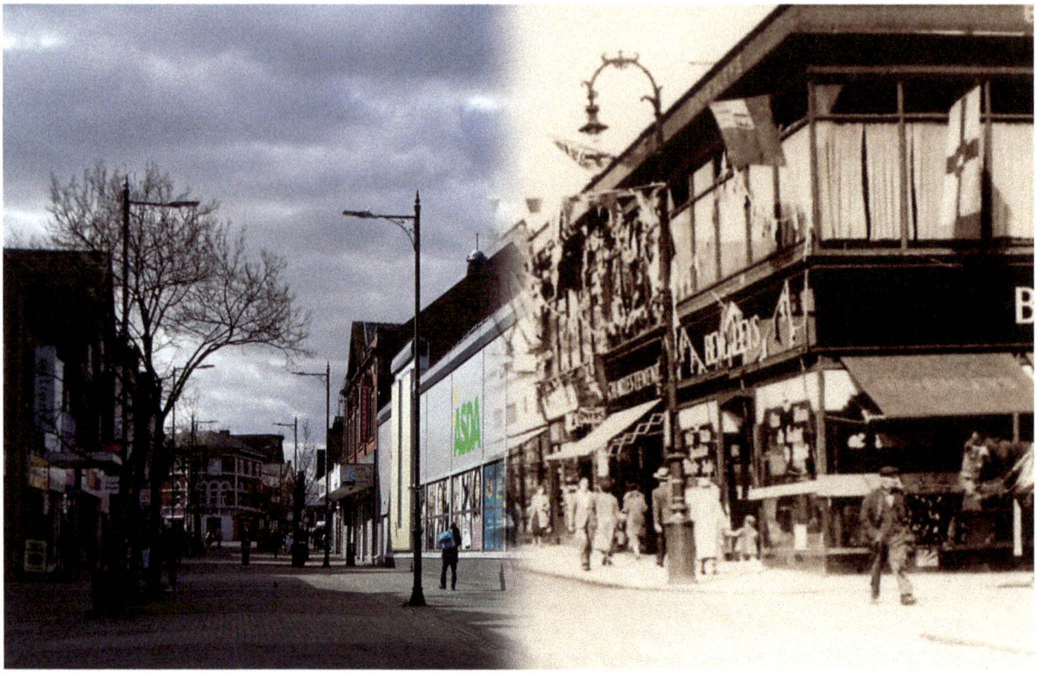

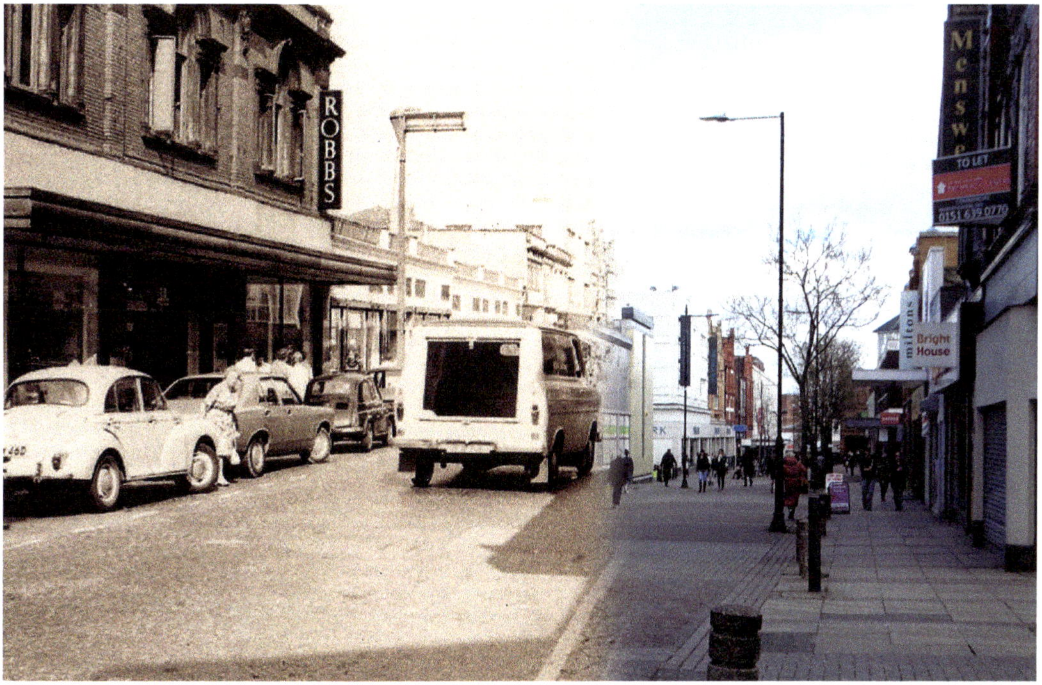

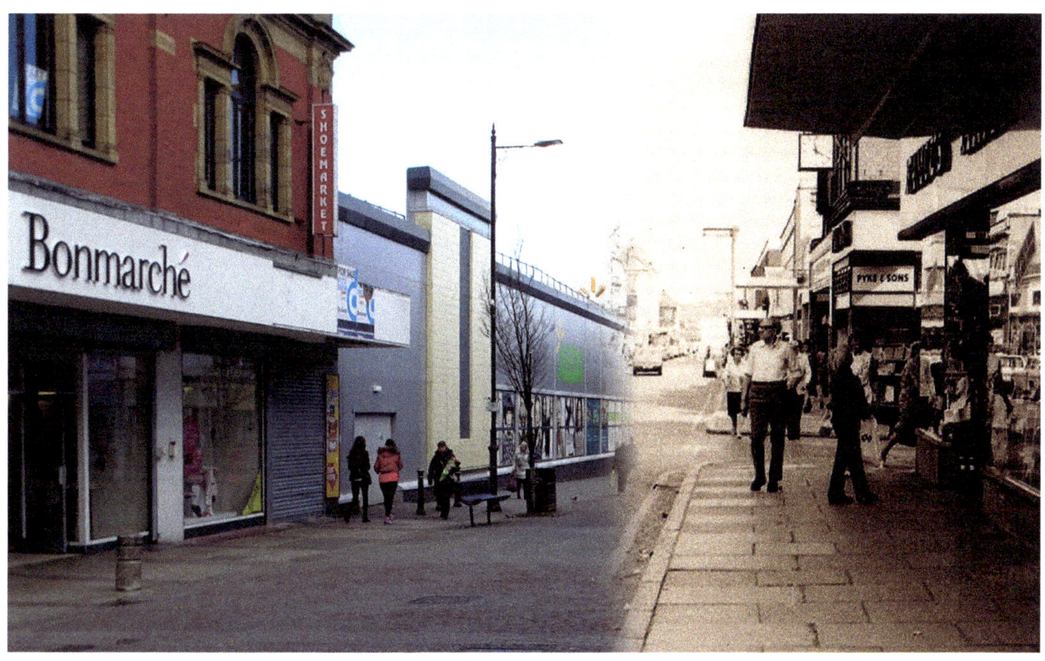

Robbs Stores, Grange Road

Robbs advertised that they had 'Everything for the Family and the Home', where 'personal service and courteous attention are household words, and where value for money is the supreme consideration at all times'. The store included a ladies' hairdressing and beauty salon and the Oakroom restaurant, which offered morning coffee, morning tea and daily luncheons at 2/9p, 3/9p and 5 shillings.

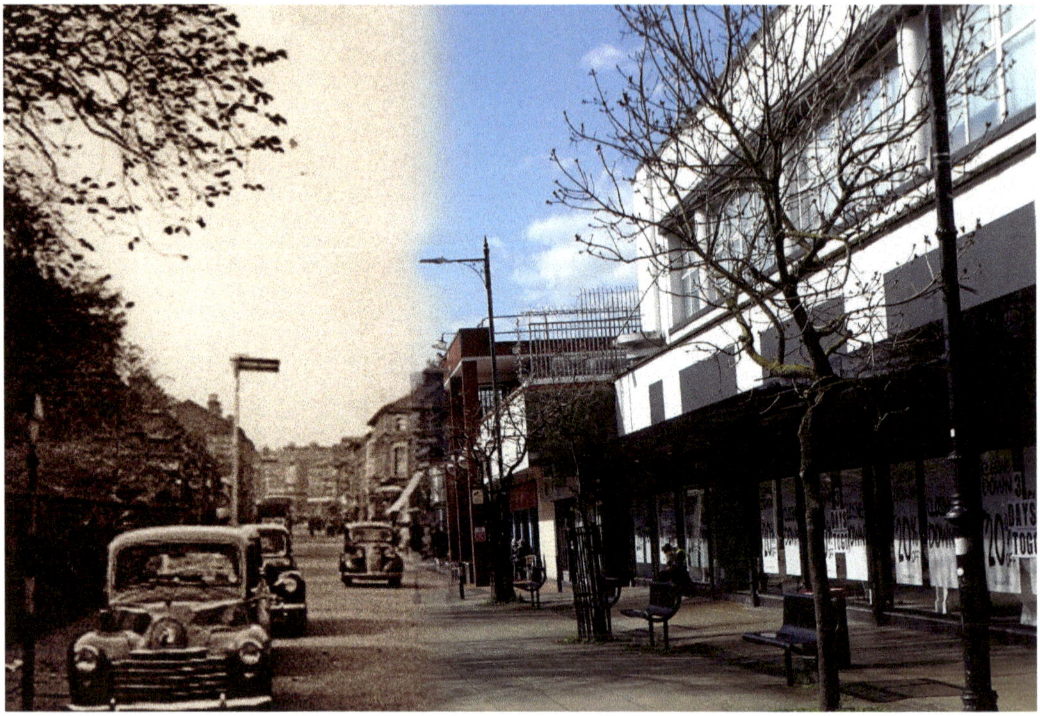

Allanson's, Grange Road

The Allanson family opened a draper's shop on the site in the 1860s and the store was developed and enlarged extensively in the 1930s when it became a public company. The building was damaged by fire during the Second World War and the company was taken over by Beatties in 1964.

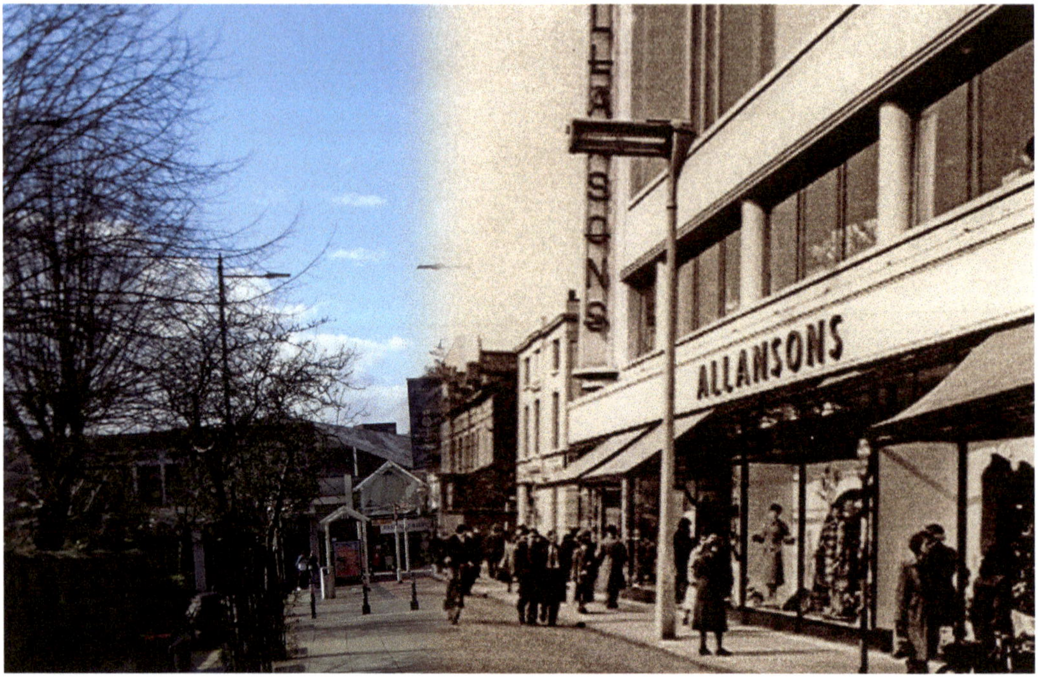

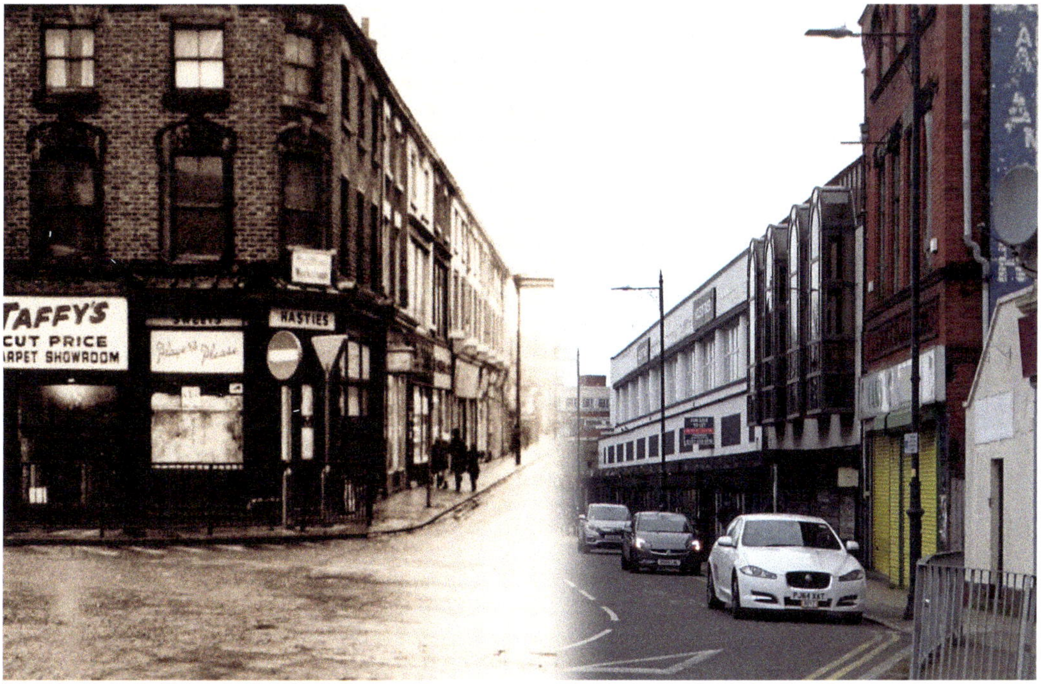

Taffy's Carpets, Grange Road

Grange Road, from Argyle Street. A branch of Taffy's cut-price carpets was situated at the end of the block and the white building further down the road still survives as Beatties department store, which sells clothes, homeware items, fragrances and gifts.

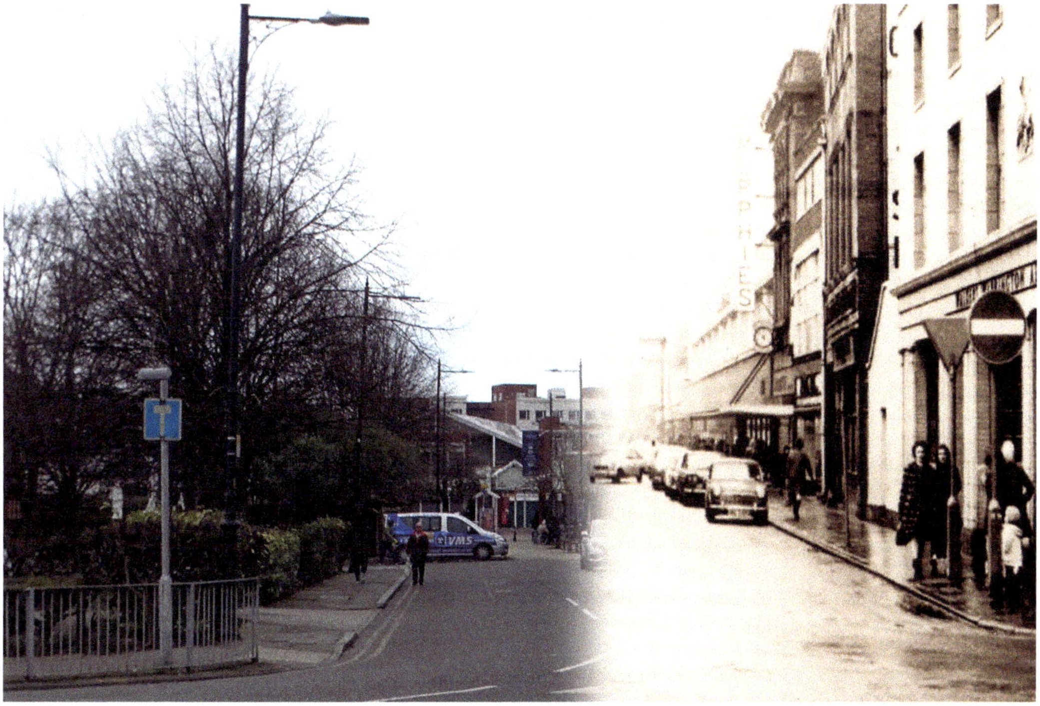

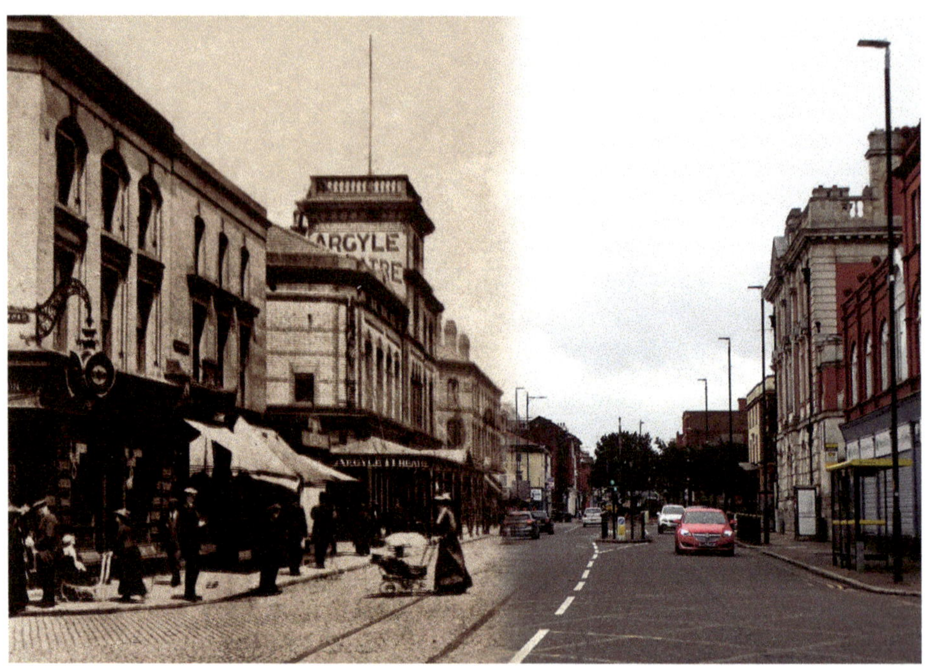

Argyle Theatre and Hotel, Argyle Street

The Argyle Theatre and Hotel was opened on 21 December 1868 by Dennis Grennell and in 1876 it was named the Prince of Wales Theatre. However, when it was managed by Dennis J. Clarke between 1888 and 1934, the name Argyle was restored and it became one of the country's most famous music halls. Charlie Chaplin, W. C. Fields, G. H. Elliot, George Formby, Stan Laurel and Donald Peers all appeared on the stage at the theatre. On 21 September 1940 it took a direct hit from German bombers and was destroyed by fire. The building on the left is the George and Dragon, which is still standing as licensed premises.

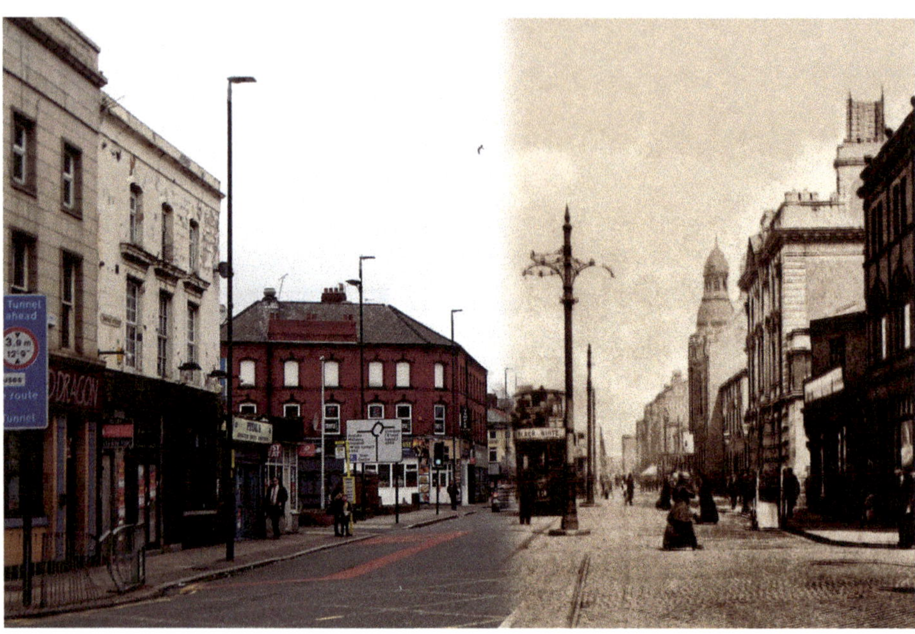

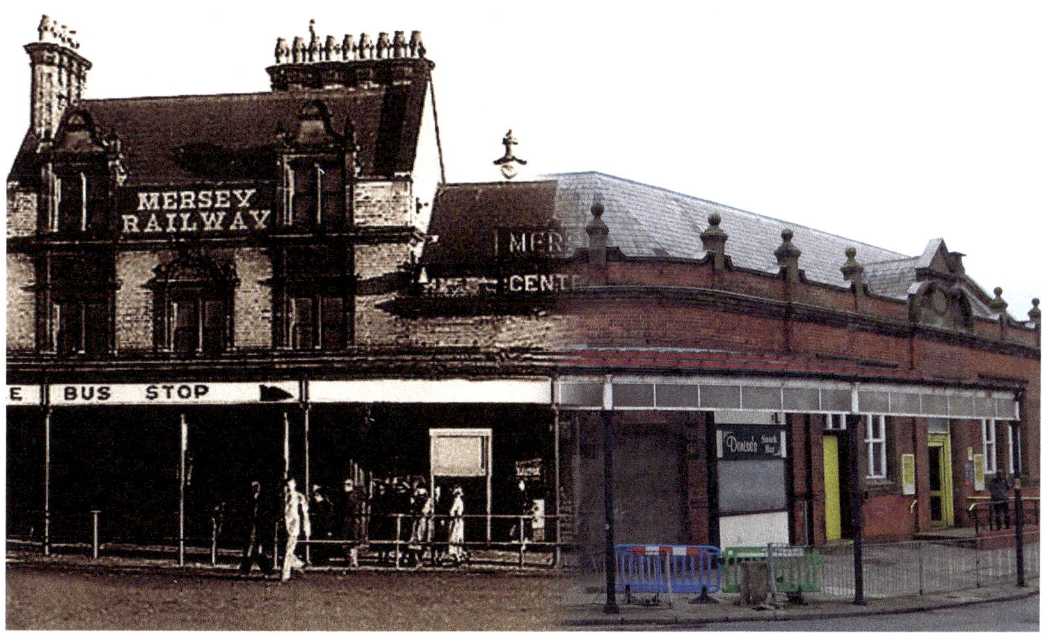

Mersey Railway Entrance

This image shows the entrance to Mersey Railway, Birkenhead Central Station, which was opened on 20 January 1886. The sign on the roof advertises 'Frequent Electric Trains to Liverpool and Rock Ferry'. The Merseyrail network now has sixty-eight stations and 75 miles of route, of which 6 ½ miles are underground. It carries approximately 110,000 passengers each weekday, or 34 million passengers per year. It is the most heavily used urban railway network in the country outside London. It is now operated by a joint venture on a contract for twenty-five years, with a fleet of trains, which are being replaced with new units in 2020–21.

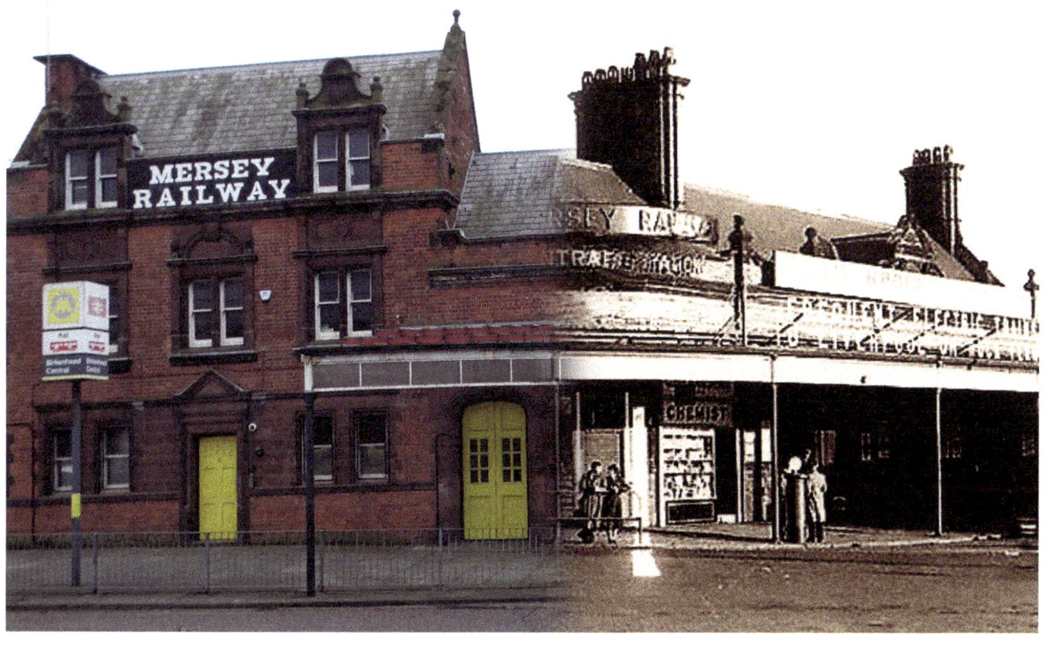

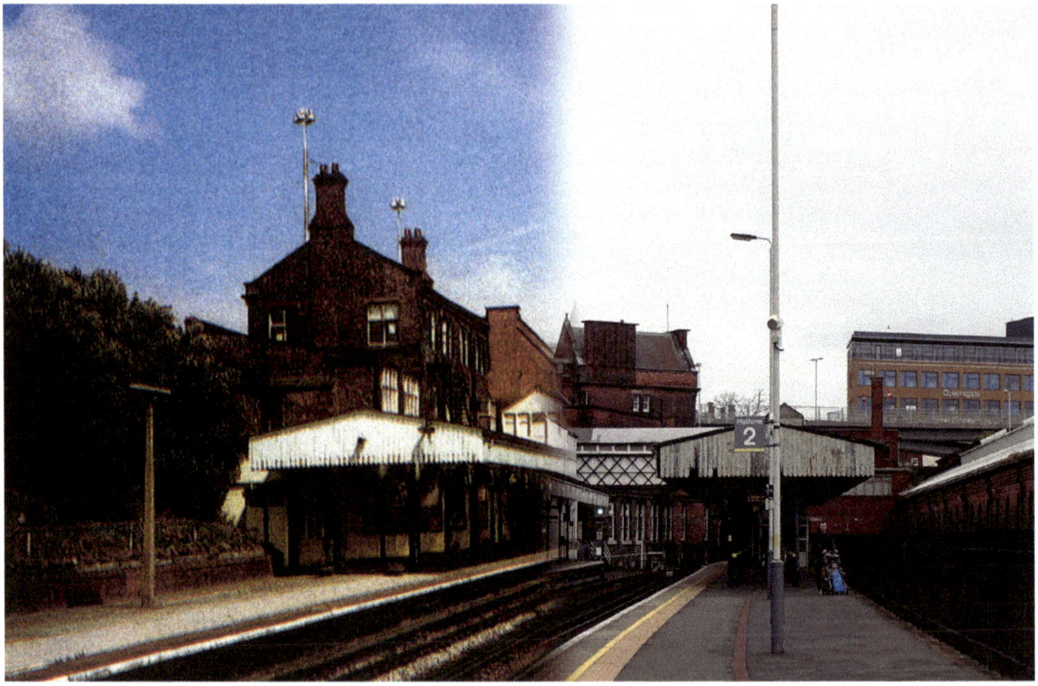

Central Station

Central Station is the nearest station on the Merseyrail network to The Grange shopping centre and Birkenhead Market and is used by people travelling from Liverpool, Rock Ferry and Chester stations.

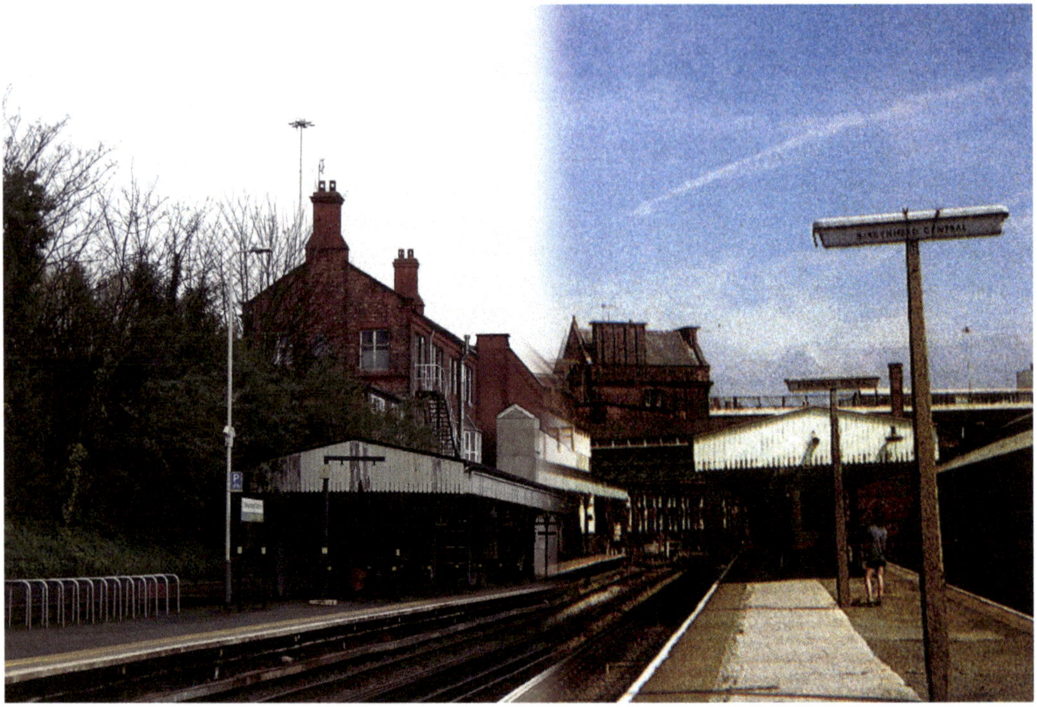

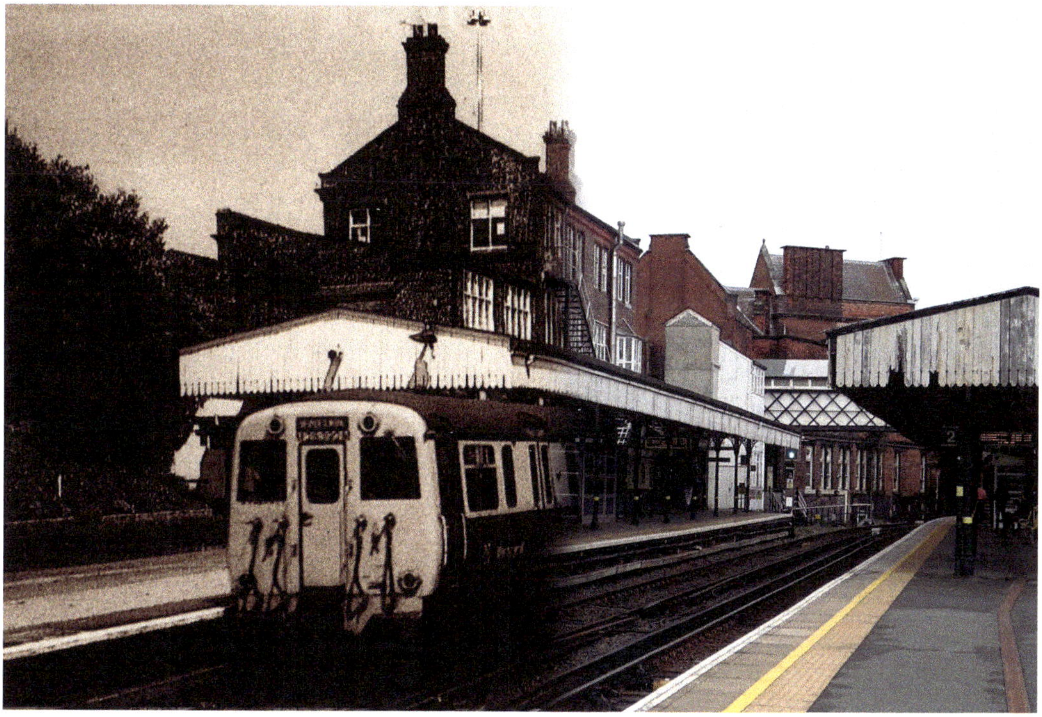

Mersey Railway

This image shows a Mersey Railway train loading passengers at Central Station bound for Birkenhead Hamilton Square, Liverpool James Street and Liverpool Central.

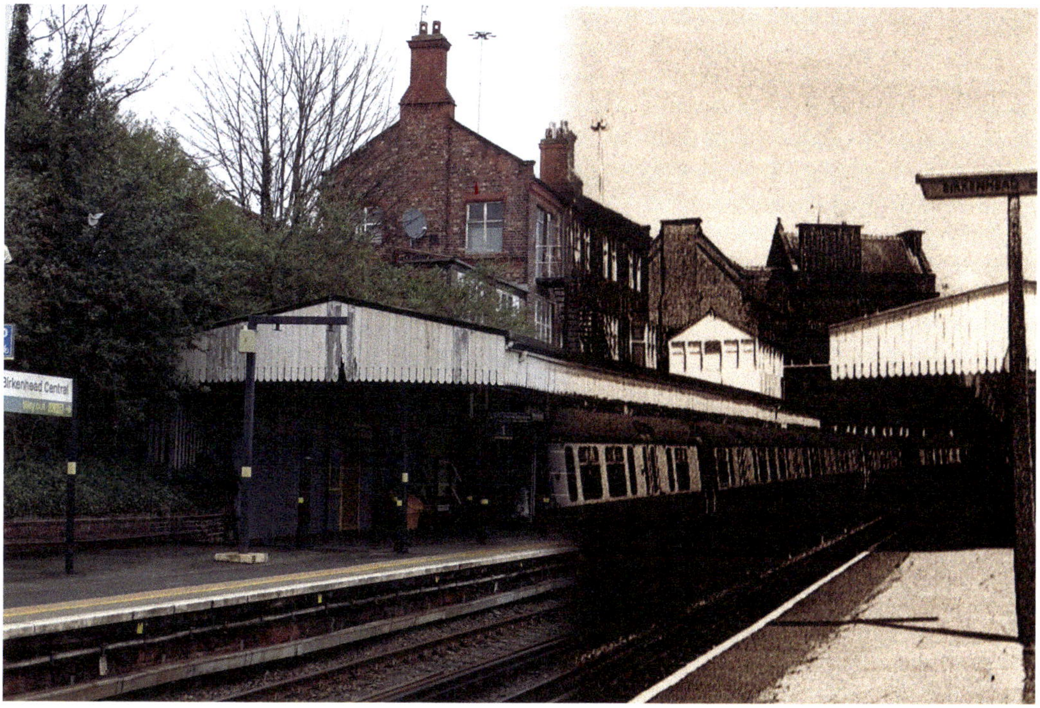

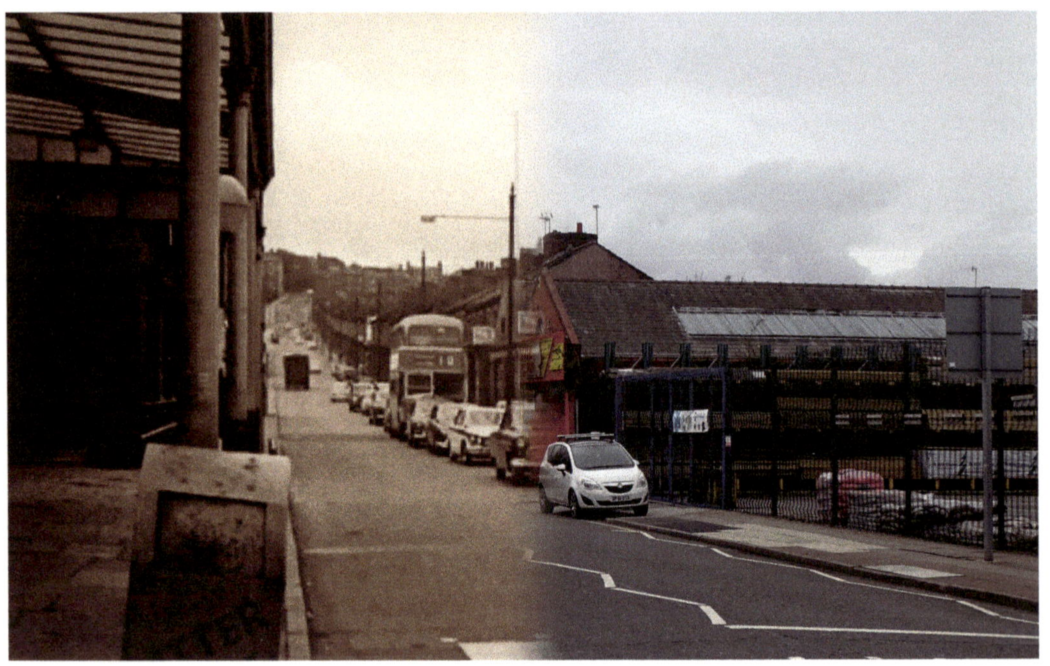

Argyle Street South

A queue of traffic on Argyle Street South, including the number 10 Birkenhead bus, which operated through Birkenhead town centre to Liscard and New Brighton from New Ferry. The service was very popular, particularly at weekends in the summer months when families travelled to the seaside resort in Wallasey.

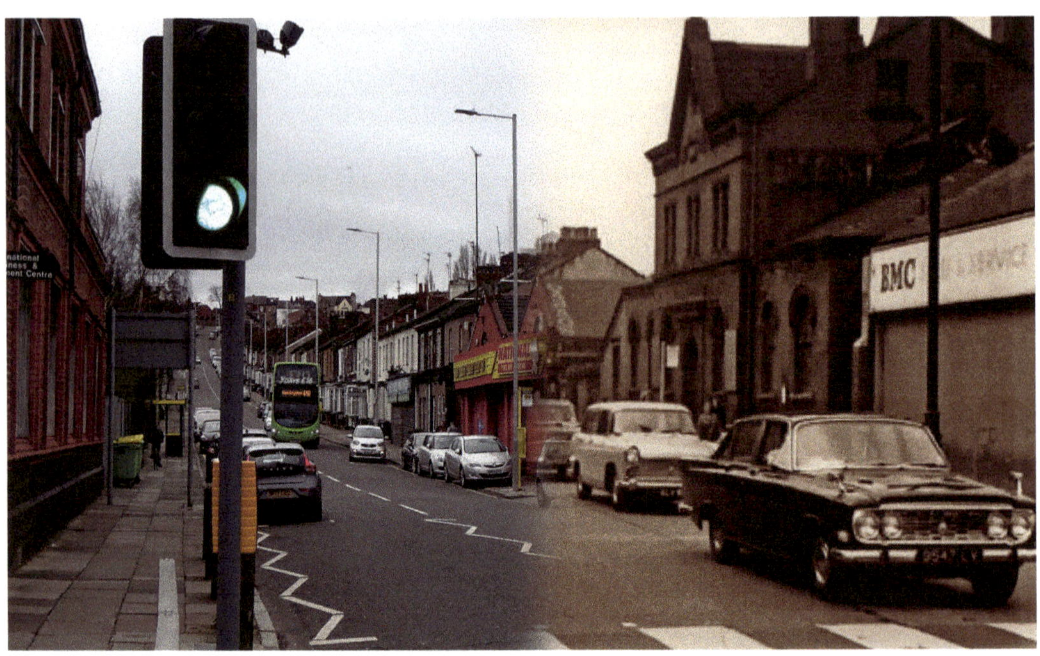

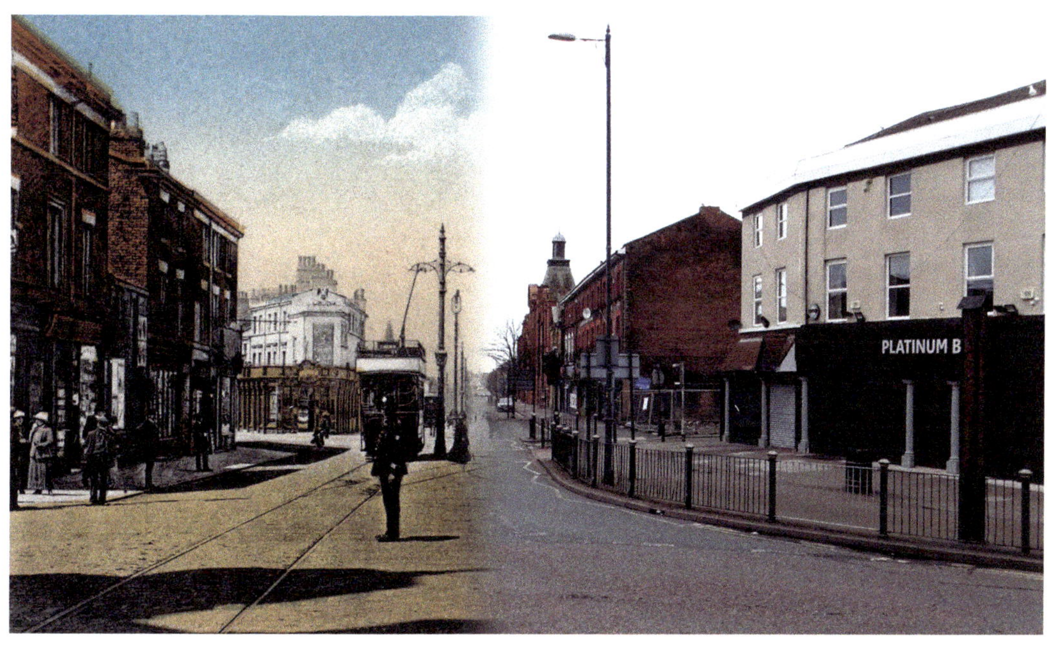

Police Officer Directs Traffic, Conway Street

Conway Street showing the Conway Arms on the left, which was situated on the corner of Claughton Road. The pub was demolished in the 1960s when the area was redeveloped and the tunnel flyover roads were constructed. The Empire Cinema was the last cinema in Birkenhead when it closed in 1991. The building next to C. Stephens, Funeral Director's was the main post office, which was moved to Argyle Street in 1908. It became The Picture House and later The Super Cinema, and was one of the first venues for the group the Beatles in the 1960s. It later became a ballroom and furniture showroom and recently a restaurant. The building with the dome was the Birkenhead Higher Elementary Technical School.

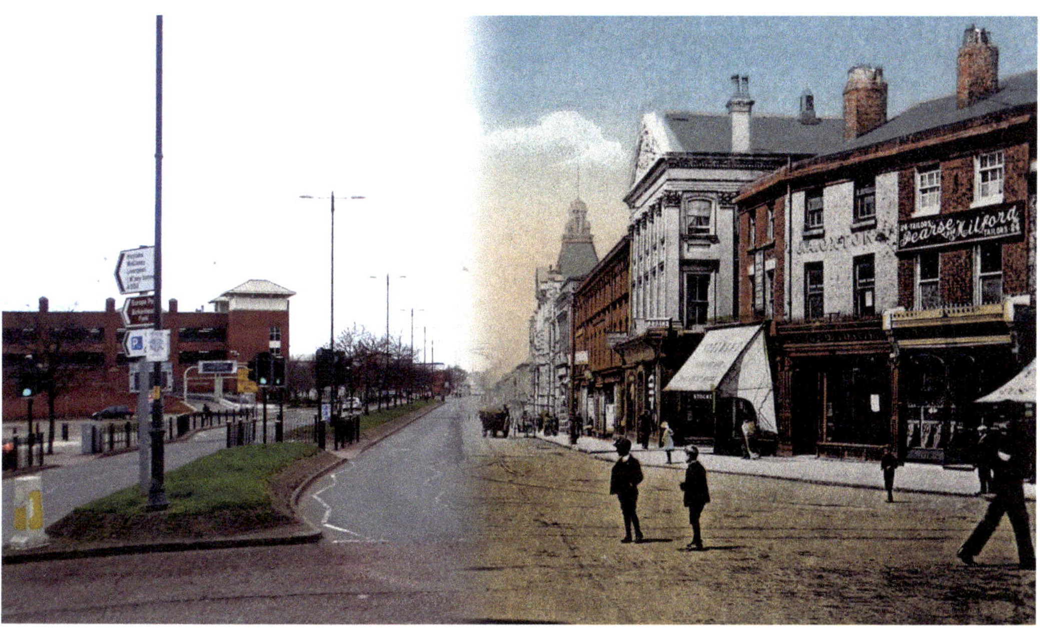

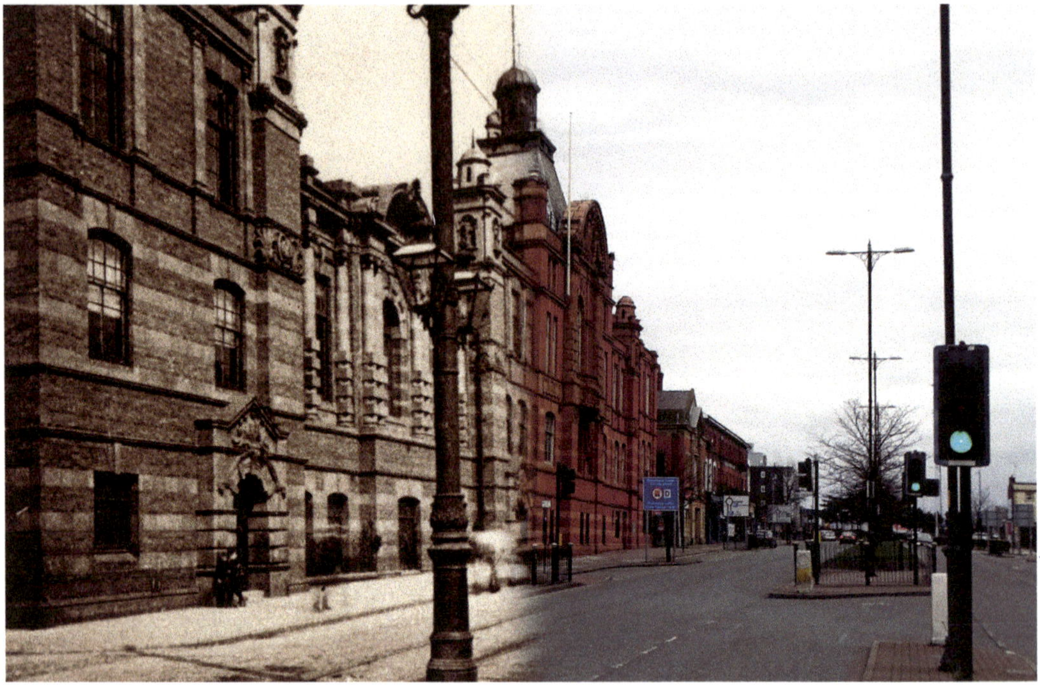

Birkenhead Higher Elementary School, Conway Street

The Technical College was named by A. A. Dobbs after one of his relatives. Mr Dobbs bought a large piece of land between Argyle Street and Park Road East, named it Parkfield, and erected a number of fine villas around 1835.

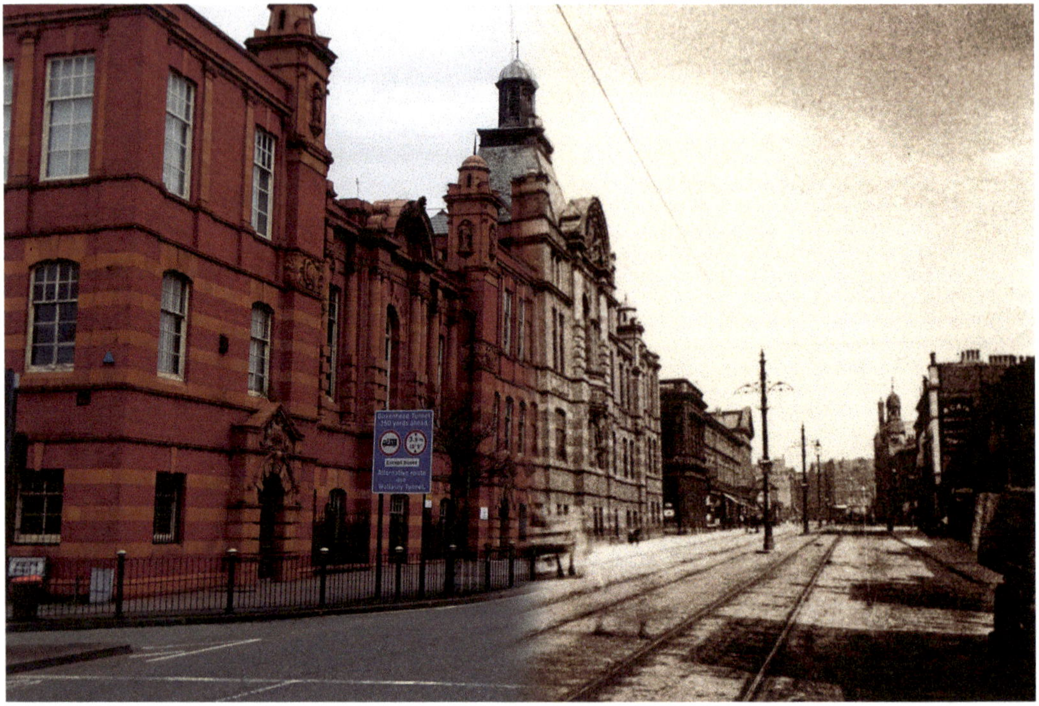

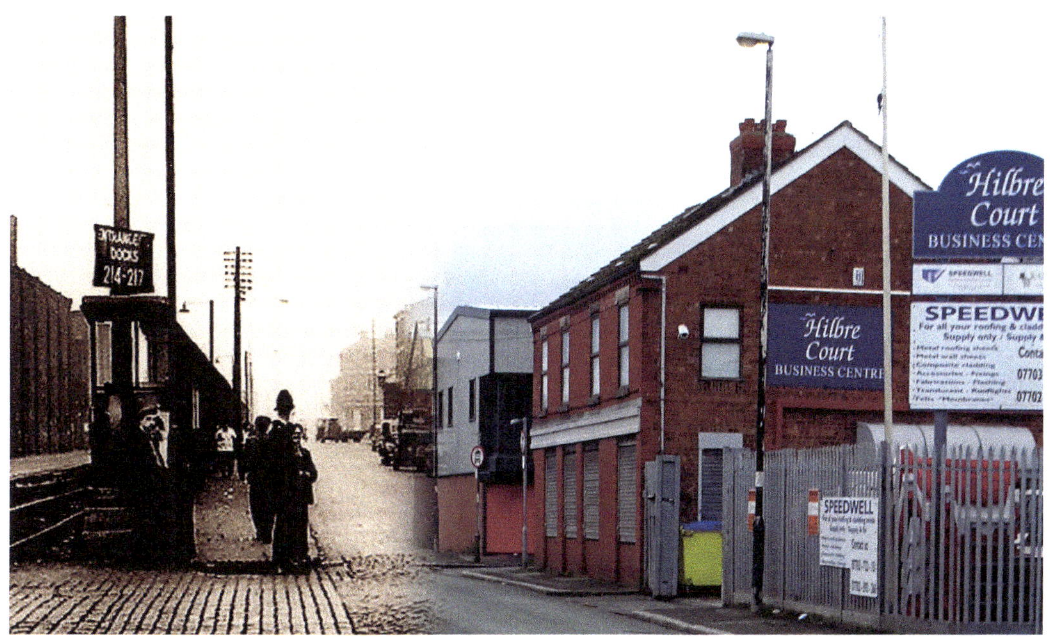

Vittoria Dock

The main entrances to the Vittoria Dock and Vittoria Wharf was from Corporation Road. In the late 1950s and 1960s several of the berths at Birkenhead docks were rebuilt, old warehouses demolished and new sheds constructed. Vittoria Dock loading berths were completely redesigned and modern warehouses built for the Clan Line and Alfred Holt & Co. Ltd. Three new export berths incorporating the most up-to-date techniques of berth design and cargo handling, a dockside apron of 35 feet wide and a lorry flow park ensured the minimum of delay in the loading of export cargoes. A modern administrative building was completed in 1967.

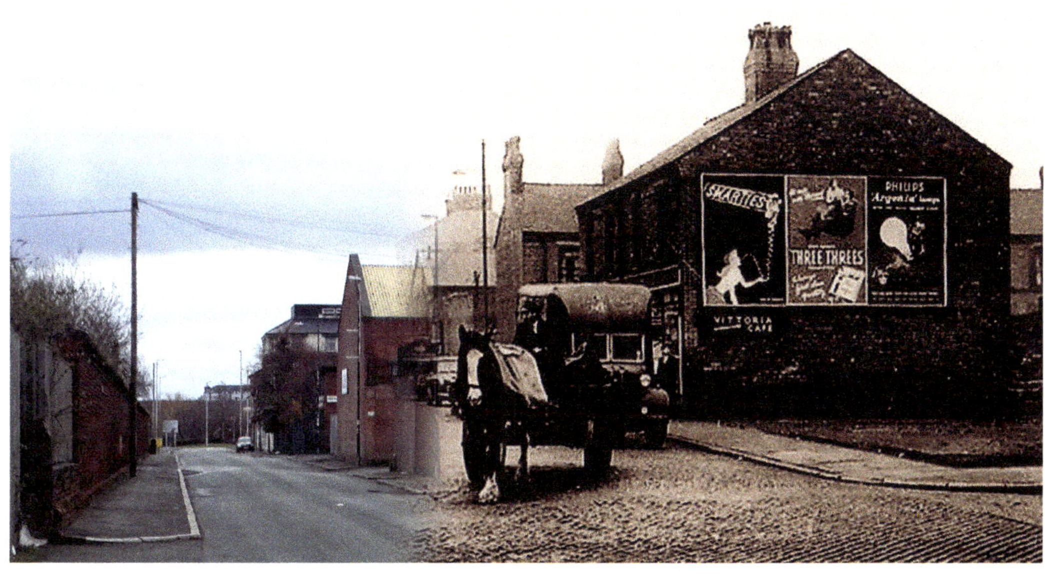

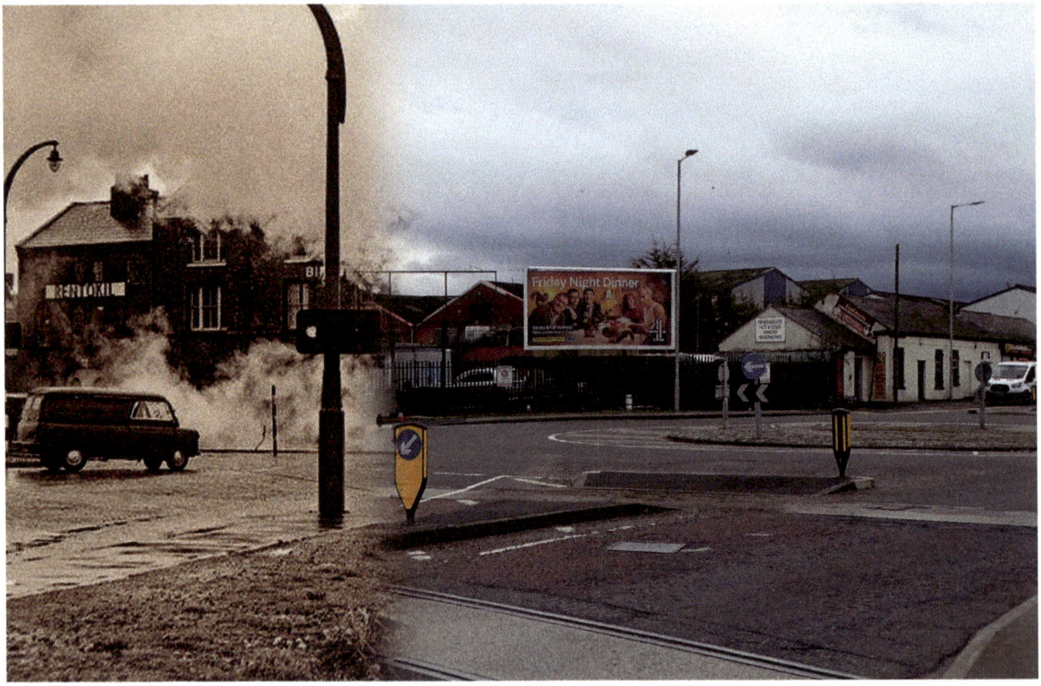

Police Officer, Birkenhead Docks

A police officer controls the traffic at the entrance to Birkenhead docks at Duke Street Bridge. This was one of the main entrances to the dock estate and it was very busy when there were a number of ships loading cargoes to ports around the world. A steam locomotive passes the Royal Duke public house at the junction of Duke Street and Corporation Road.

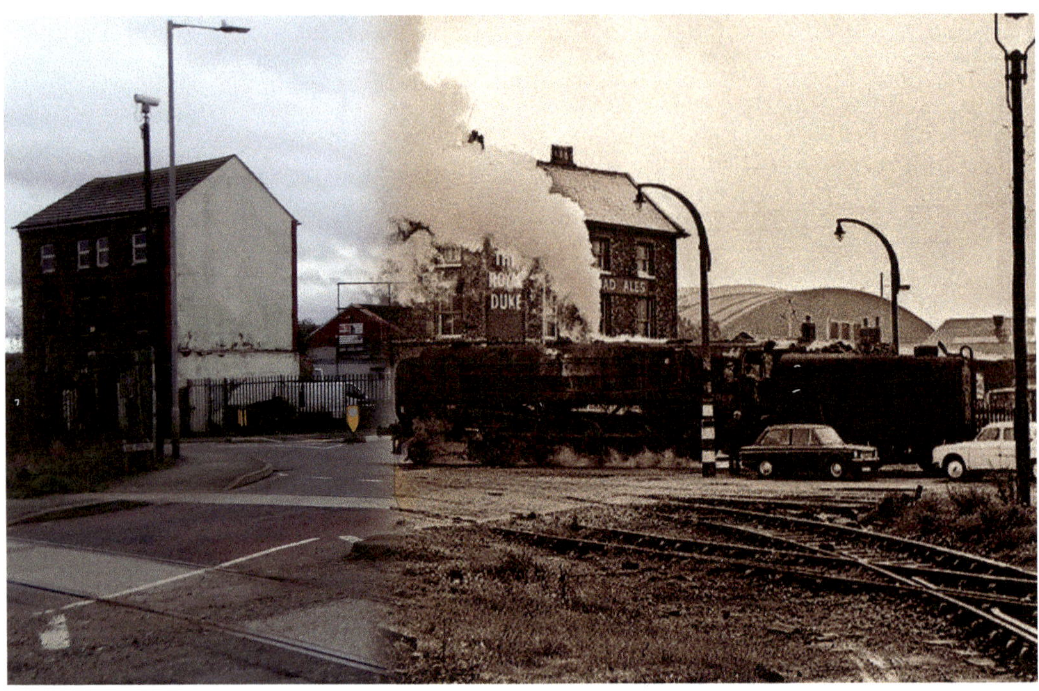

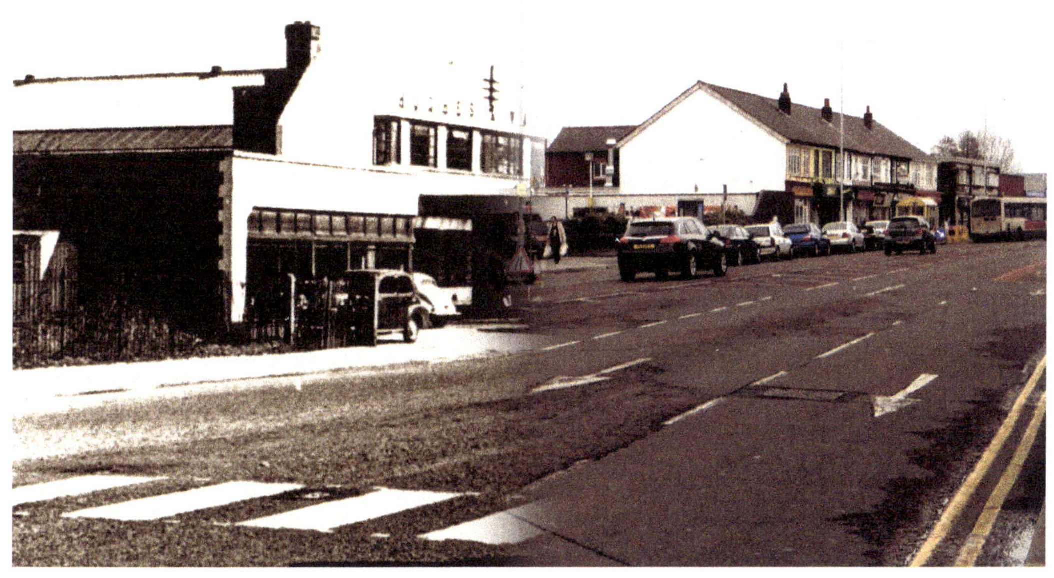

Hughes & Watts Garage

Hughes & Watts operated a garage in Woodchurch Road until the 1950s, when the premises were taken over by Kirby's Motor Engineers. The company sold the site to Sainsbury's who built a supermarket which was opened in 1982.

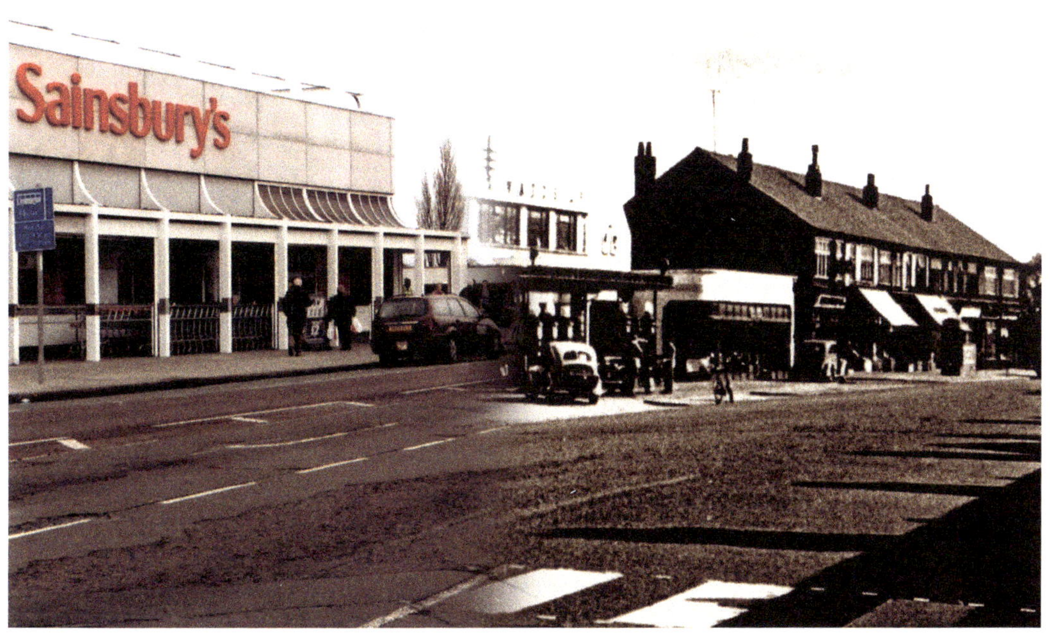

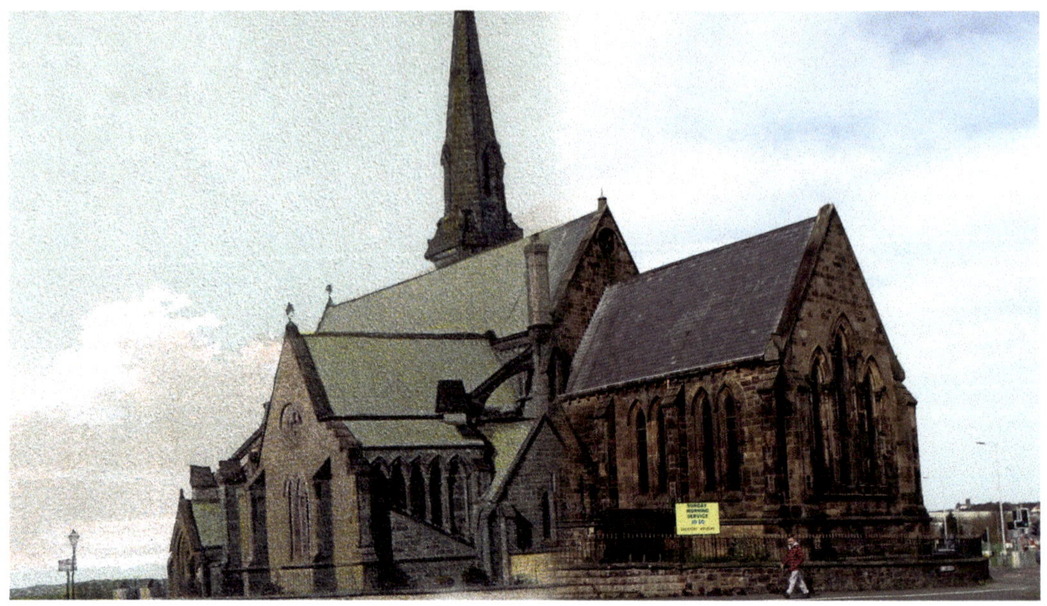

St James', Church, Laird Street

St James' Church was built in 1858 at the junction of Laird Street and Hoylake Road. It was built to serve the Dock Cottages which were built by the Birkenhead Dock Co. in 1845 to house the families of their workmen. Each block was four storeys high and each flat was provided with fresh water. The cottages were originally named Queens Buildings and survived for a century before they were demolished and Ilchester Square was built on the site. The final section of Ilchester Square was demolished in 2009 and a new housing development is under construction next to Birkenhead North railway station. There are also plans to build more houses on a site close by, where local authority properties were demolished several years ago.

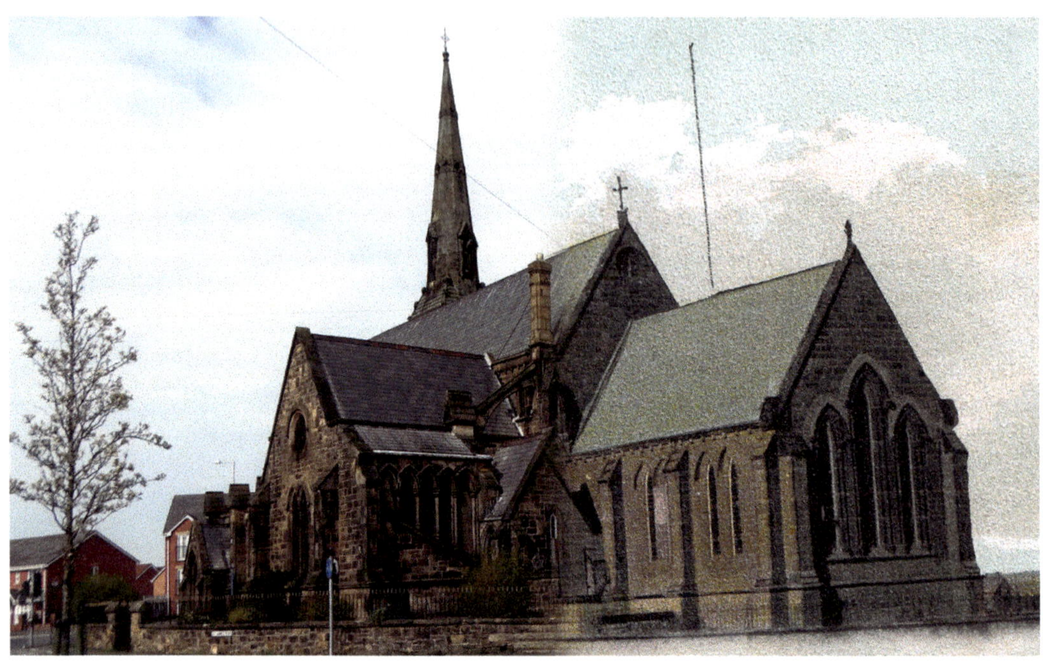

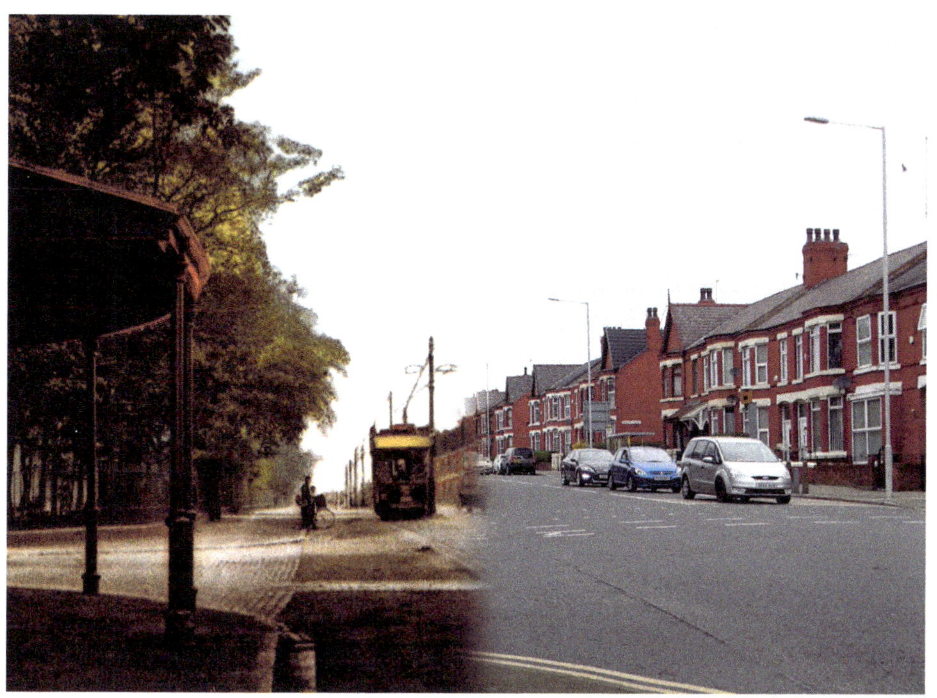

Park Road North

A tram stops in Park Road North, near Birkenhead Park and Birkenhead Park railway station. Horse buses were operating in Birkenhead as early as 1848, when a service ran between Woodside Ferry terminal and Oxton. On 30 August 1860, Birkenhead's first tramway was inaugurated by George Francis Train. It operated from Woodside to Birkenhead Park, a distance of 1 ½ miles, via Shore Road, Argyle Street and Conway Street.

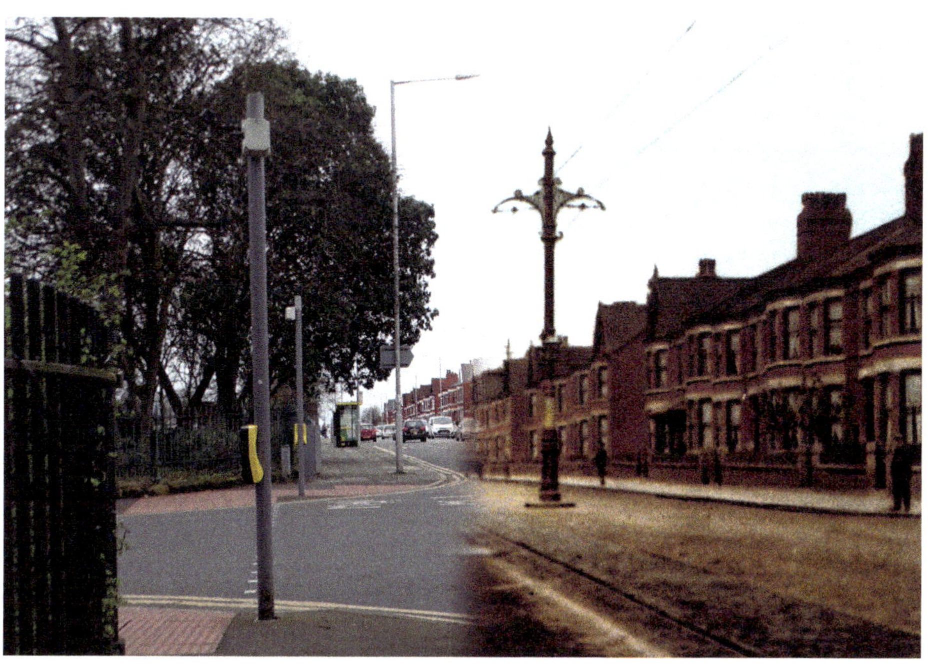

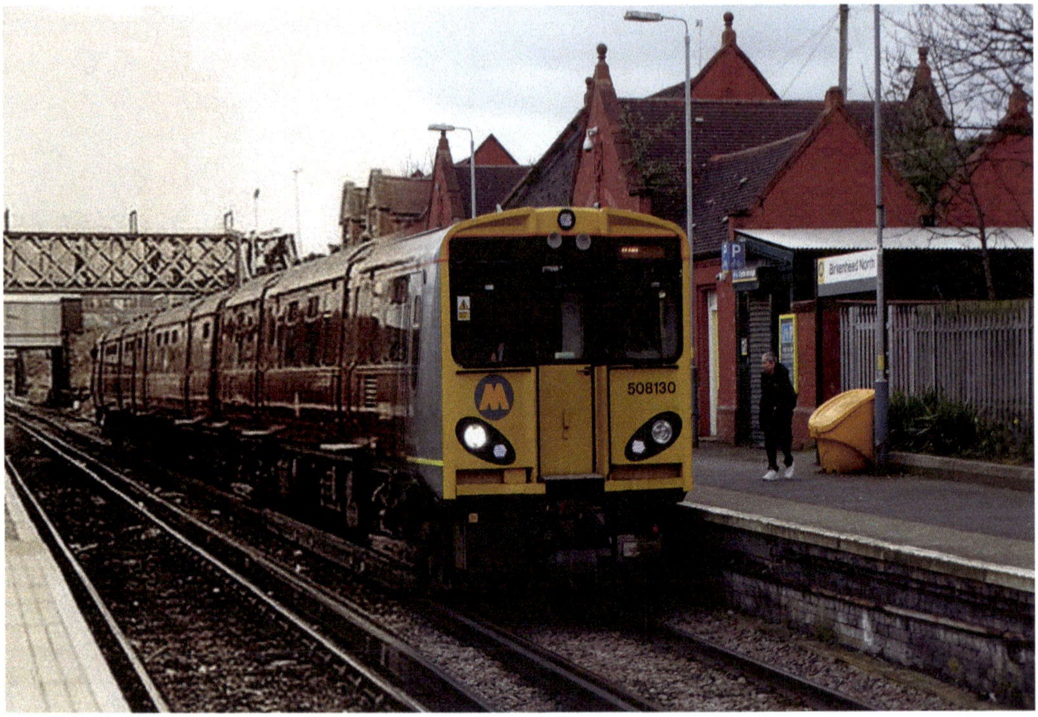

Birkenhead North

A Mersey electric train arrives at Birkenhead North from Liverpool Central. Trains from Liverpool Central to New Brighton and West Kirby pass through Birkenhead North station. Lifts and facilities for elderly and disabled persons have recently been installed at the station.

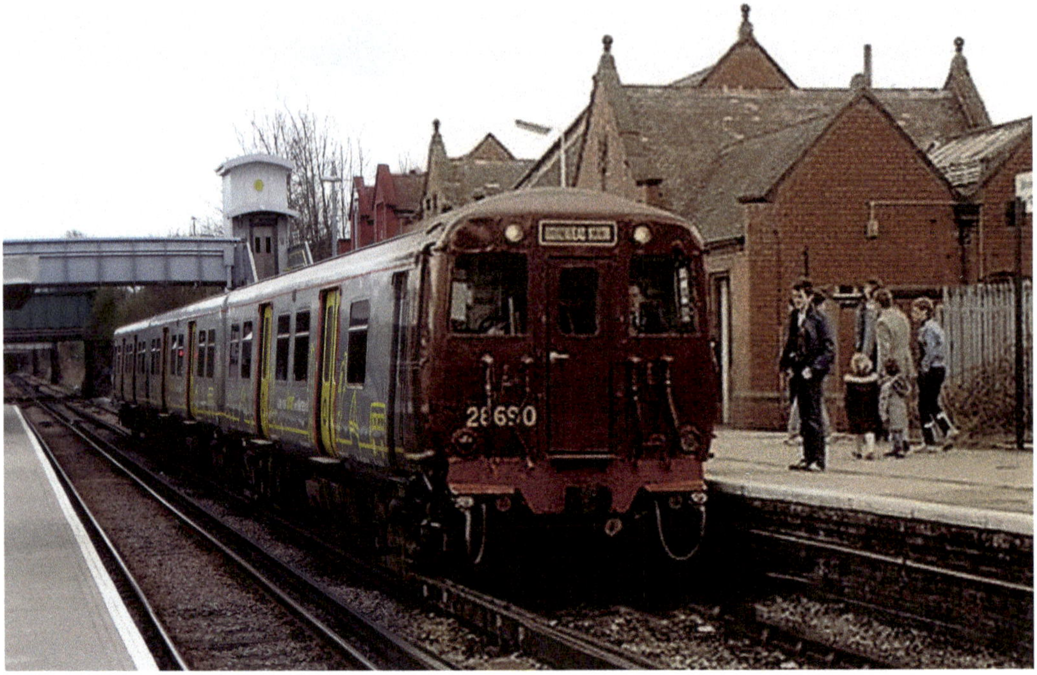

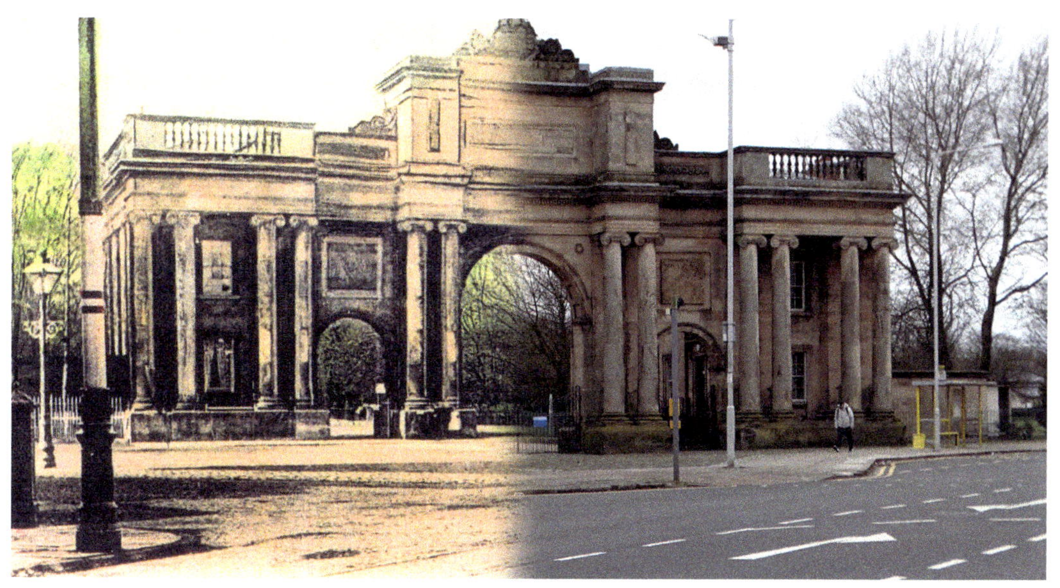

Entrance Gate at Birkenhead Park

The entrance gate in Birkenhead Park was designed by Lewis Hornblower and is on the junction where Park Road North meets Park Road East. The frontage measures 125 feet, with a central carriageway through an arch of 18 feet span, which is 43 feet in height. The original gates featured the armorial bearings of Birkenhead Priory. Opposite the gate is the Laird School of Art in Park Road North, which was opened on 27 September 1871 and was the first public school of art outside London. It was given to the town by John Laird and operated until 1979, when it merged with the Birkenhead College of Technology in Borough Road.

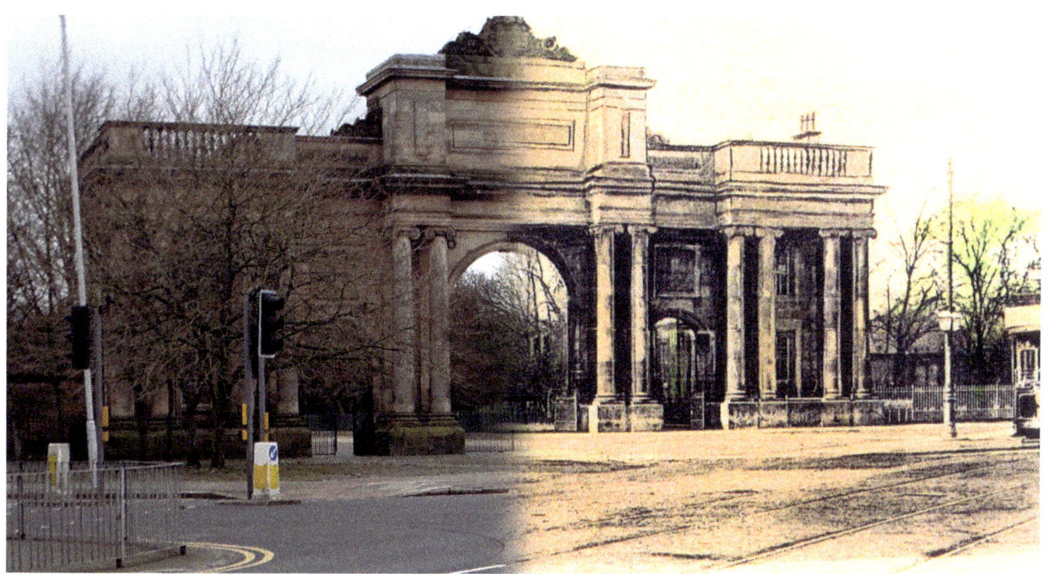

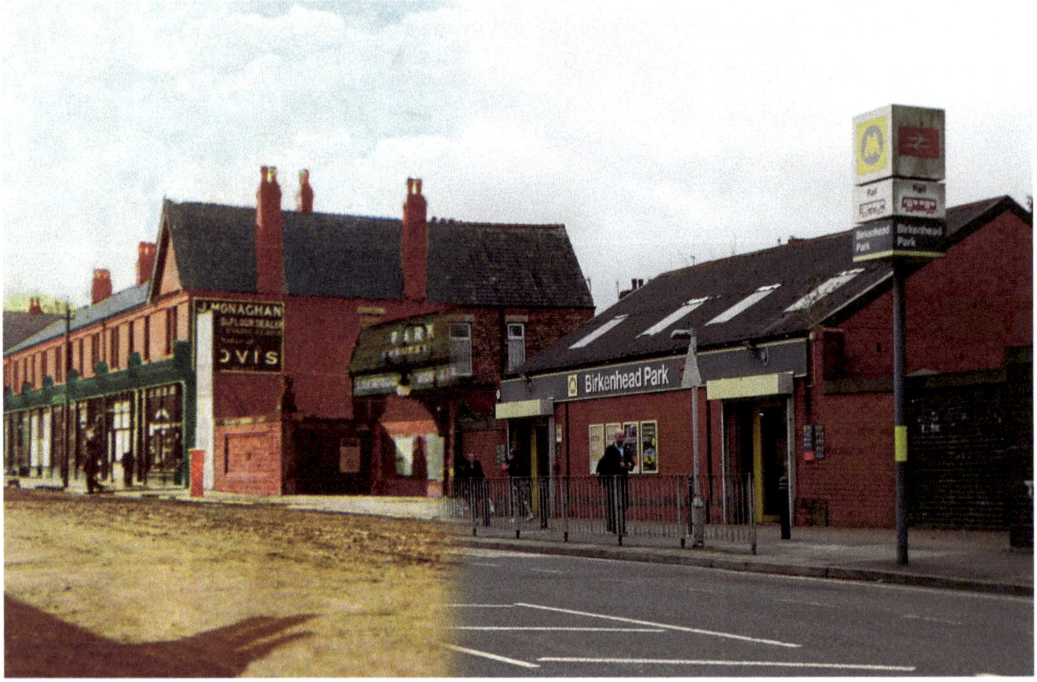

Birkenhead Park Railway Station, Duke Street, *c.* 1930

The station entrance and building were destroyed in 1941 when the whole area with its proximity to Birkenhead docks was a target for German bombers. The platform signal box was demolished in 1988 when the track signalling system on the Mersey Railway network was restructured.

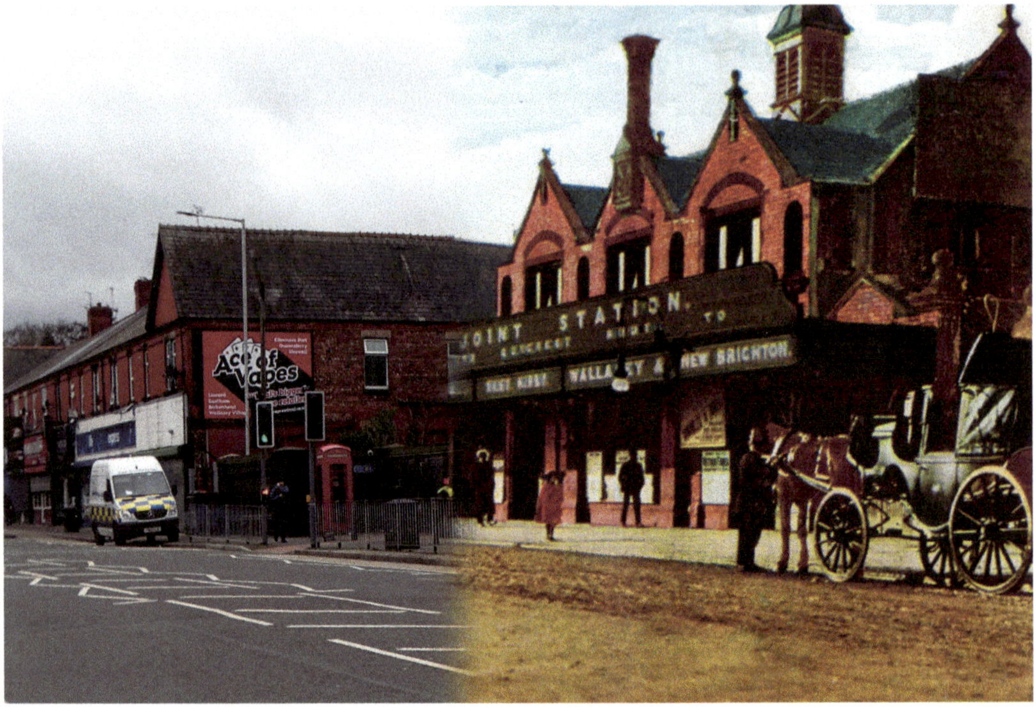

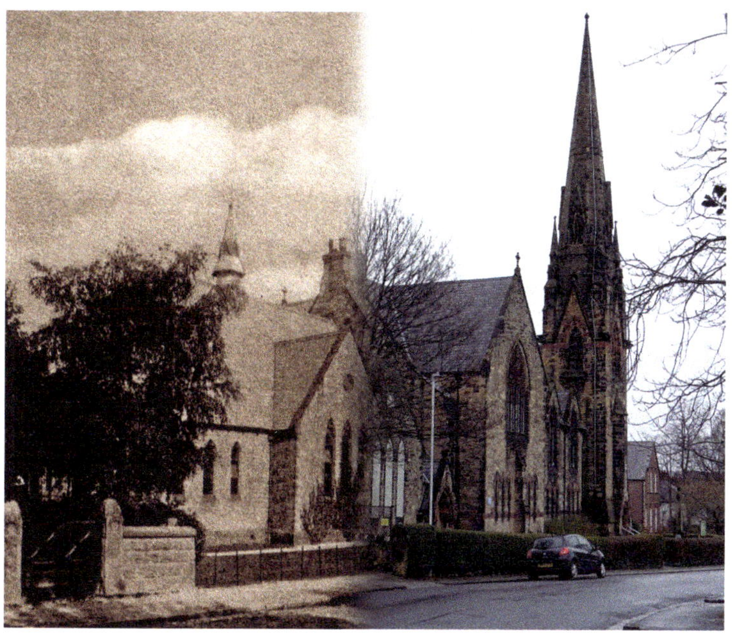

Trinity Church, Claughton

Trinity Church in Claughton is a combined United Reformed and Methodist church. The church is recorded in the National Heritage List for England and is designated as a Grade II building. It was originally known as Trinity Church, when built between 1865 and 1866, and was designed by W. and J. Hay. It was initially a Presbyterian church, and was united with Palm Grove Methodist Church in 1977. The church was constructed in rubble stone with dressings in red and yellow ashlar, and has slated roofs. It has a nave with a south porch, north and south isles, north and south transepts, a hall with a north porch at the east end, and a north-west tower with a spire.

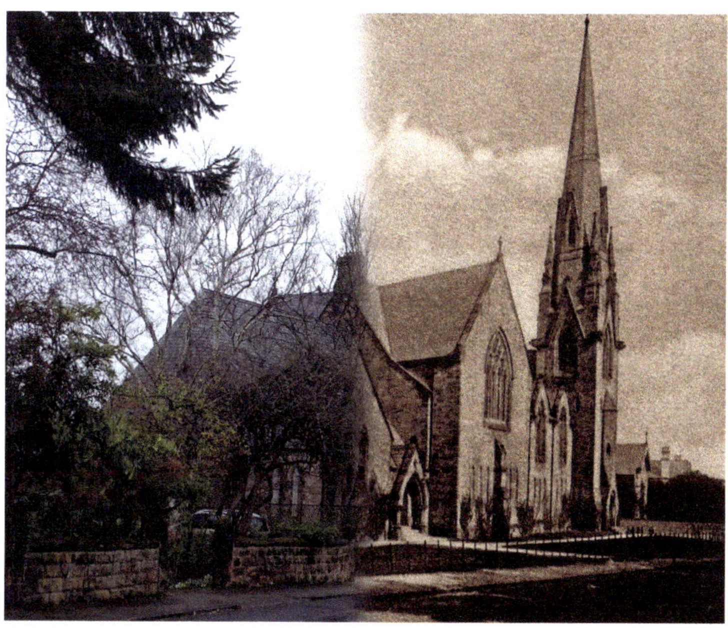

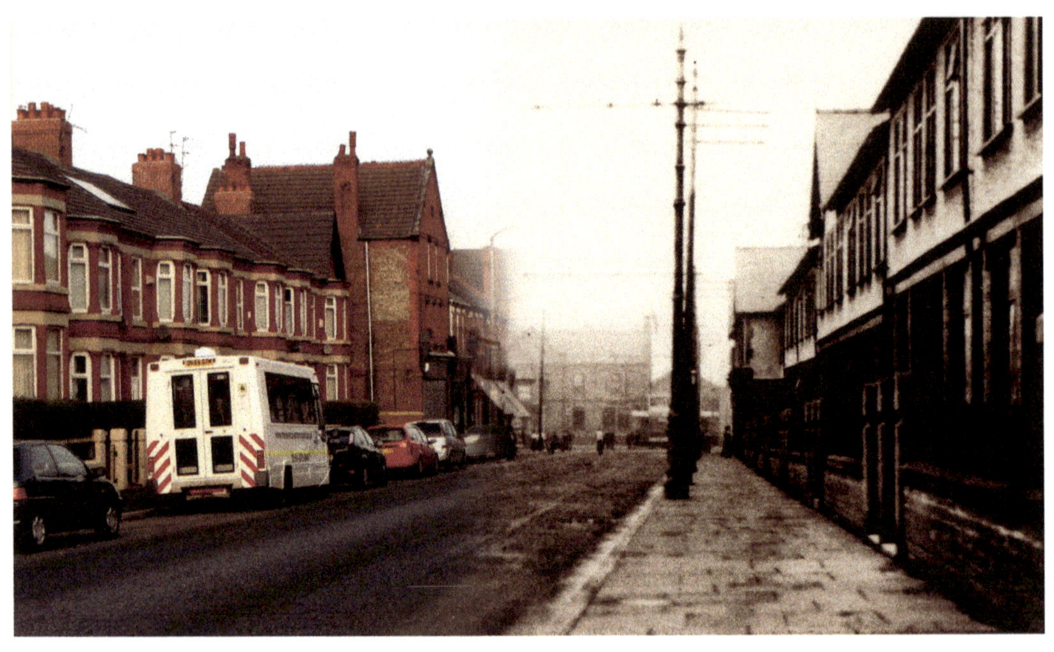

Mallaby Street

Mallaby Street leads down from Birkenhead Park to Laird Street. It was once a popular shopping centre containing a bakery, chemist, travel agent and other small shops and businesses.

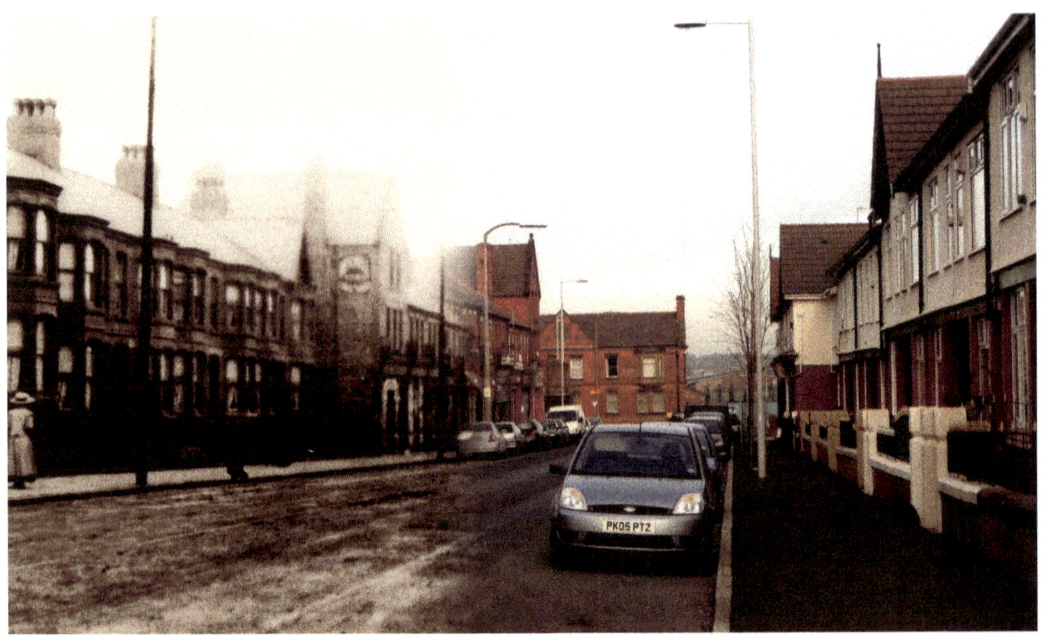

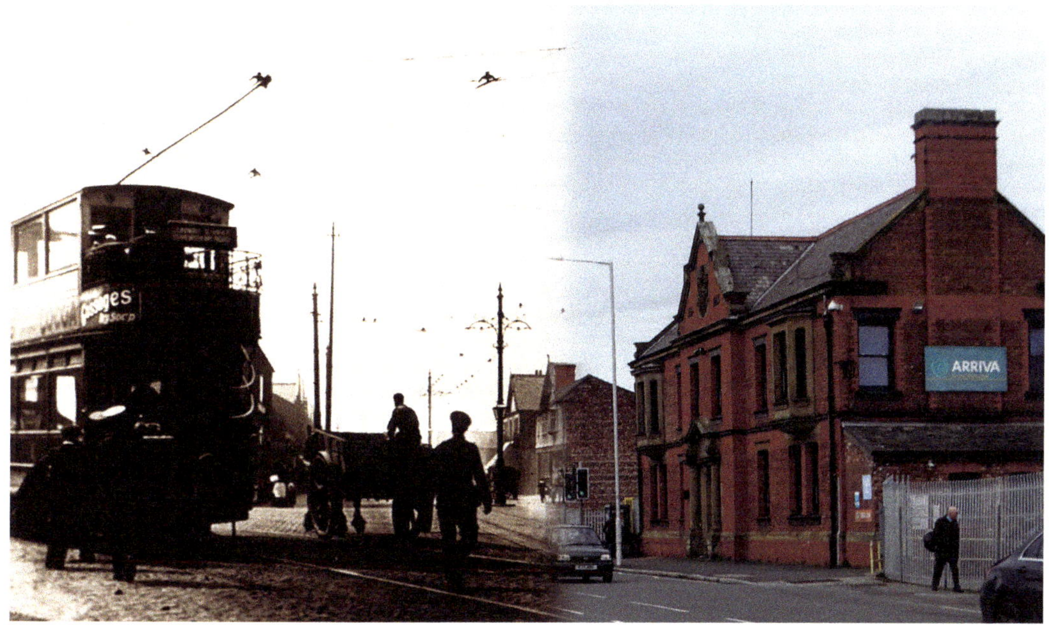

Tram Terminus, Laird Street, 1910

The Tramways Office was opened on 28 July 1903 following the introduction of the new electric trams and various routes across the borough. Forty-two trams could be stored at the depot and this was later extended to accommodate sixty vehicles. An extension was built in 1927 when the new buses were introduced and the depot is still used as the depot for Arriva plc, Wirral.

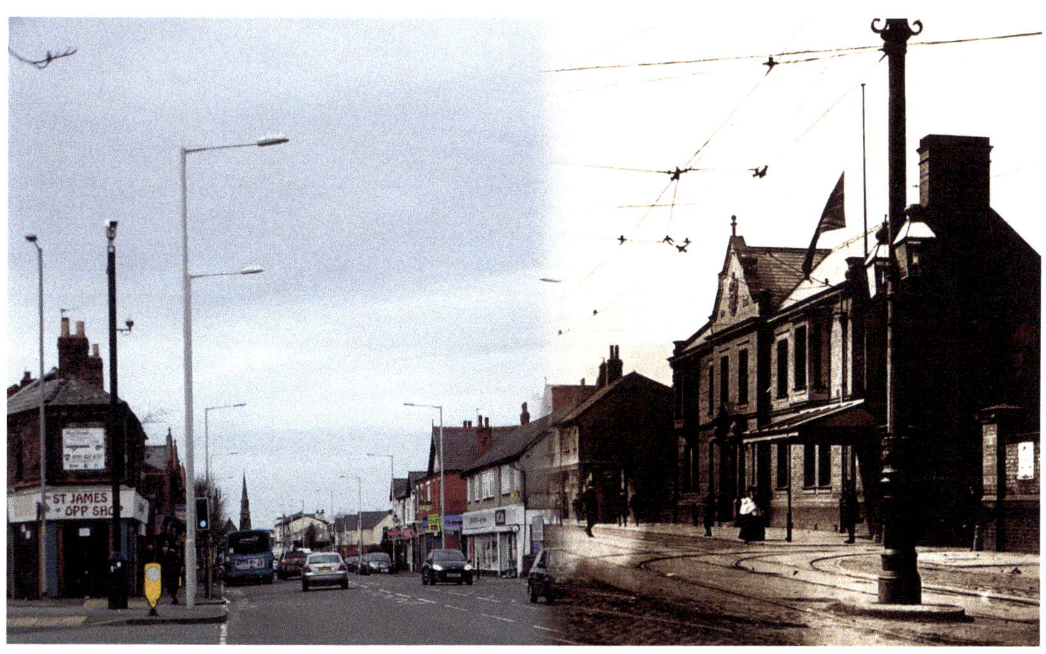

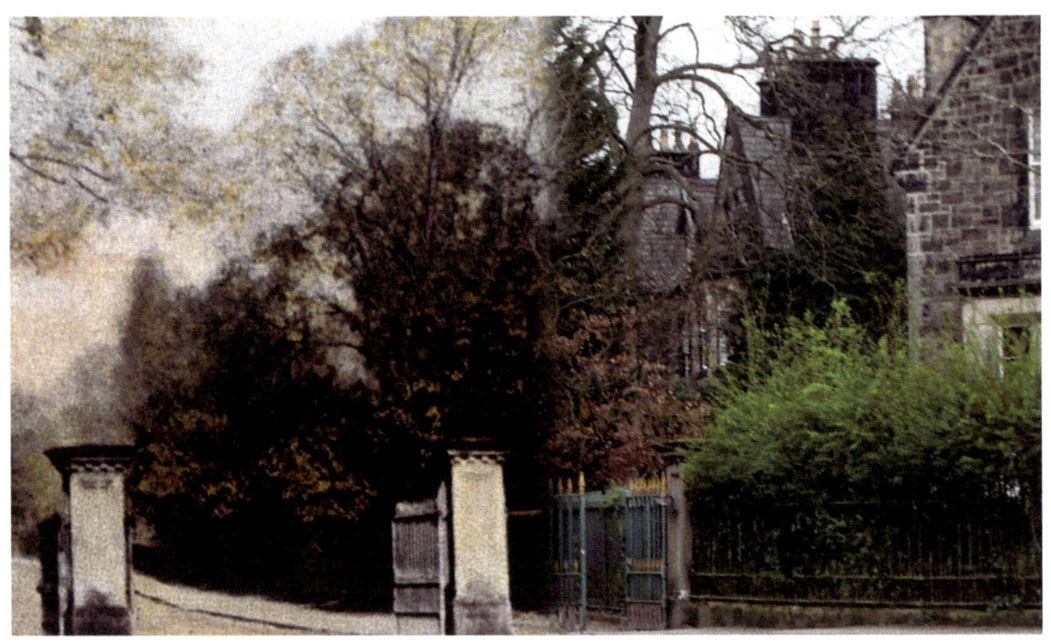

No. 1 Cavendish Road was originally a lodge to Birkenhead Park, and later used as a house. It was designed by Lewis Hornblower and John Robertson. The house is in stone with a Welsh slate roof and is in Tudor style. It has two storeys and has a gabled bay on the left and a projecting gabled porch.

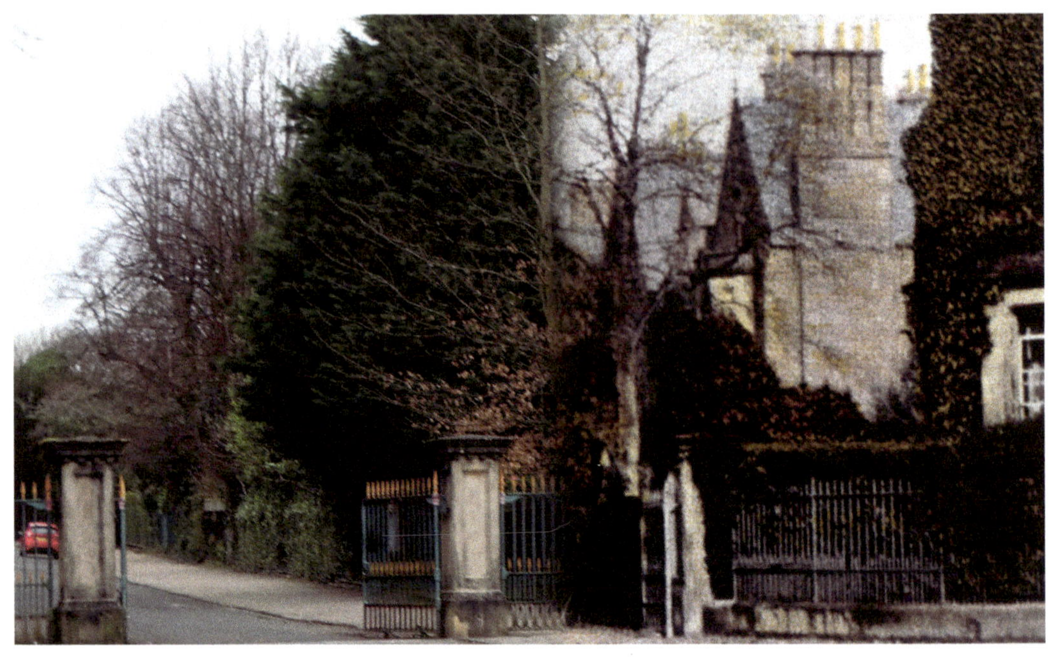

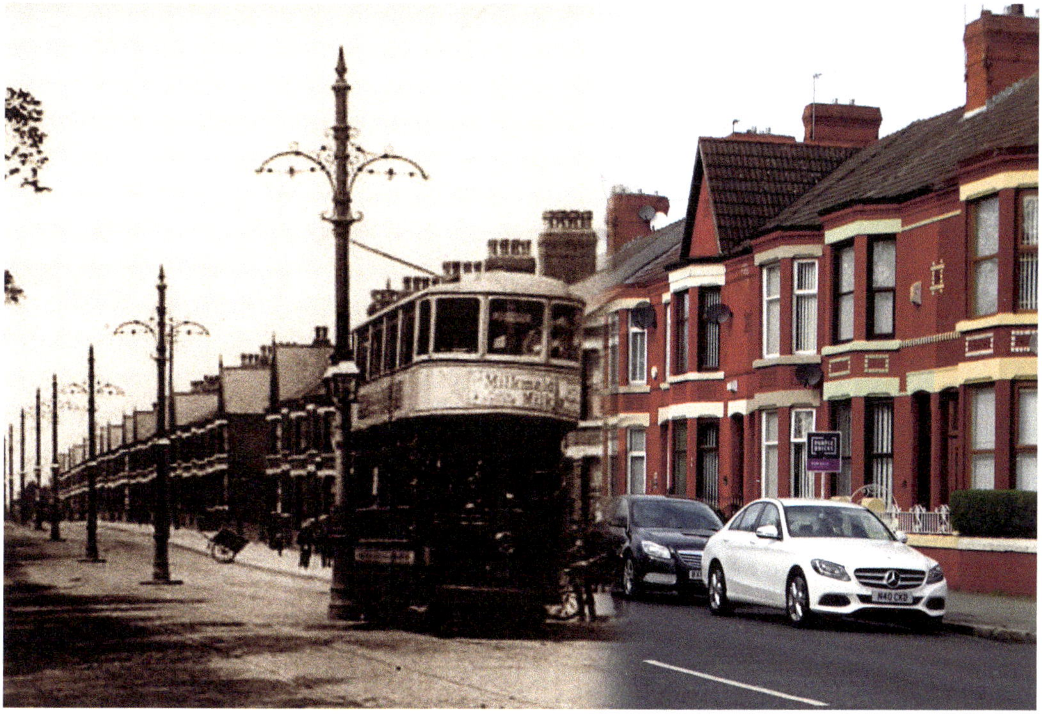

A Woodside-bound tram stops in Park Road North to allow passengers to alight.

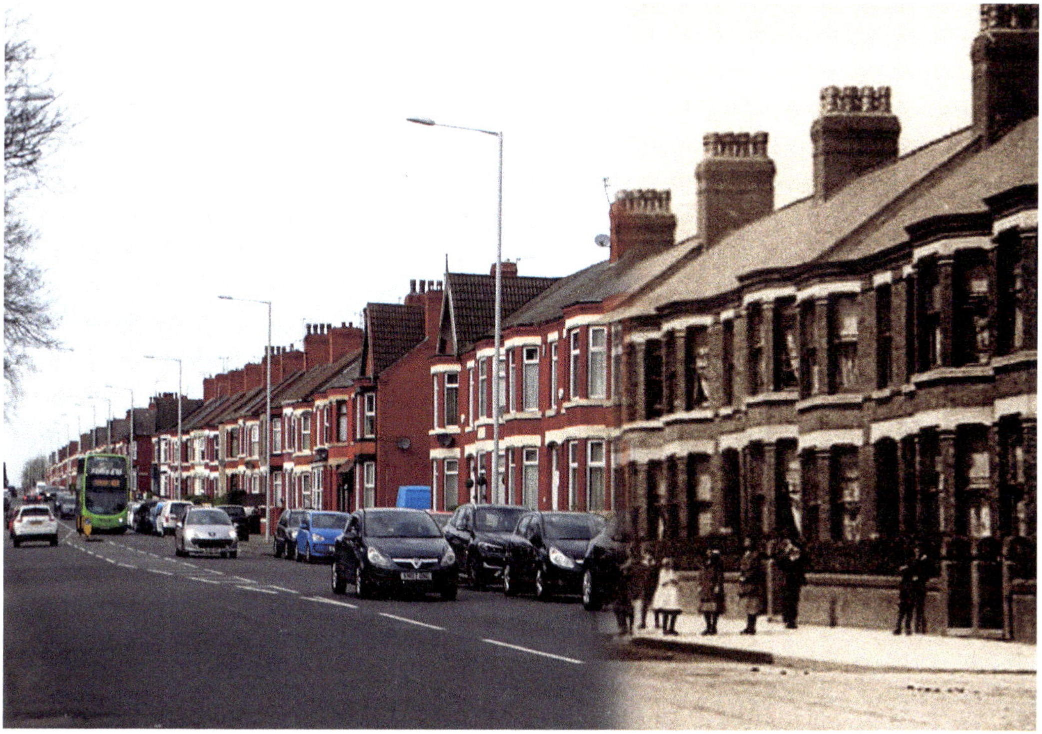

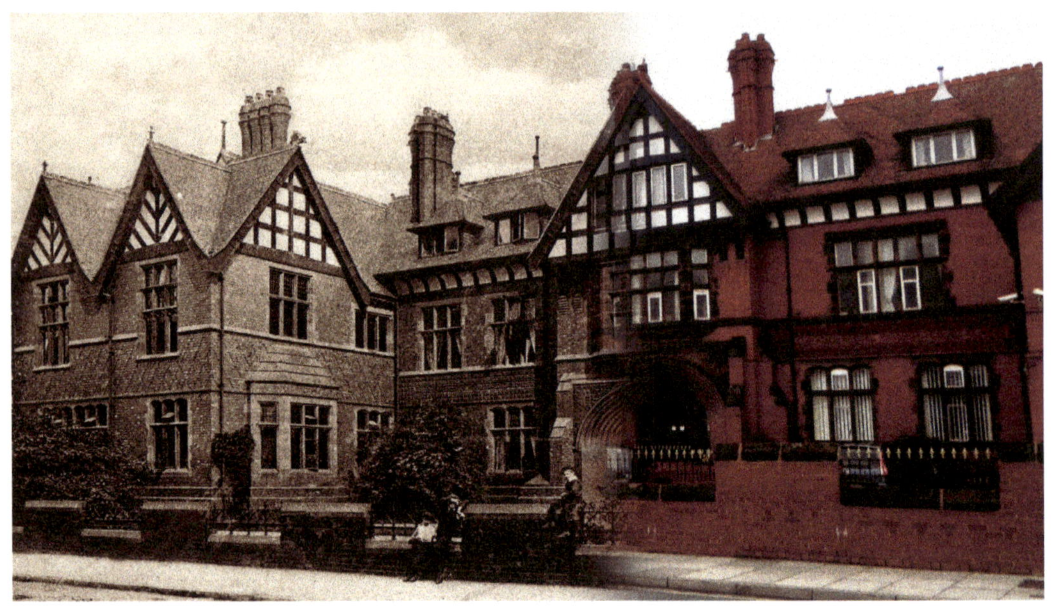

Birkenhead Children's Hospital

The Wirral Dispensary and Hospital for Sick Children was originally opened in Wilkinson Street in 1869, moving to Oxton Road in 1872 and to the Woodchurch Road site in 1883. From 1898 until just after the Second World War the hospital was known as the Birkenhead and Wirral Children's Hospital. It was supported by voluntary subscriptions until the formation of the National Health Service in 1948, when it came under the control of the Birkenhead HMC, and subsequently in 1974 of the Wirral Area Health Authority. It closed in January 1982, when the services were transferred to the new Arrowe Park Hospital.

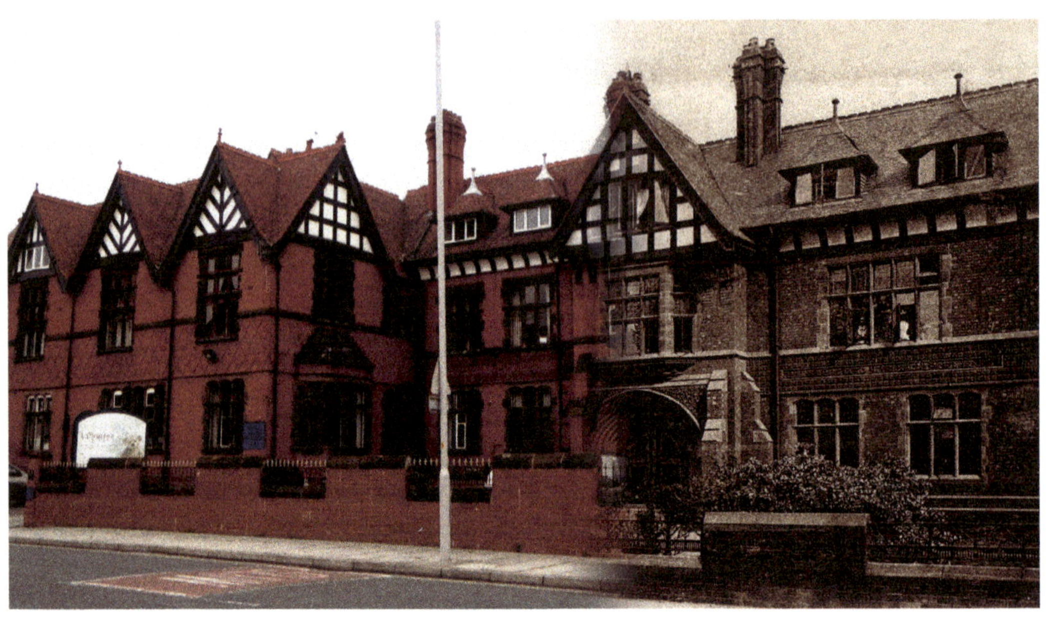

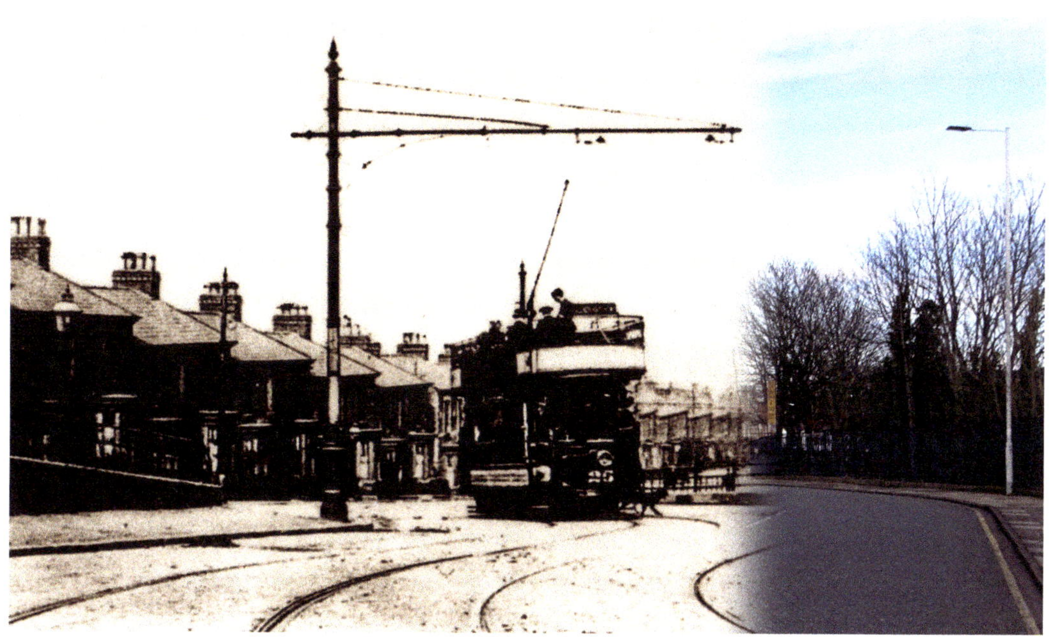

Pearson Road

Pearson Road, Tranmere, is at the top of the hill leading down Argyle Street South to Borough Road and Birkenhead Central station. The residents have a view down to Cammell Laird's shipyard, the River Mersey and Liverpool docks. It was often used as a playground for local children in the winter after a heavy snowfall.

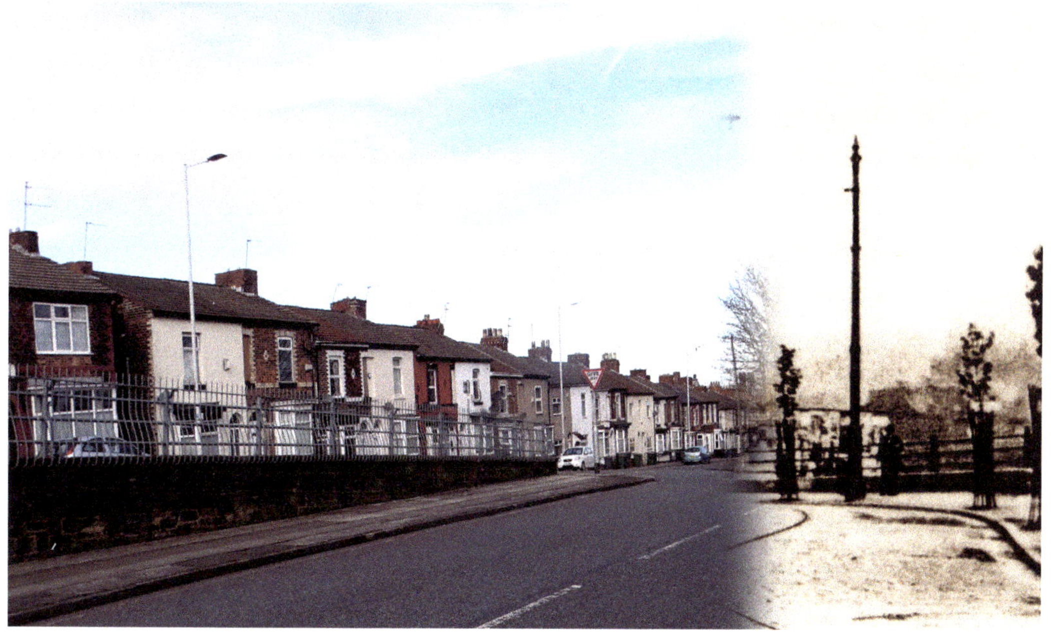

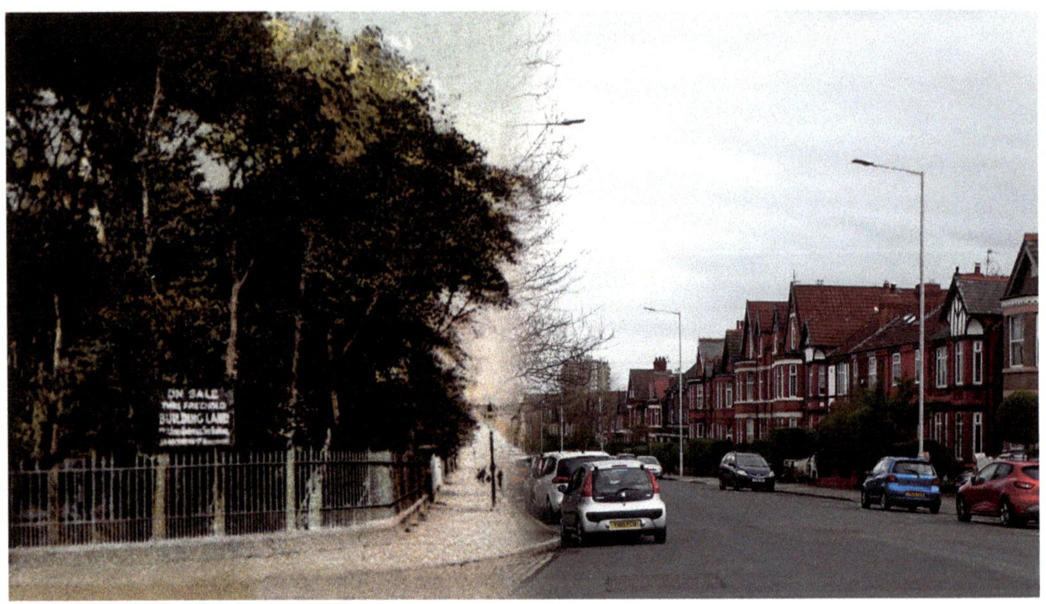

Park Road East

Four houses on the 1875 Ordnance Survey map were newly built when the map was surveyed. They were named Claremont, The Laurels, Elmslea and Thornbury. The first recorded occupants in 1876 were, respectively, Robert Thompson, shipowner; Charles Timmis, grocer; Edward Deurden, lard manufacturer; and William Wild, cotton broker. At some point, possibly during the Second World War, Claremont and The Laurels were amalgamated into one property, known as The Laurels. In 1948, The Laurels were used by a Royal Engineer field squadron, not to be confused with 113 Assault Regiment Royal Engineers which was at Harrowby Road Drill Hall. In late 1964 the building was acquired by the Education Department and became an annexe to the Laird School of Art.

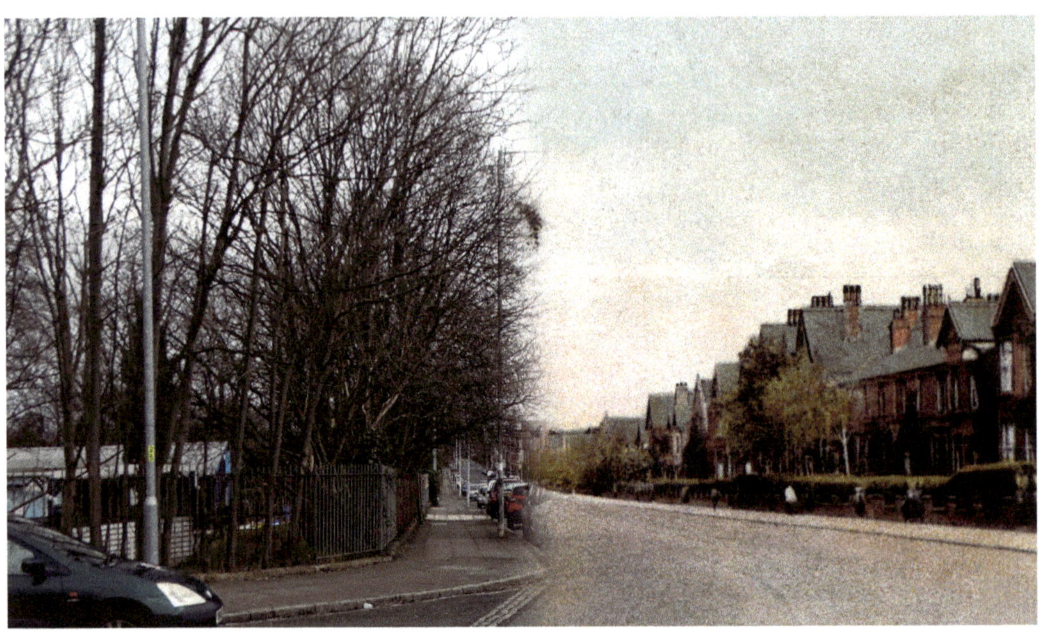

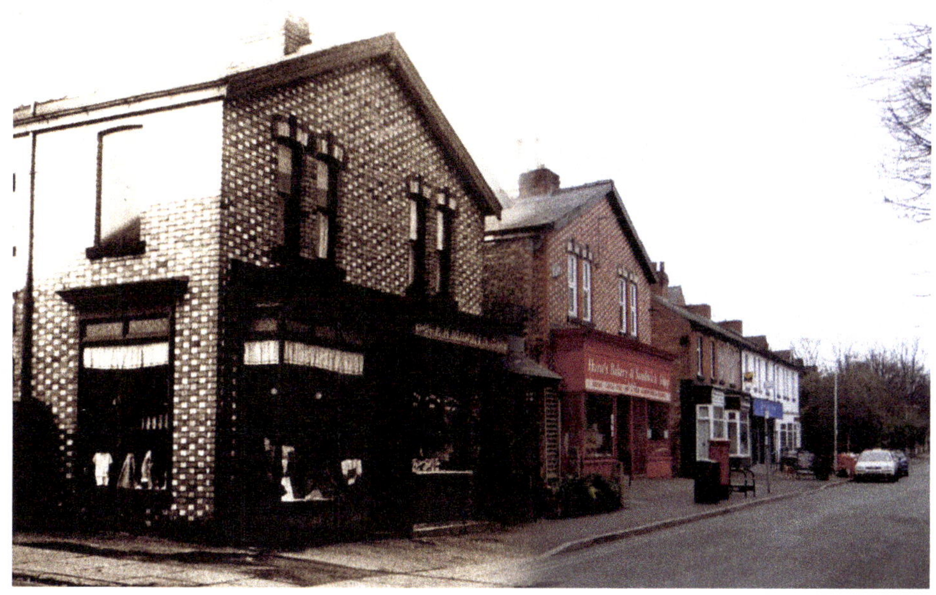

Shops, Wellington Road

Shops in Wellington Road, at the junction with Silverdale Road, Oxton, Birkenhead. Wellington Road was named after the Duke of Wellington. However, it was known by that name before his death, and it must be concluded that it was named in his honour rather than in his memory. At the time of his death in 1852 there were only two houses recorded there. One was the home of Richard Scolefield, who was a wool broker, and the other was owned by William Tyson, described as a shareholder of joint stock. By 1871 the two houses were named as Apsley Villa and Field House. Apsley House was the London home of the Duke of Wellington and Apsley Villa is still standing. However, Field House was destroyed by bombing in the Second World War.

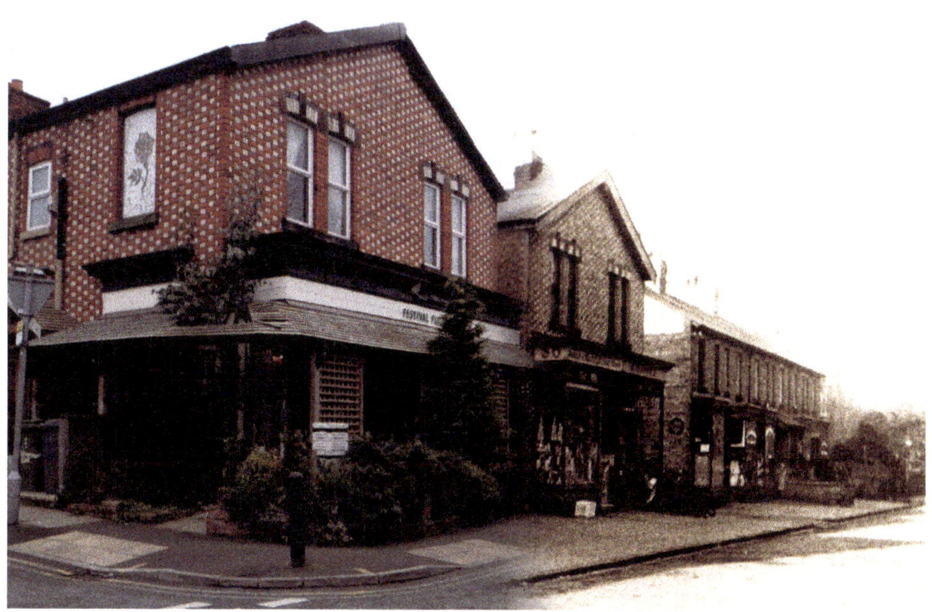

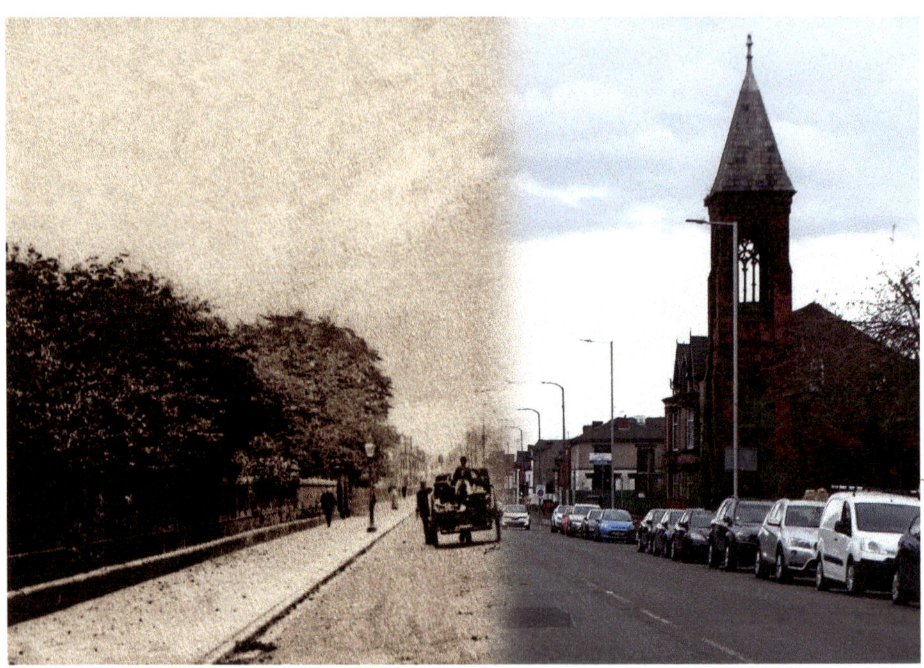

Park Road South, 1911

The church on the right was the Catholic Apostolic Church, built in 1875 and purchased by the Church of Christ and opened on 12 May 1951. It was destroyed by a serious fire in June 2009. No. 2 Park Road South is a house, later used as offices, in stone with a Welsh slate roof. Nos 8 and 10 are a pair of houses, also with Welsh slate roofs, in two storeys and attics. Nos 90 and 92 are a pair of ashlar-faced houses with a concrete-tiled roof in two storeys and with a six-bay front with the central two bays projecting forward.

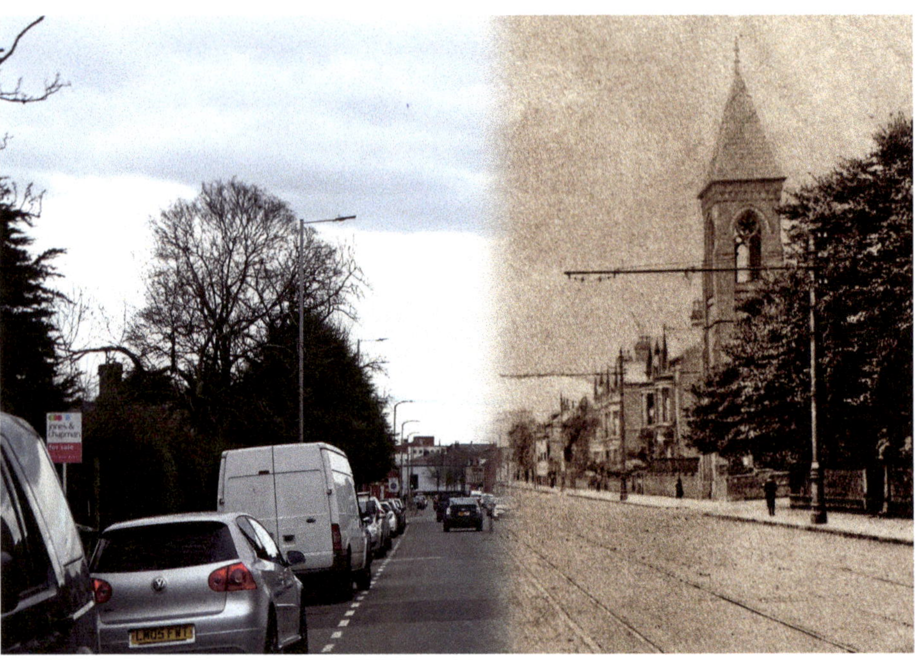

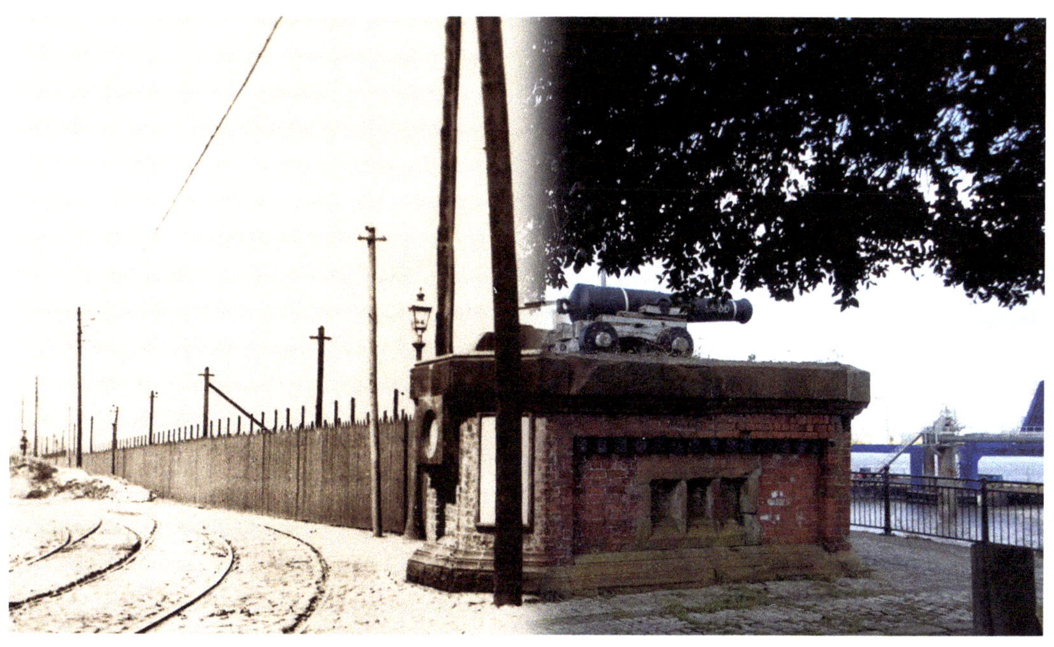

One O'clock Gun, Morpeth Dock

On 18 July 1969 the 102-year tradition of firing the gun at one o'clock ended. The Naval Hotchkiss gun at Morpeth Dock had been loaded by Mersey Docks & Harbour Board staff employed at nearby Woodside Landing Stage, but a restructuring had meant that they were no longer available to carry out these duties. The actual firing had been by remote control from Liverpool University's Tidal Institute, better known as Bidston Observatory. The original cannon was a relic of the Crimean War and it was first proposed to discontinue the practice in 1932. This did not happen, although firing was suspended during the Second World War.

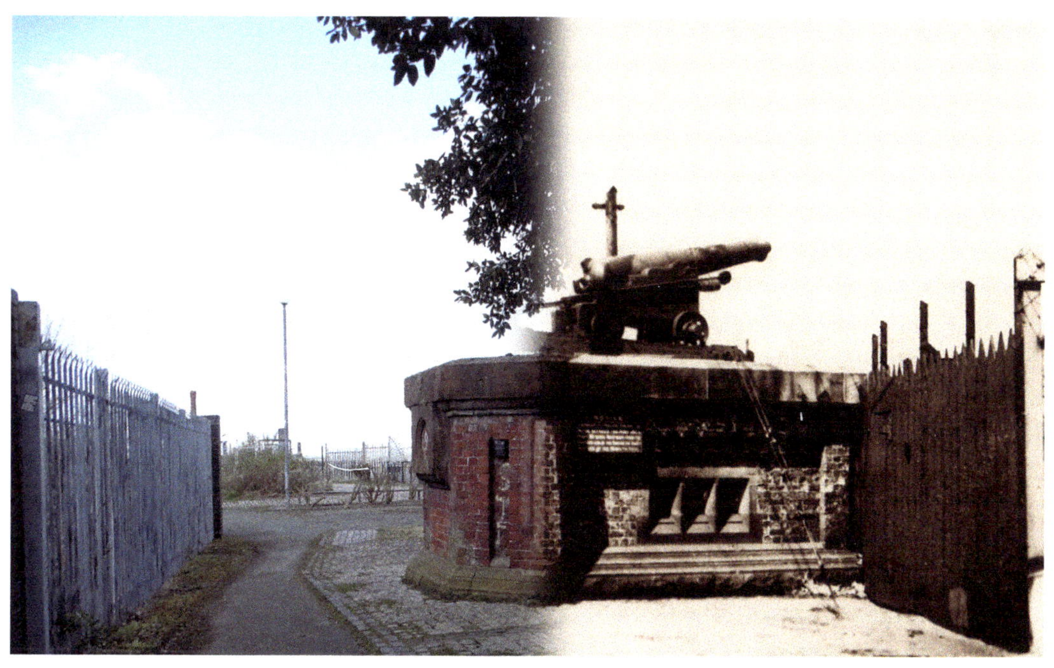

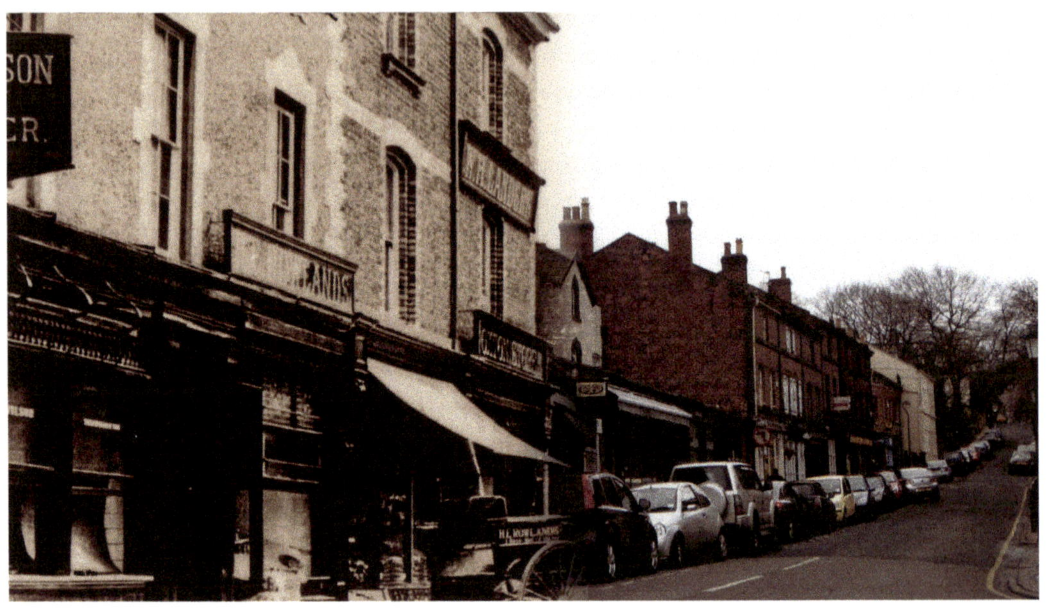

H. E. Rowland's, Rose Mount

The poulterer H. E. Rowlands with delivery carriage parked outside their premises at Rose Mount, Oxton. The other shops are Arthur Rowlands, fruiterer; Selves, confectioner; J. S. Cooke, boot repairer; F. Tutty, ironmonger; Miss White, milliner; J. Fletcher, grocer; Bertha Young, draper; M. Crowhurst, confectioner; M. Jones, greengrocer; M. Wharton; E. Parker, newsagent; and C. Cameron, confectioner.

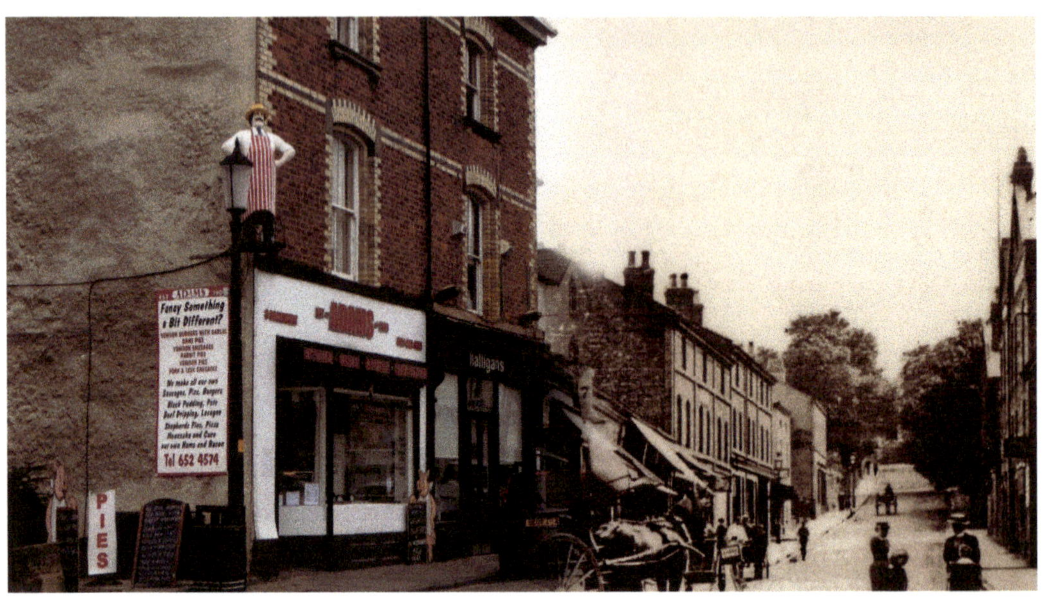

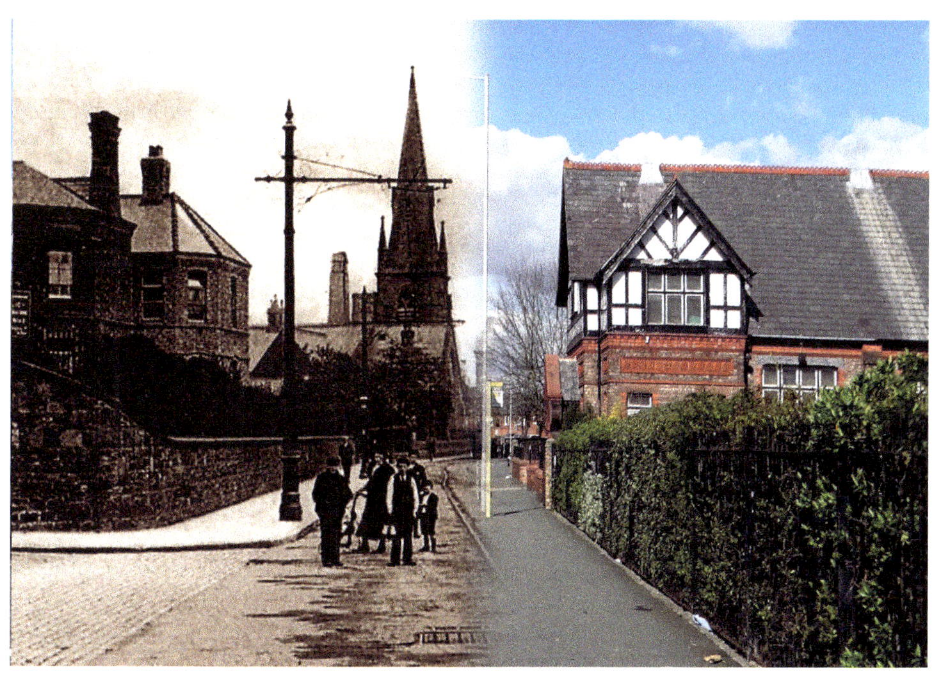

St Catherine's Church, Tranmere

St Catherine's Church was founded in 1831 on land donated by W. Hough. Previously worshipers had to walk to St Andrew's Church in Bebington. In the 1870s the building was altered and improved, with the addition of a spire. The Birkenhead Union Workhouse is on the left of the photograph, which was opened in 1864. On the right is the St Catherine's Church Institute, which was erected in 1892 and comprised of two halls seating over 600 people. The workhouse is now St Catherine's Community Hospital, and the Institute is a public hall.

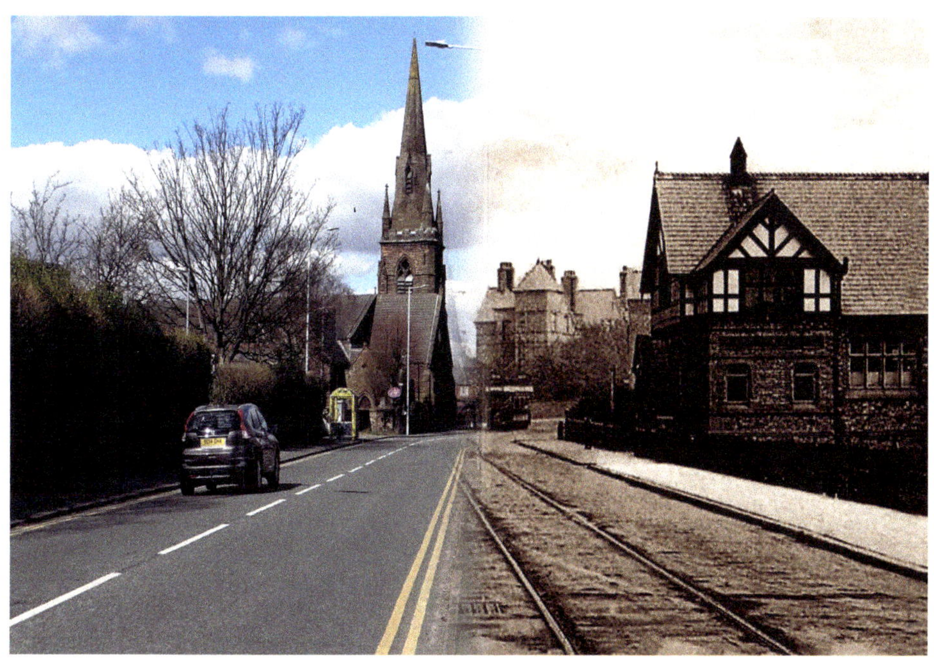

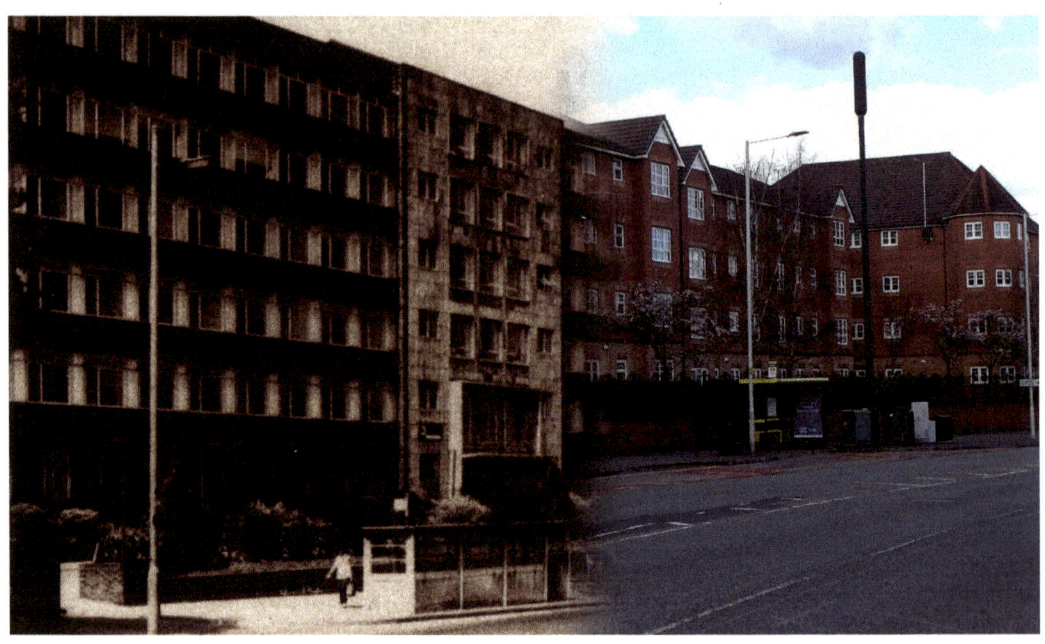

Birkenhead Technical College, Borough Road

A Technical School was proposed as far back as 1866, and plans were prepared in 1913. The First World War followed and land was finally acquired in 1930. The Second World War again delayed plans, which were finally agreed by the Minister of Education in 1949. Her Majesty Queen Elizabeth the Queen Mother laid the foundation stone on 3 May 1950 and the building was handed over on 5 October 1954. The college offered full- and part-time day and evening courses in a wide range of technical and commercial subjects, with emphasis given to courses related to the main industries and occupations in the area. It survived until 2005, when it was demolished and replaced by a housing development.

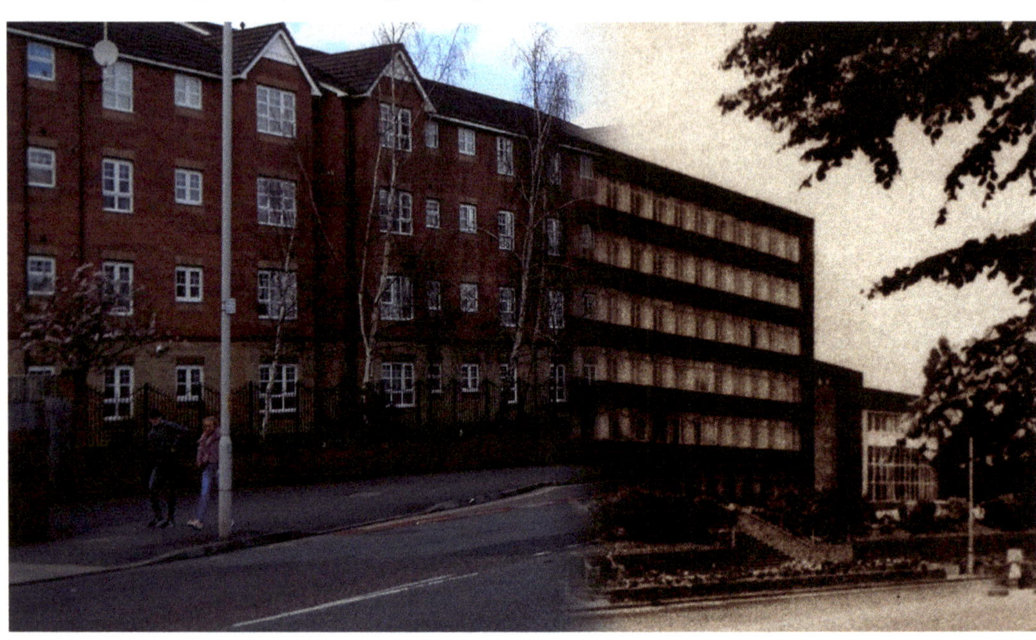

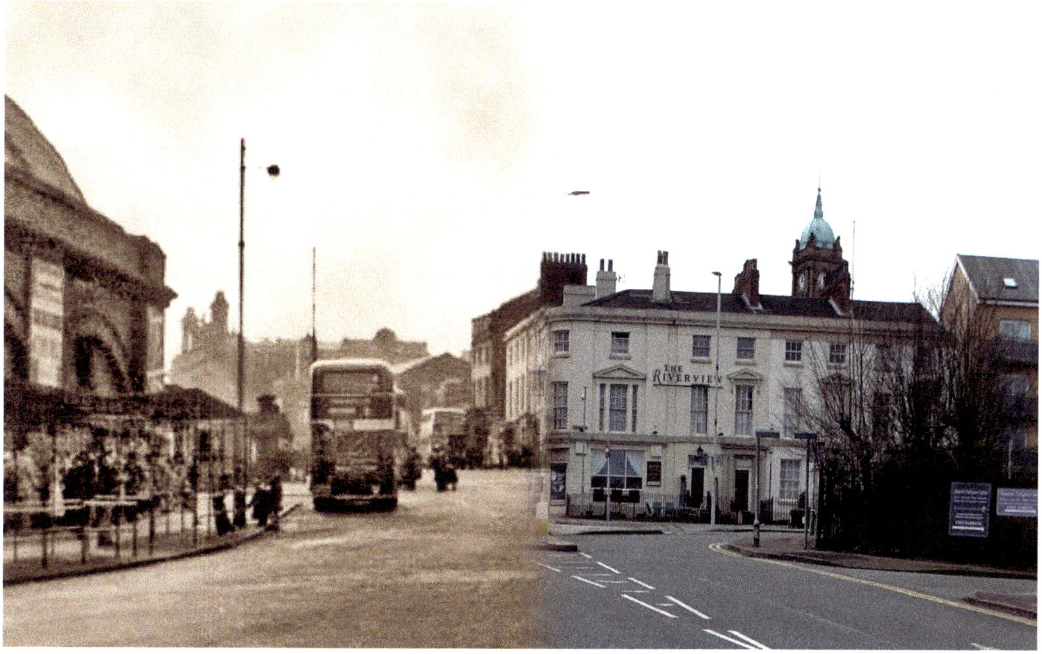

Crosville Buses Loading Passengers, Woodside

Birkenhead Corporation and Crosville buses connected with Birkenhead ferries from Liverpool and trains arriving at Woodside Mainline station and Hamilton Square railway station. This view is from Woodside bus station looking towards Birkenhead Town Hall. Woodside railway station is on the left, with a Crosville bus leaving the terminal bound for Chester.

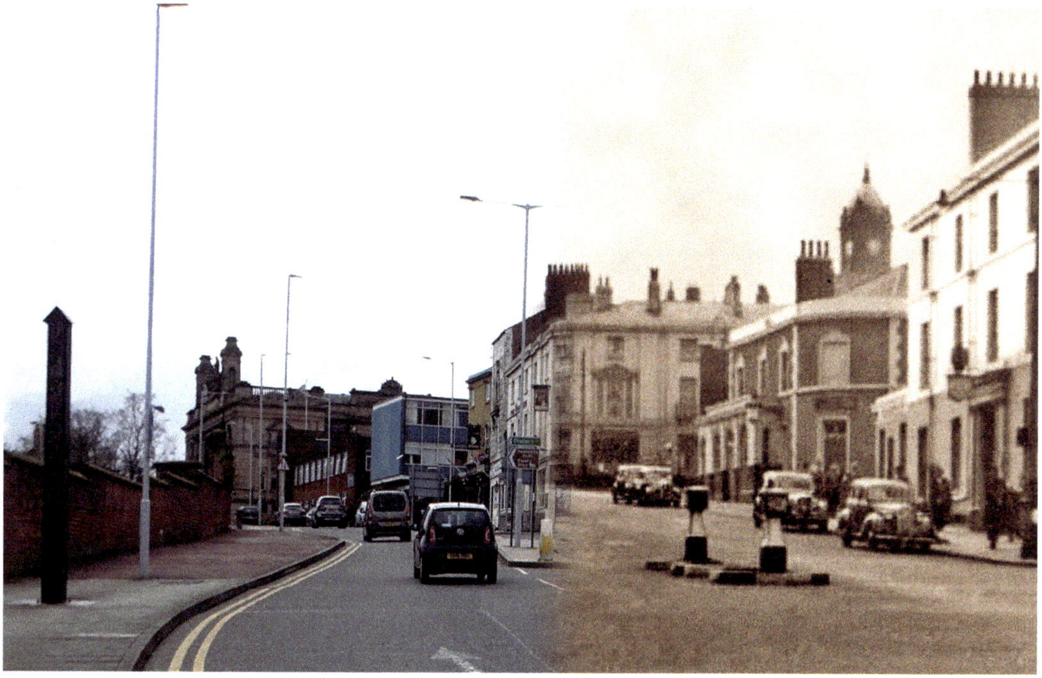

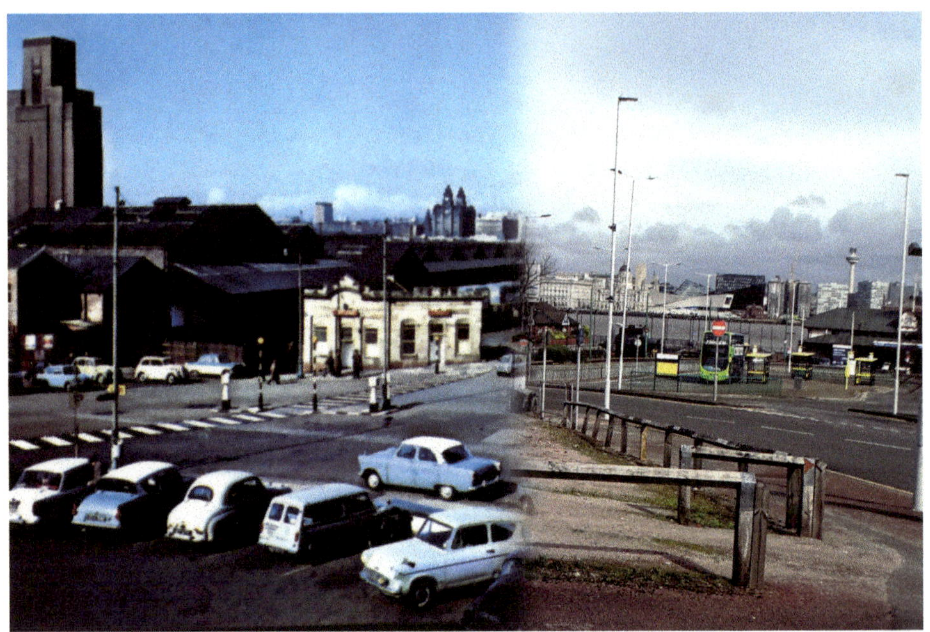

Bus Station and Ferry Entrance, Woodside

The Three Graces at Liverpool Pier Head can be seen across the River Mersey and the ventilation tower of the Mersey road tunnel is on the left. The photograph is taken from the front of the Woodside Hotel, which was built in 1834 to replace an earlier building of the same name. It was damaged by fire on 4 June 2008 and 13 August that year and was declared structurally unsafe. The hotel was then demolished, without planning permission, in October 2008.

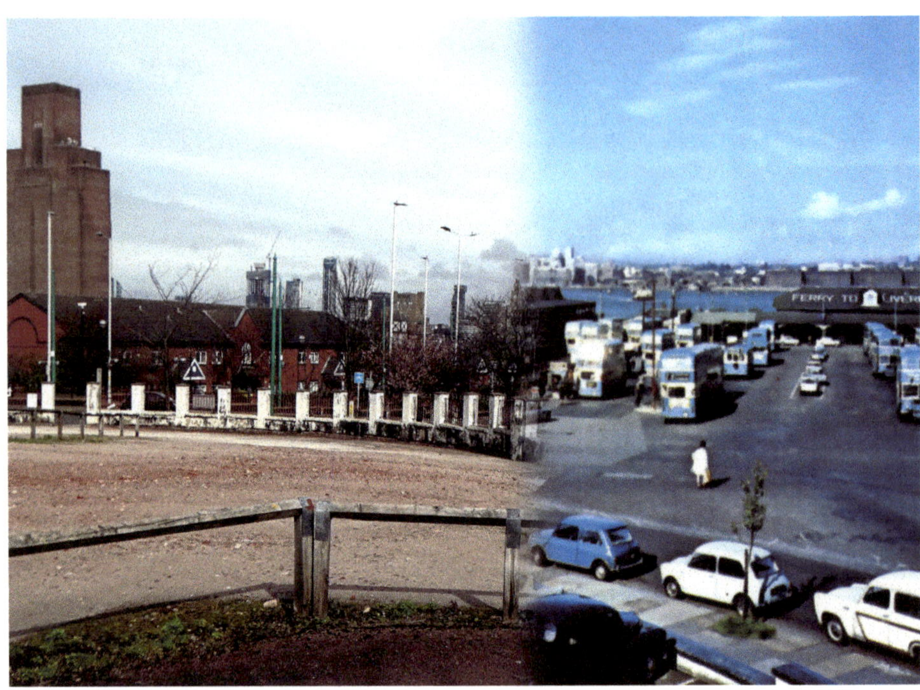

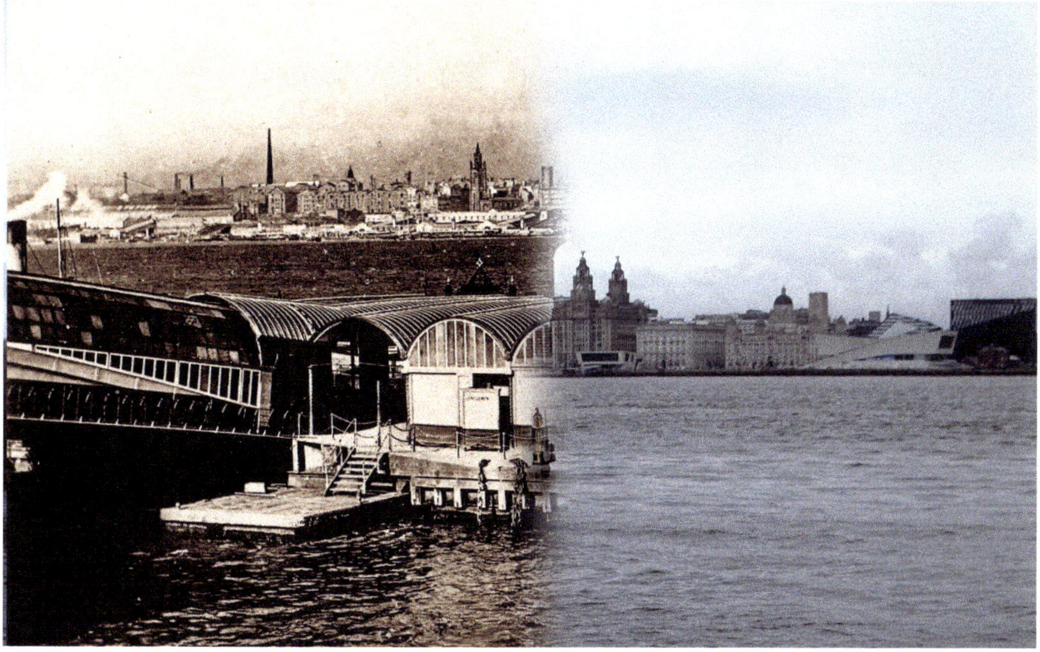

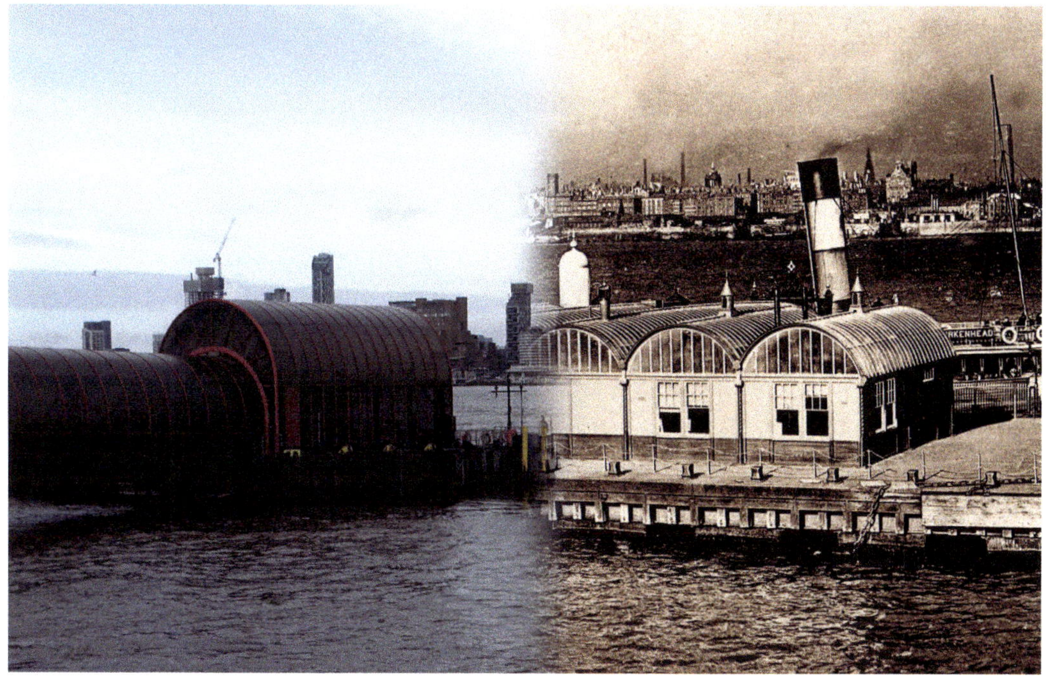

Woodside–Liverpool Ferry, Woodside Landing Stage

The floating stage was installed in 1862 and a floating roadway was built six years later to enable vehicles to travel across the river. However, the service had difficulty coping with the increasing demand in the early years of the twentieth century and it was announced that a vehicle tunnel would be built under the river. The Mersey Tunnel was opened in 1934 and the vehicle ferry service was closed in 1939.

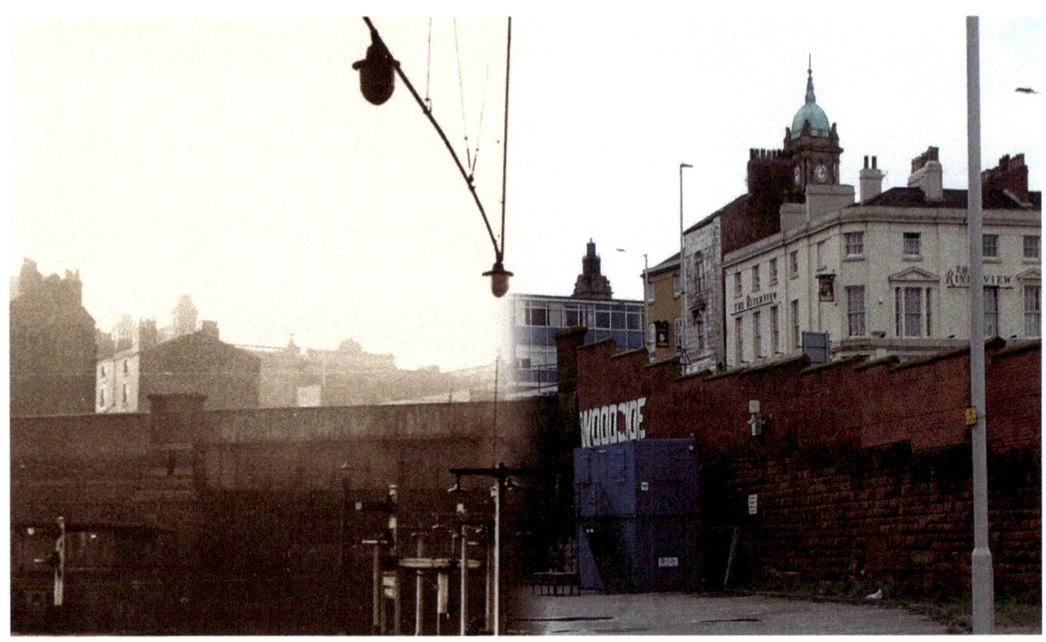

Woodside Railway Station

The station at Monks Ferry was closed in 1878 and the passenger services were transferred to Woodside station. The station was opened on 1 April that year when it became the terminus for the Birkenhead to Chester line. Work on the Chester & Birkenhead Railway began in 1838 and a single line was opened in September 1840. The Birkenhead terminal was built in Grange Lane, which was an equal distance from Woodside, Monks Ferry and Woodside ferries. Woodside station survived until 6 November 1967, when it was closed. A section of the site is now a car park for buses.

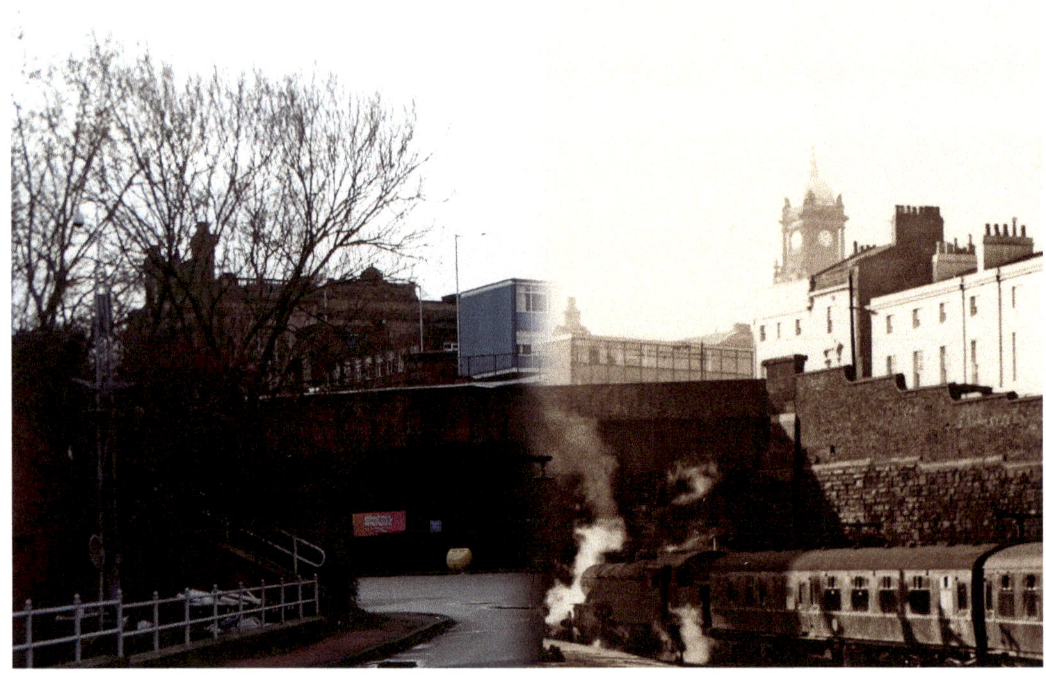

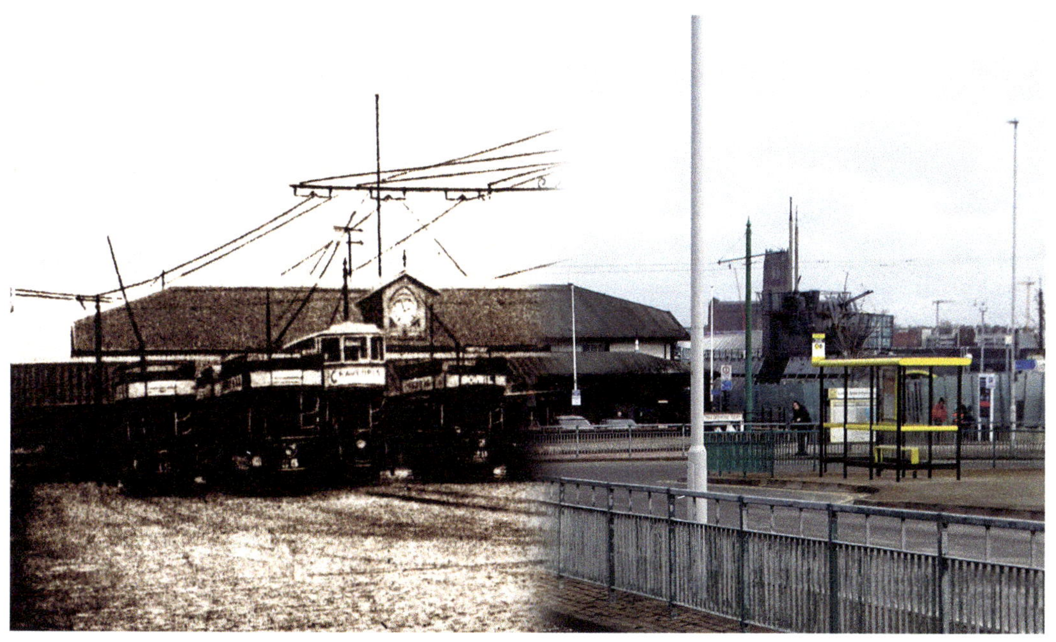

Woodside Ferry Terminal

In 1990 Mersey ferries announced that the 'Ferry 'cross the Mersey' would be at the heart of the new range of services where passengers would be able to step on board at Liverpool Pier Head, Wallasey (Seacombe) or Birkenhead (Woodside) for a fascinating forty-five-minute river cruise. A lively commentary brings to life the stories of the river and the ferries which are the oldest of their kind in Europe, as well as the unfolding river scene, including, of course, one of the most memorable waterfronts. Passengers have the choice of staying on board for the round trip or getting off at Seacombe, Woodside or the Pier Head. There are now interesting attractions at all three terminals.

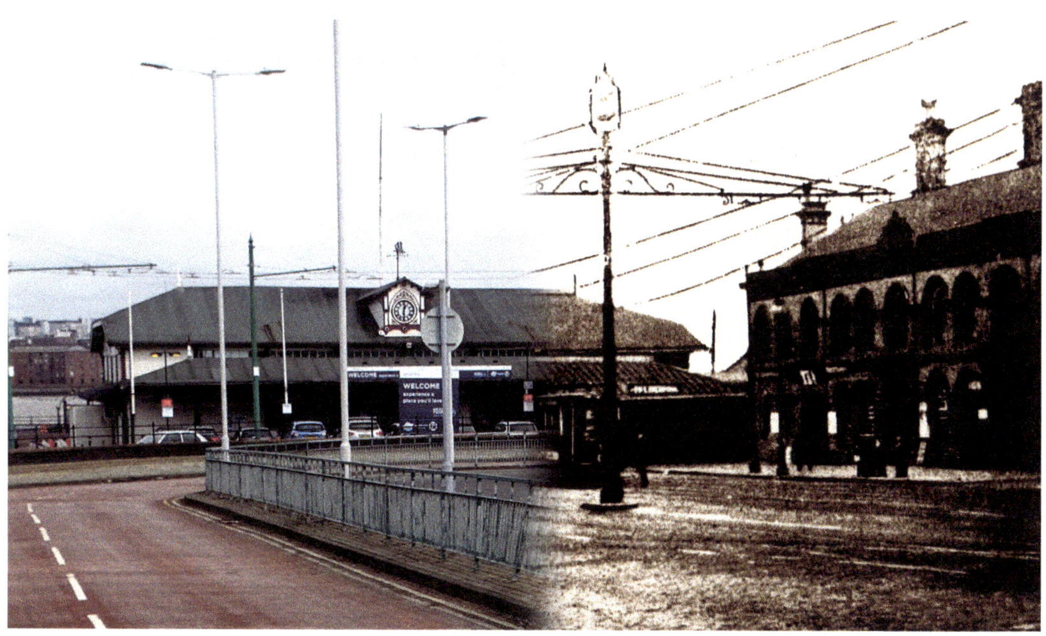

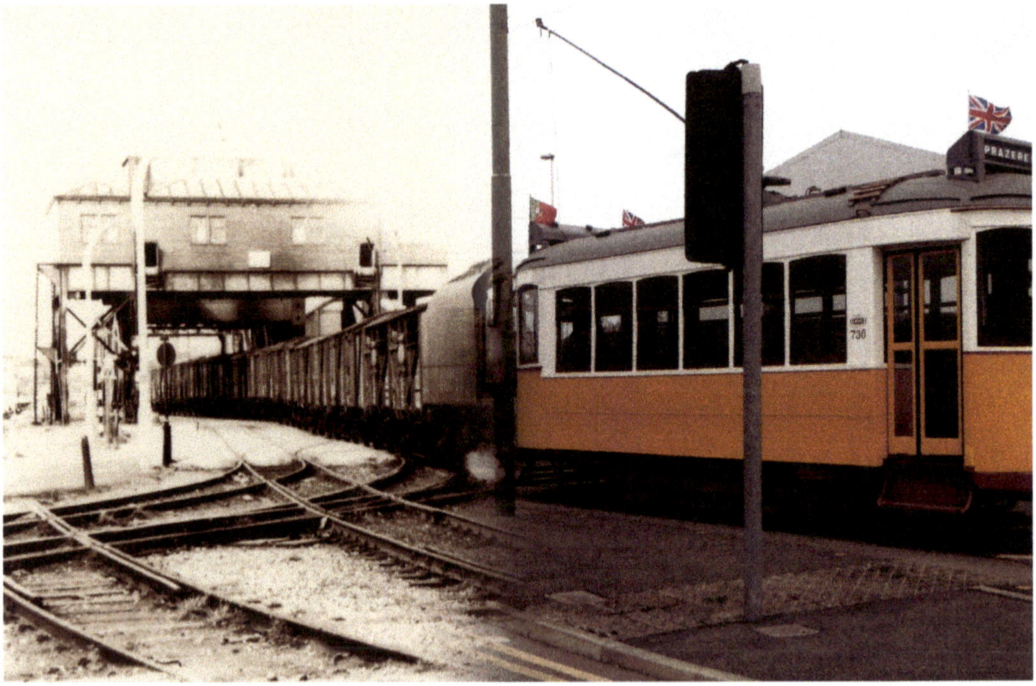

Egerton Bridge

Locomotive 92160 leads a freight train over Egerton Bridge on 9 September 1966, and a tram which now operates from Woodside to the tram depot in Taylor Street as a tourist attraction at weekends.

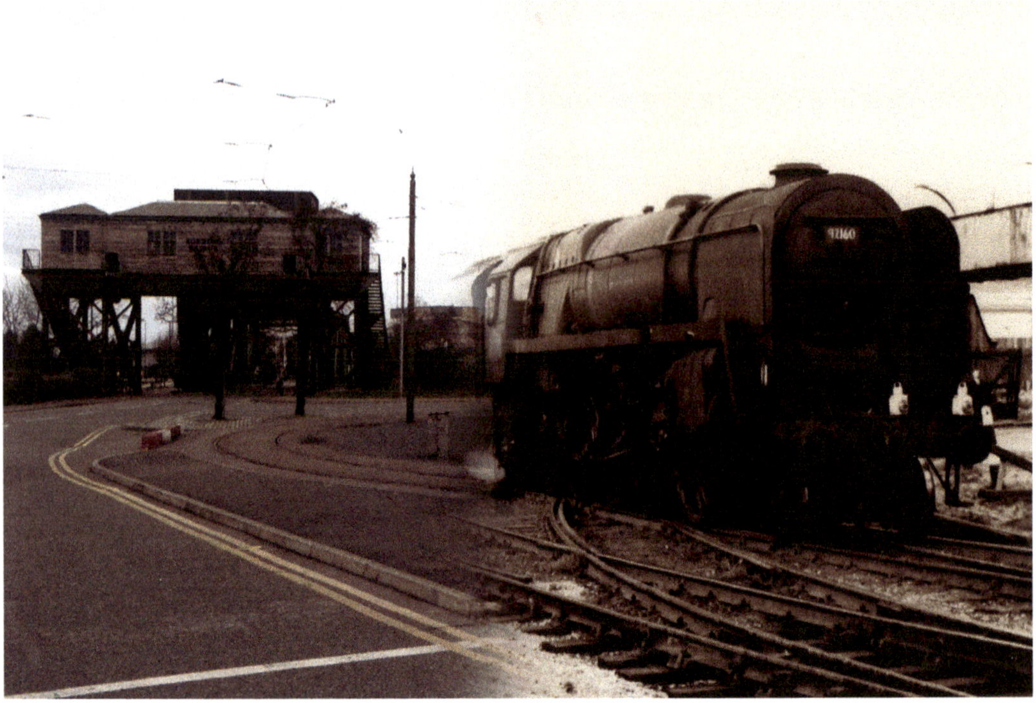

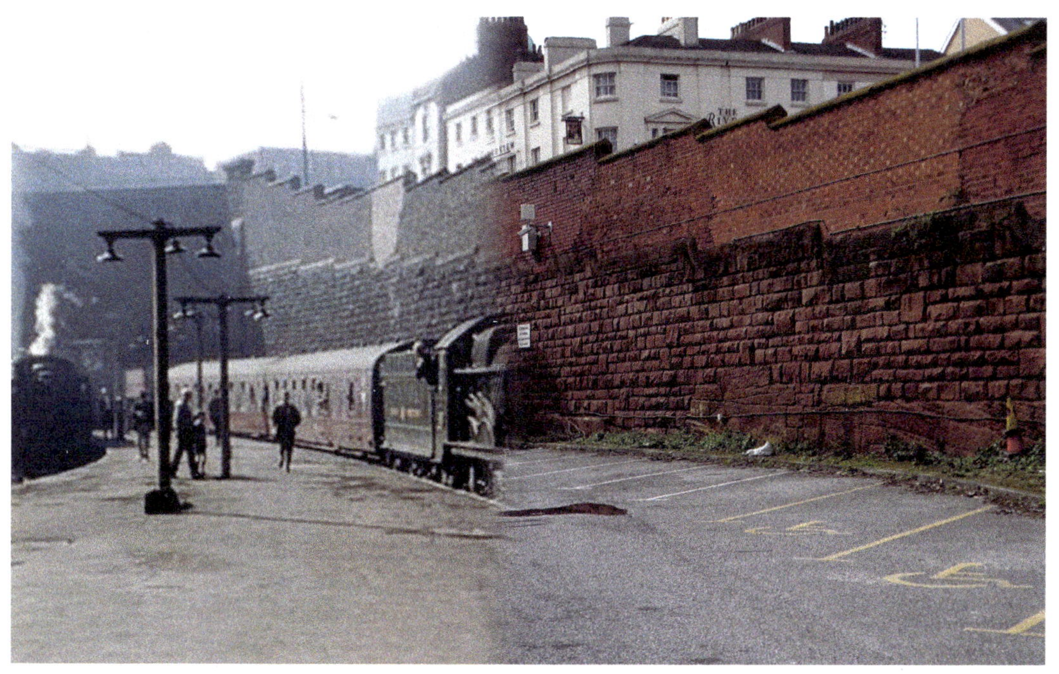

Woodside Station

A train from Chester arrives at Woodside station. The railway linked London with the South West and west of England, the Midlands and most of Wales. Trains ran from Birkenhead Woodside station to Chester and London Paddington. The town hall and the Birkenhead police headquarters can be seen behind the bridge. The police headquarters in Mortimer/Chester Street was opened on 30 October 1953 by Sir David Maxwell Fyfe, then Secretary of State for the Home Department, and it was extended by the addition of an extra wing in 1956.

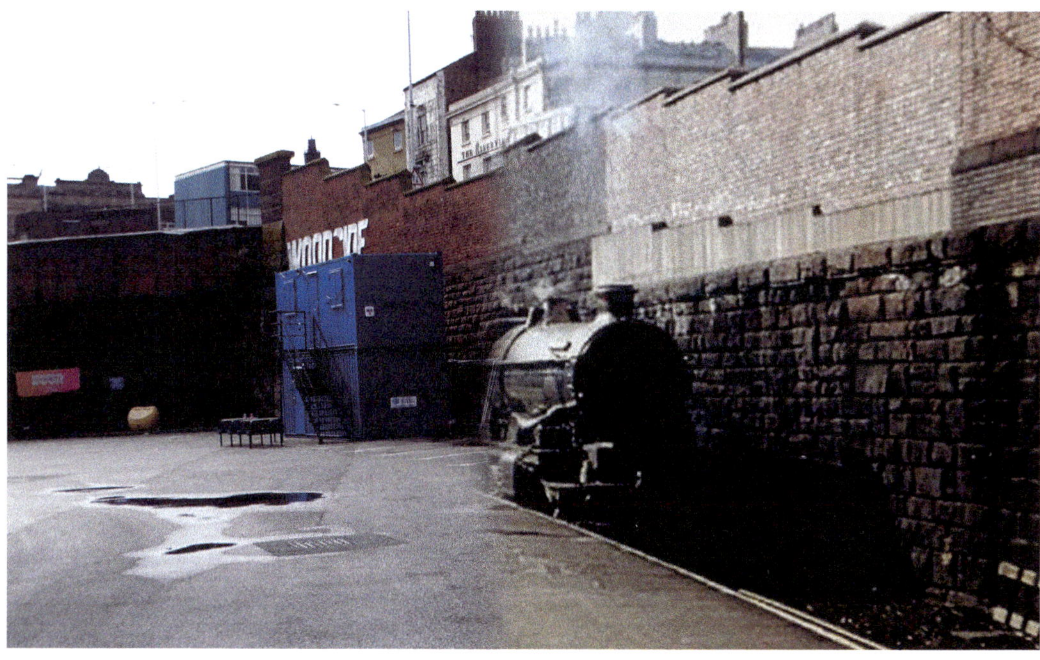

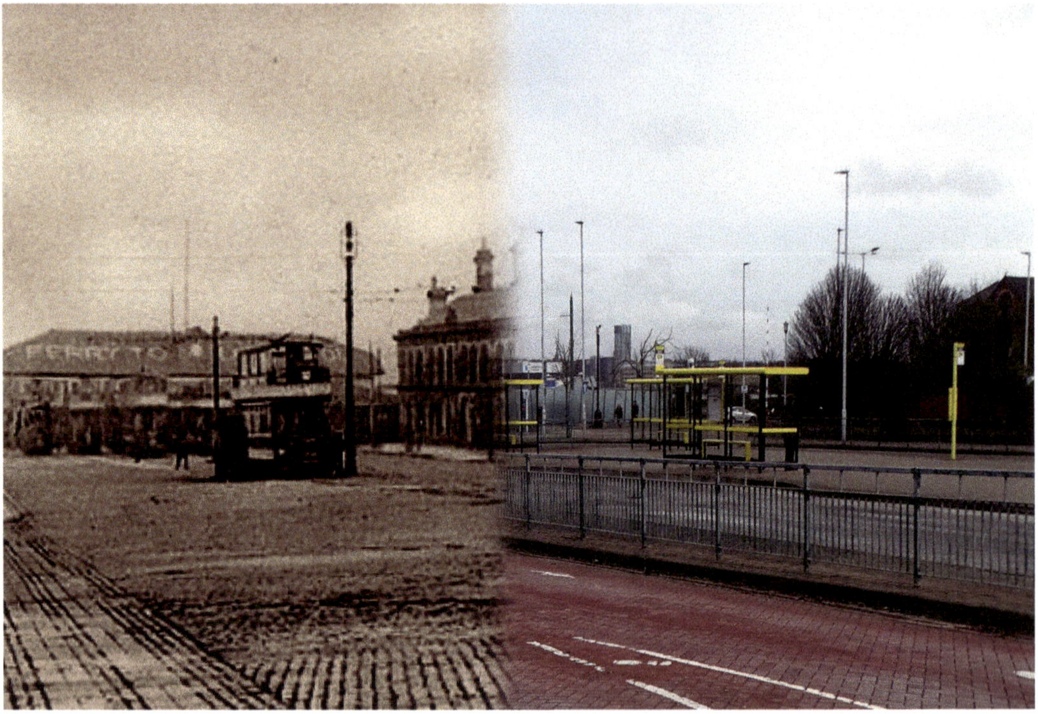

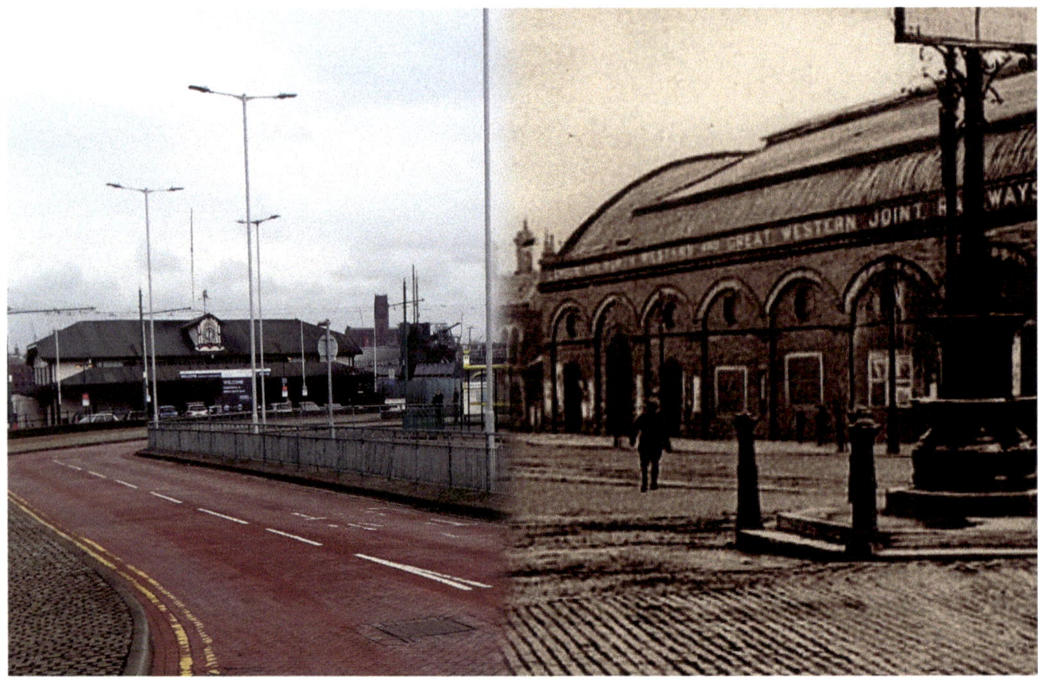

Woodside Ferry Terminal and Tram Station

As a wooden construction on brick foundations, the 1864 booking hall is a listed building. It remains unaltered, and was refurbished from 1985 in the original style, with many of the original timbers being replaced.

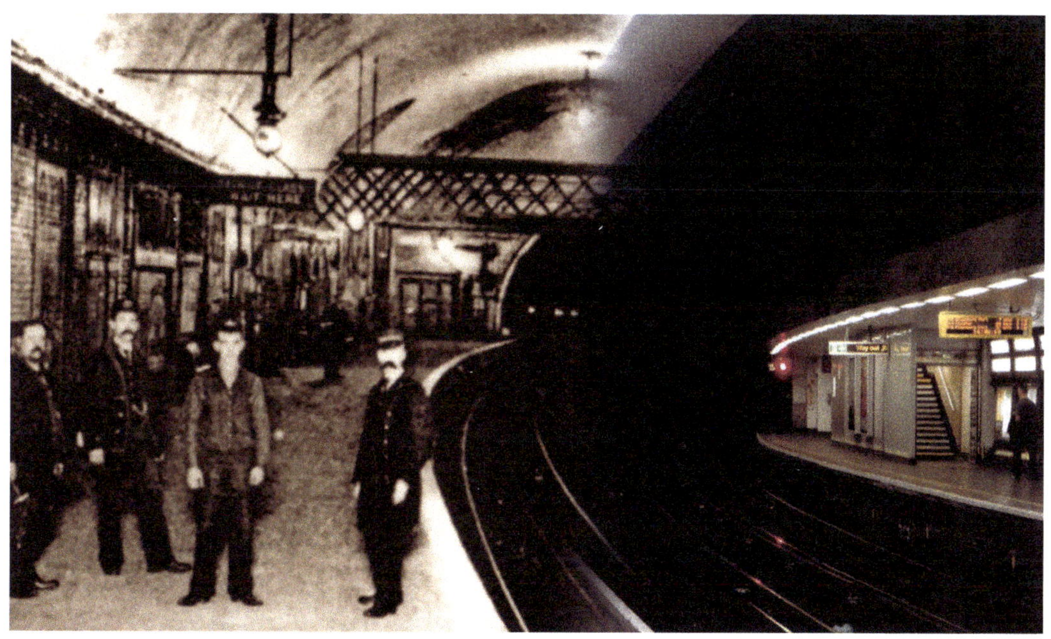

Platforms 1 and 2, Hamilton Square Station

The Prince of Wales opened the line from James Street in Liverpool to Hamilton Square and Green Lane in 1886. The track was extended to Birkenhead Park, West Kirby and New Brighton in 1888, Rock Ferry in 1891, and the following year Central station, in Liverpool City Centre, was opened. The trains were propelled by steam engines initially, with the steam and smoke polluting the underground stations. The railway was on the verge of bankruptcy due to the low patronage caused by the choking atmosphere created by the steam engines. However, in 1903 the system was electrified, becoming the world's first electric railway.

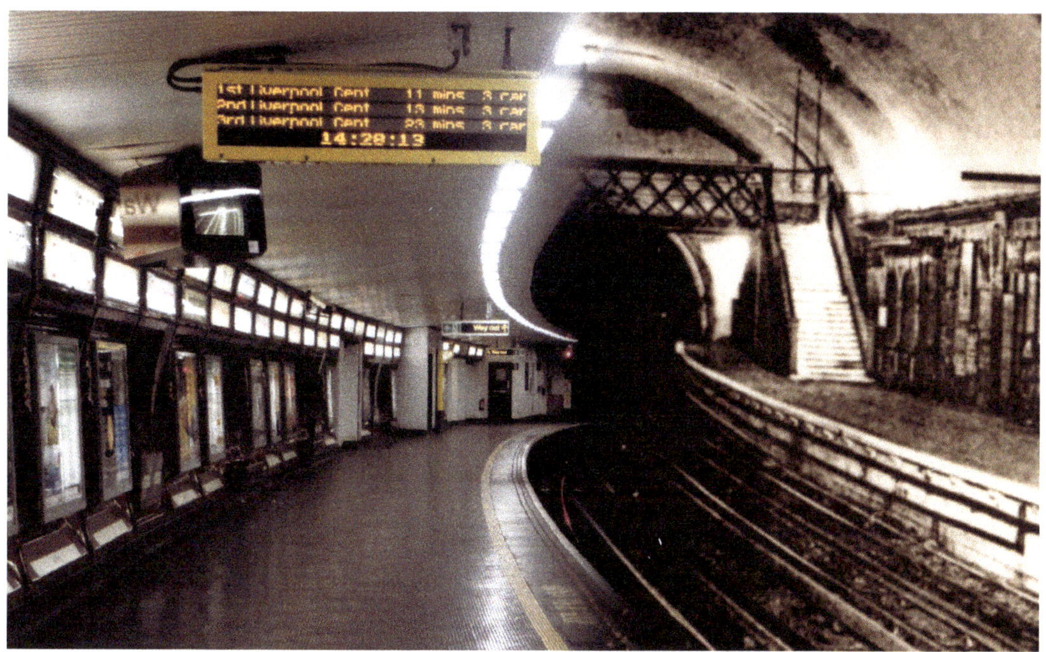

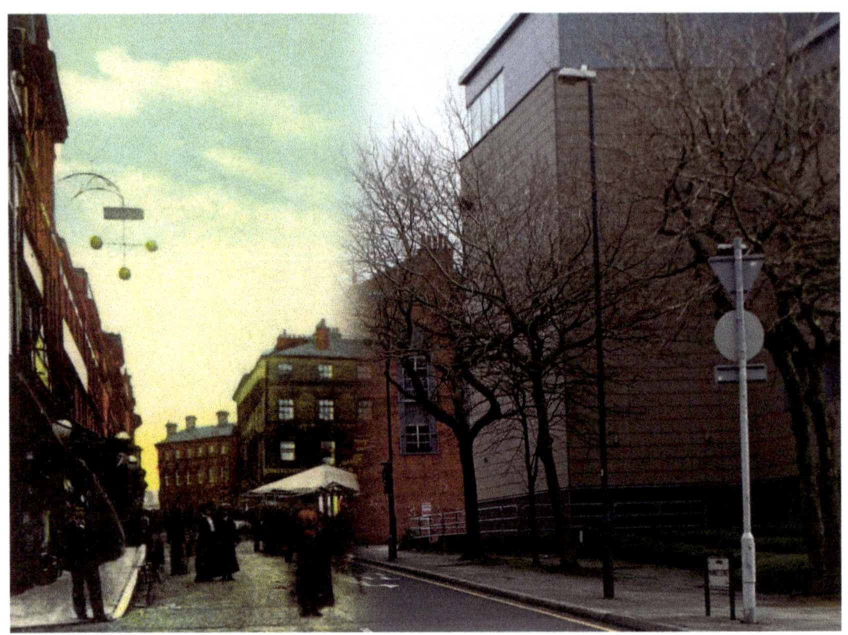

Outside Stalls, Birkenhead Market

The market was opened on 12 July 1845, replacing one built ten years earlier. The work was completed by Fox, Henderson and Co., who later worked on the Crystal Palace. The building was 430 feet long and 131 feet wide, and was situated between Hamilton and Albion Street. The market housed forty-two shops and eighty stalls, and was constructed of brick, glass and iron with a wrought-iron roof, supported by cast-iron columns. The building was extended in 1909 and was partly destroyed by fire in 1974. A new market was later erected in 1977 near the shopping centre in Grange Road.

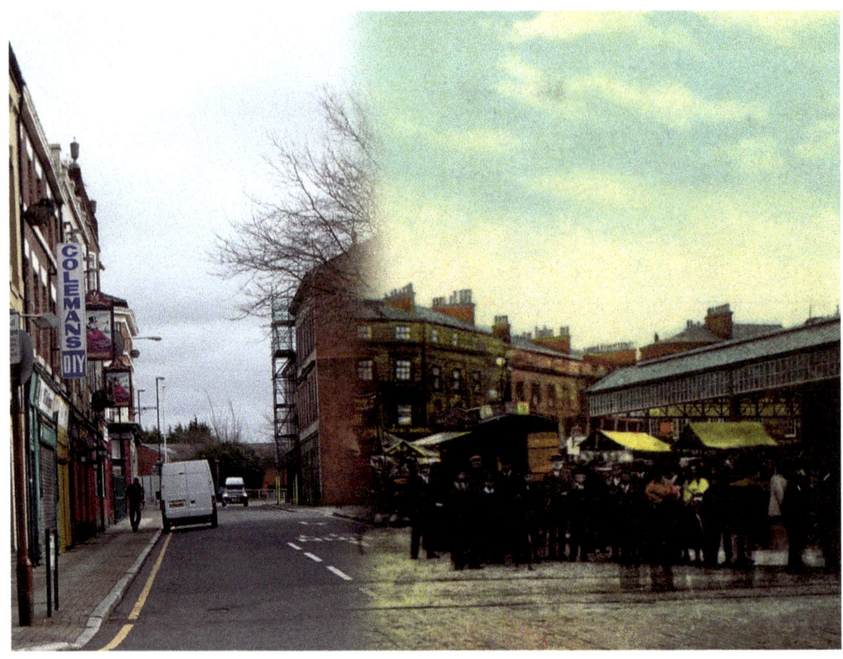

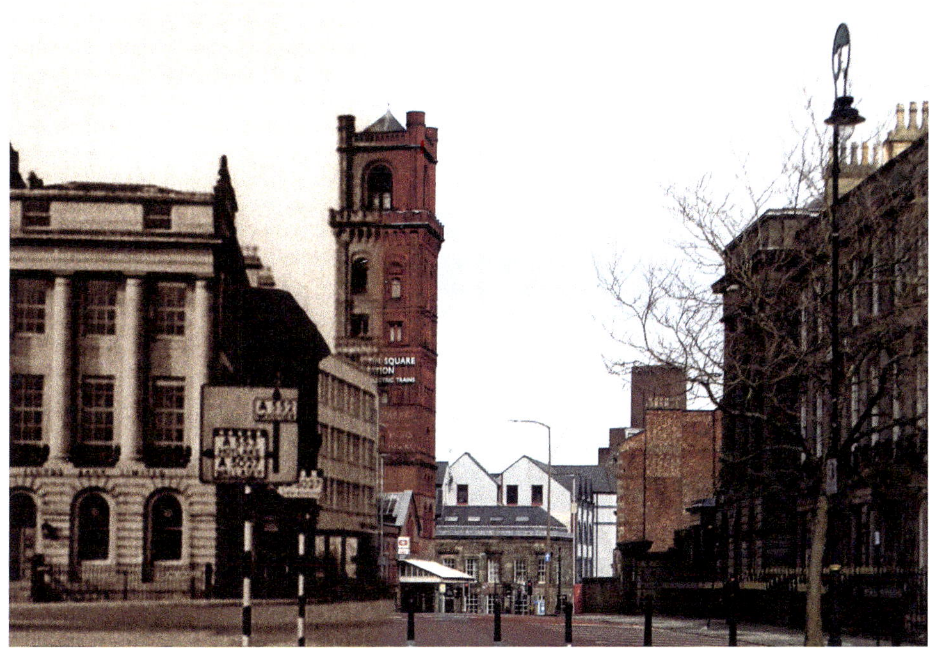

Hamilton Square and Station Entrance

Three lifts, each capable of carrying 150 passengers from top to the platform in thirty seconds, were provided at the station. Leaving James Street, the railway dips down under the riverbed, and rises again to Hamilton Square, where the station is 110 feet below the street level. The river section of the journey from James Street, Liverpool to Hamilton Square takes two and a half minutes, and the journey from the Liverpool Terminus to Rock Ferry, a distance of 3 ½ miles, with four intermediate stops, takes eleven minutes.

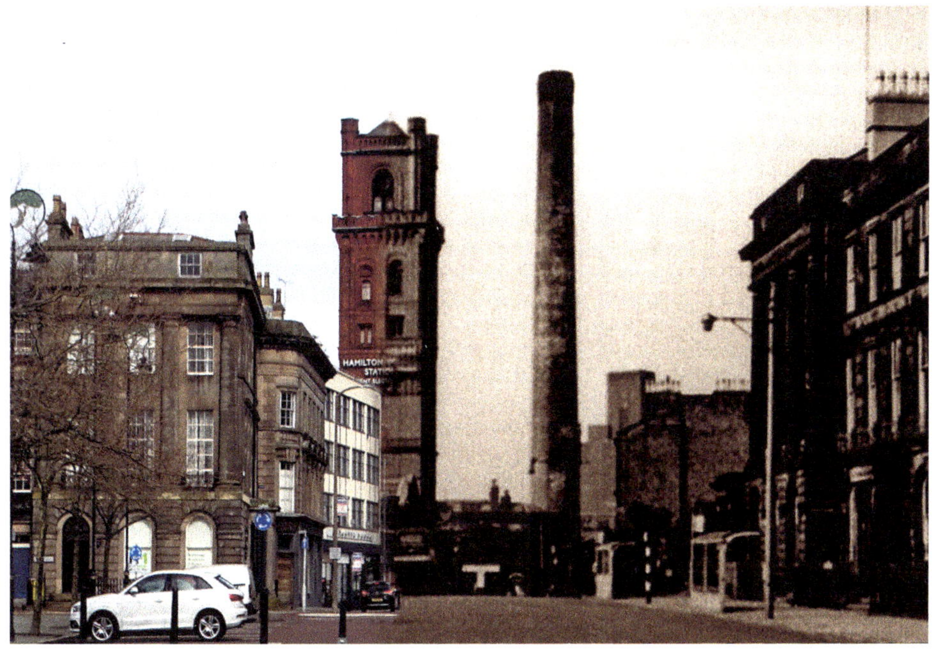

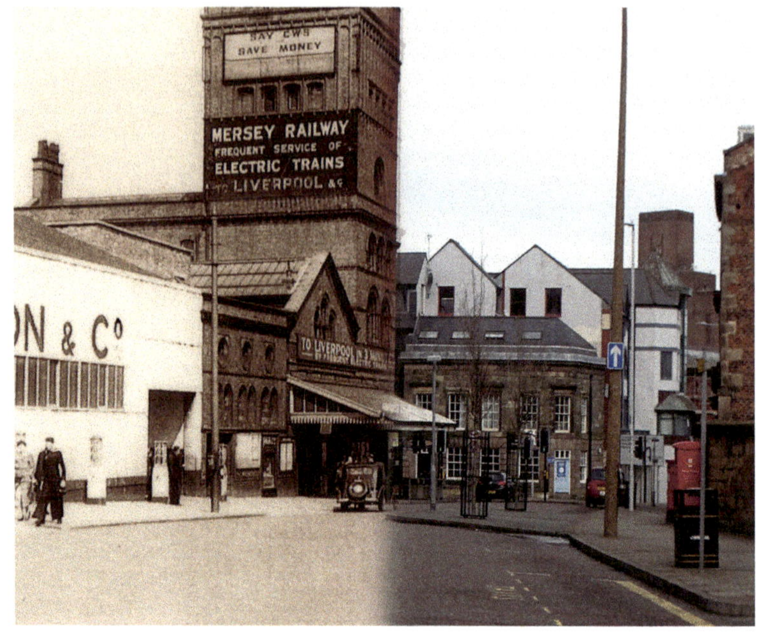

Hamilton Square Station Entrance

The railway divides into two branches at Hamilton Square, one line running to New Brighton and West Kirby and the other to Rock Ferry. Originally a junction was formed at Rock Ferry with the L&NW Railway and the Great Western lines, which ran to Crewe, Bristol, Holyhead and main destinations in England and Wales. The station entrance was designed by G. E. Grayson in Italianate style. It is built in brick and terracotta, and consists of a tall hydraulic tower, a pedimented booking hall, and a three-bay single-storey block on the left.

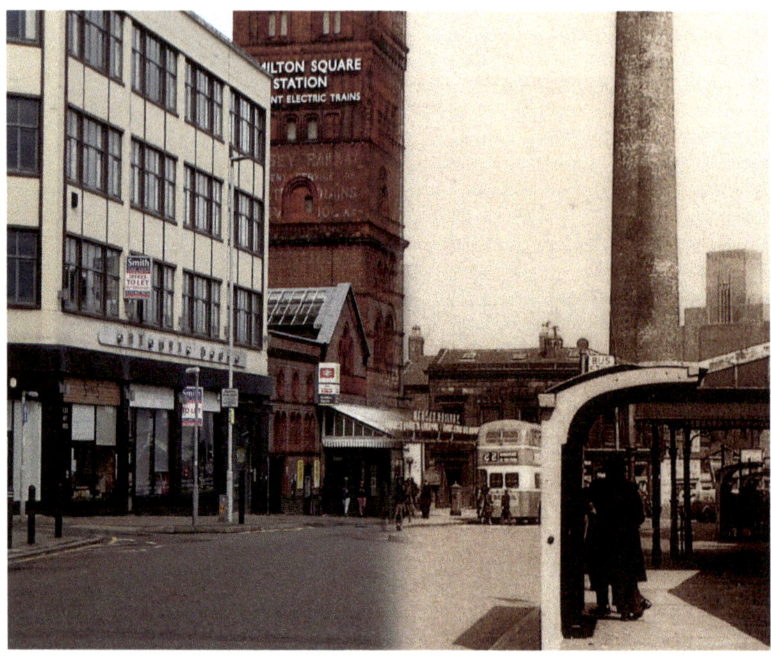

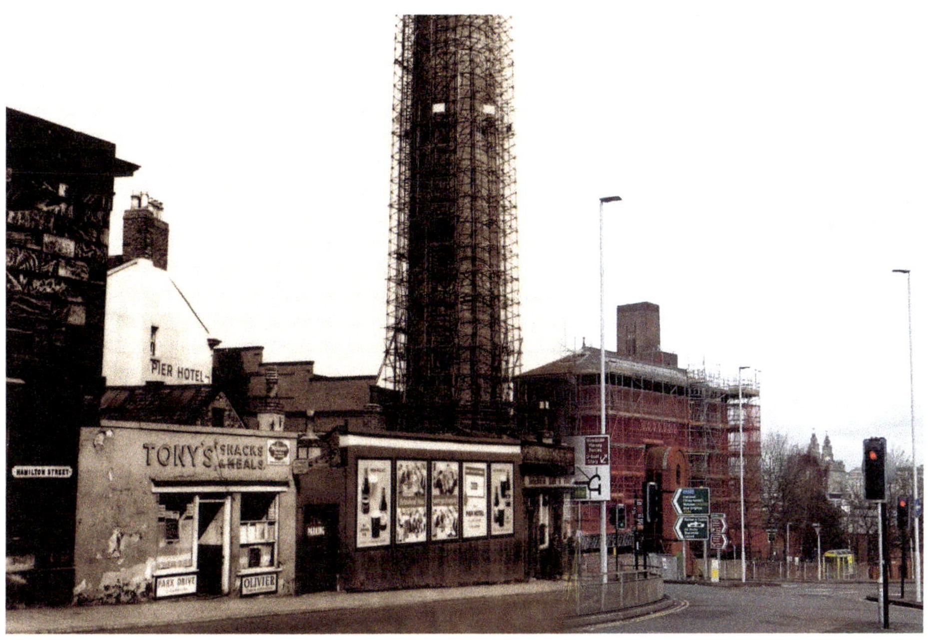

Shore Road Pumping Station

Shore Road Pumping Station at Woodside contained the pumps which removed water from the Mersey Railway tunnel under the River Mersey. It was capable of raising 18,000 gallons of water per minute from a separate drainage tunnel. The pumping station was built in the 1870s and the pumps were originally driven by steam beam engines. These were later replaced by electric pumps but one of the original pumps, the Giant Grasshopper, remains on display. However, the museum has now been closed to the public. The building was designed by James Brunlees and Charles Douglas Fox.

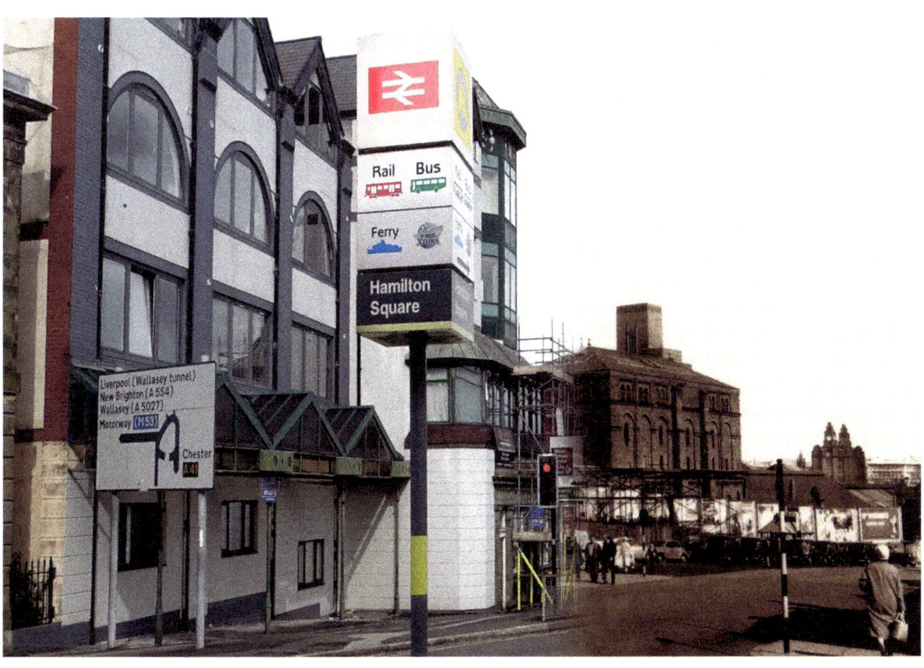

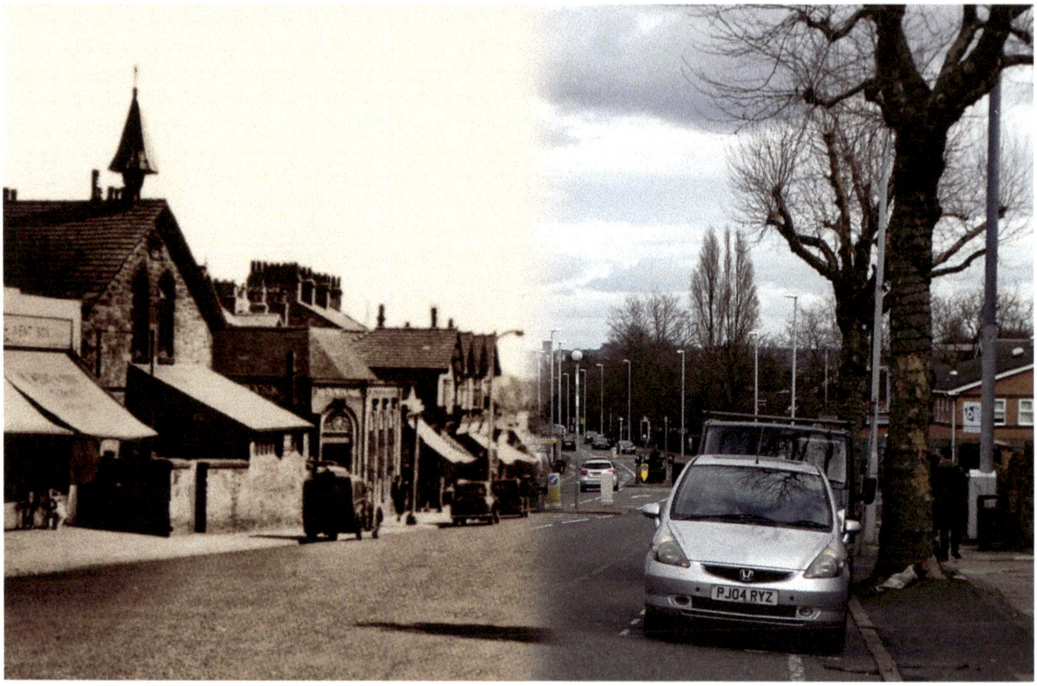

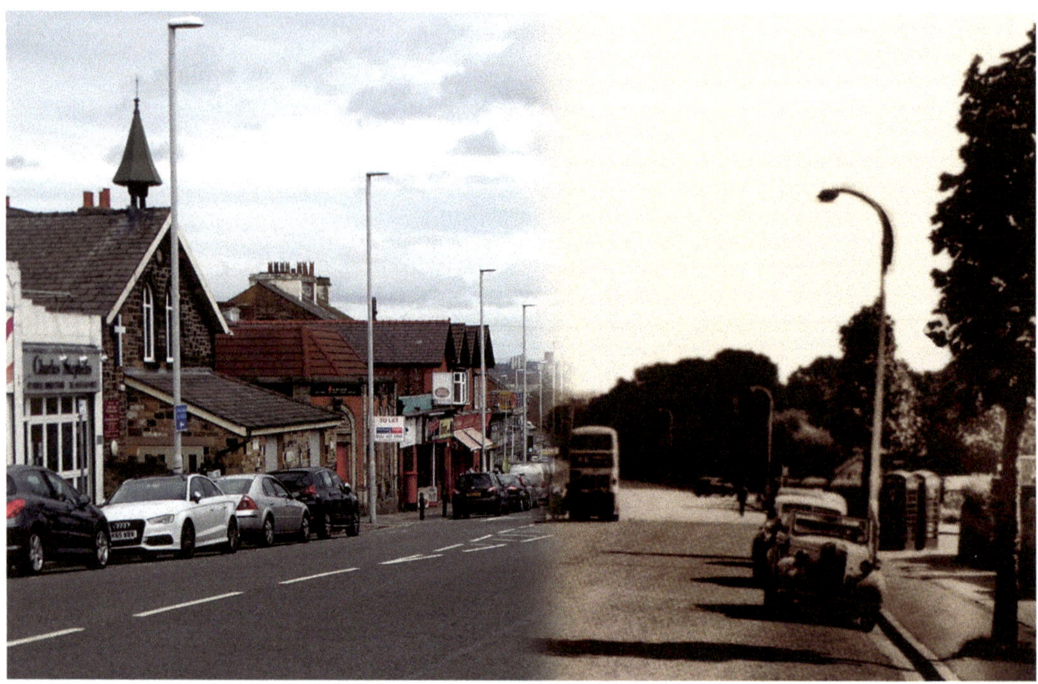

Claughton Village

Looking down Upton Road at Claughton Village towards Birkenhead. The stationery and tobacconist's shop were owned by Miss Harriet Bedford, who was also the sub-post mistress. St Bede's Mission Church was originally the Claughton Mission Room until it became the church and school in 1887. The school was transferred to Bidston Avenue in 1921.

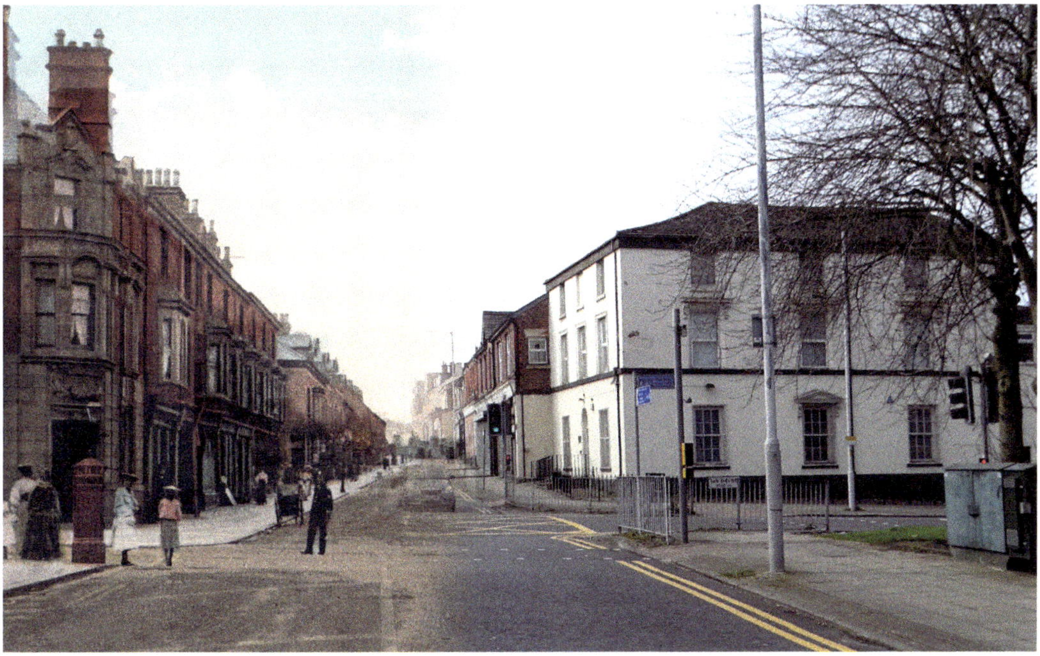

Junction of New Chester Road and Bedford Road, Rock Ferry

Bedford Road was named after Prime Minister Lord John Russell, whose family seat was at Bedford. To the left is a branch of the London and City Midland Bank with William Pollard's boot and shoe shop on the right. Parr's bank is shown on the right of the photograph, with a police officer directing traffic. The London and City Midland Bank building is still standing but the boot and shoe shop has vanished and the police officer has been replaced by traffic lights.

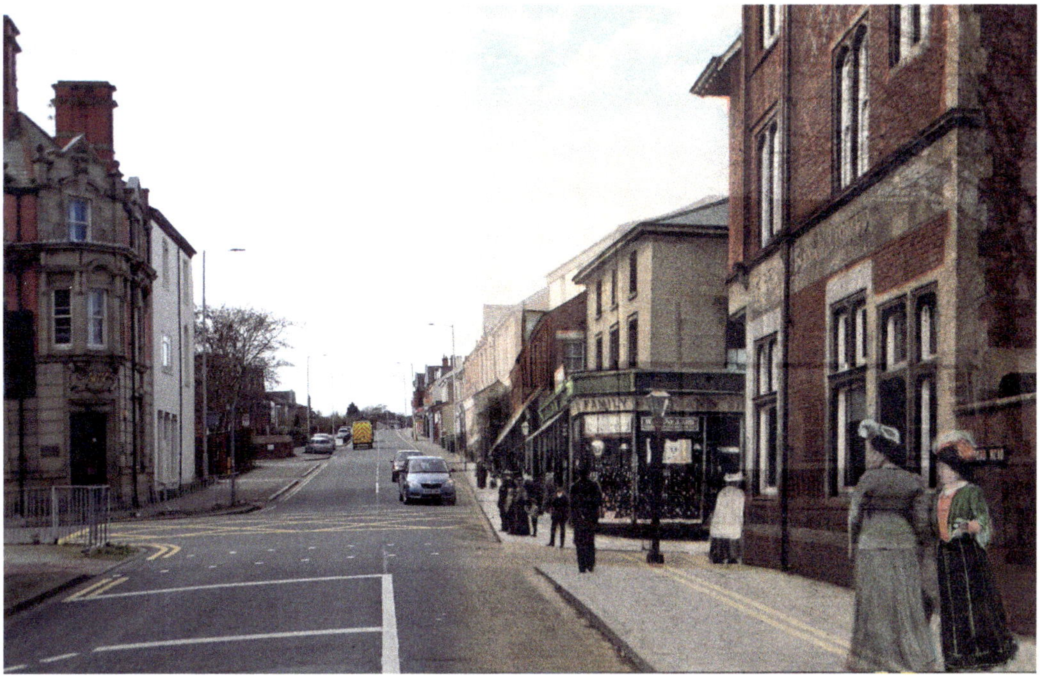

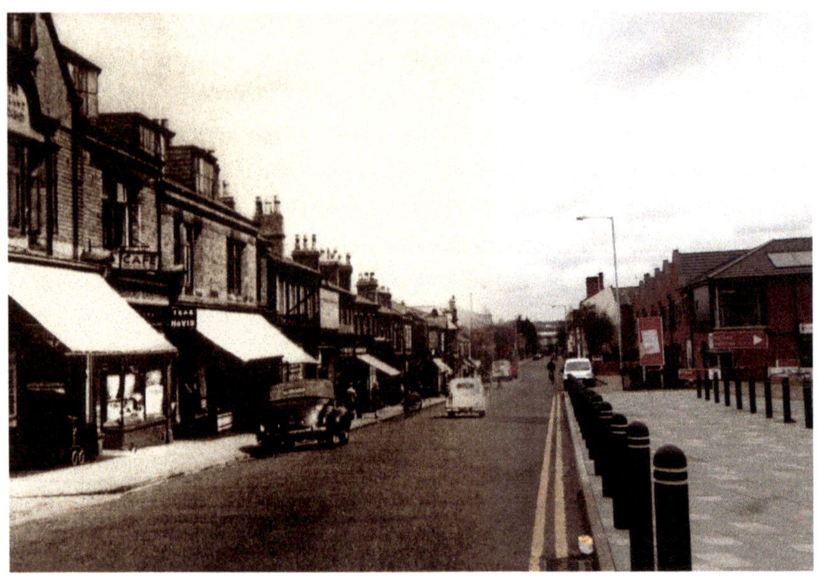

Bedford Road, Rock Ferry

There are records showing that a ferry operated from Rock Ferry as early as 1357, and it was claimed that it was used by William IV as Duke of Clarence and the term 'Royal' was used for various establishments such as the Royal Rock Hotel and the Royal Rock Beagles, established in 1845. The villas at Rock Park were built in the middle of the nineteenth century and many large dwellings around the Old Chester Road were constructed. It's proximity to the Cammell Laird Shipyard meant that Rock Ferry grew as the shipyard developed. However, in the 1960s shopping trends changed and many of the shops lay empty and dilapidated, and this was reflected in the number of businesses which closed in the road. Bedford Road had supported a wine merchant, a jeweller, two tailors, three banks and two bookshops. Wirral Borough Council embarked on a regeneration programme of the area in the 1990s, and many properties of character were demolished and lost.

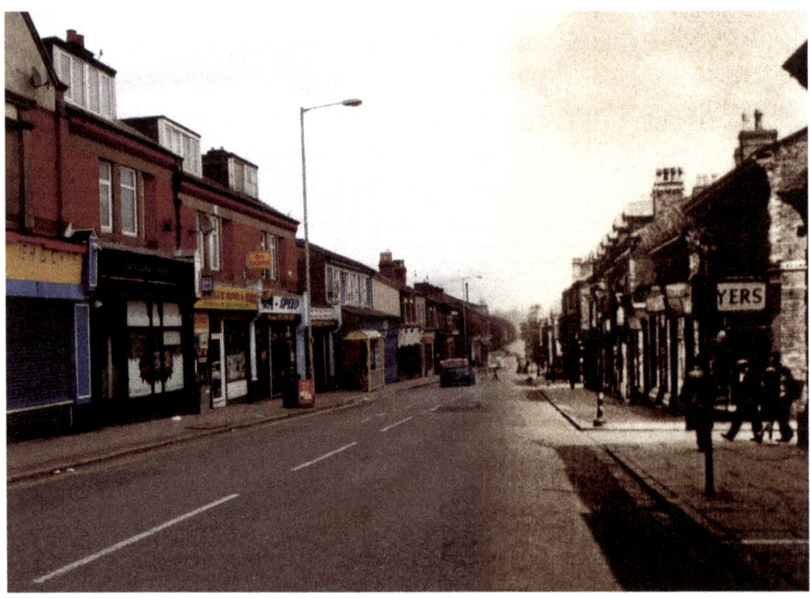

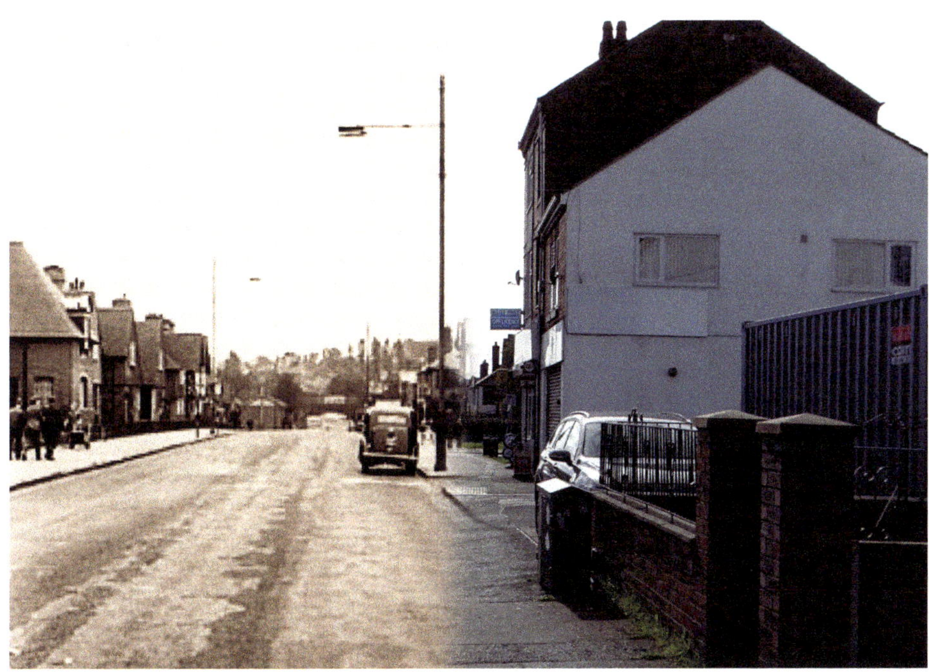

New Ferry Bypass

The re-routing of the A41 road onto the New Ferry by-pass has resulted in a decline in through traffic in the town centre. Electric trains operate from Bebington and Port Sunlight stations to Chester, Ellesmere Port and Liverpool. The community-led New Ferry Residents Association has been successful in obtaining funding for a variety of projects since it was formed in 1999. A farmers' market operates in the village hall once in a month and the association is campaigning for improvements to the shopping centre.

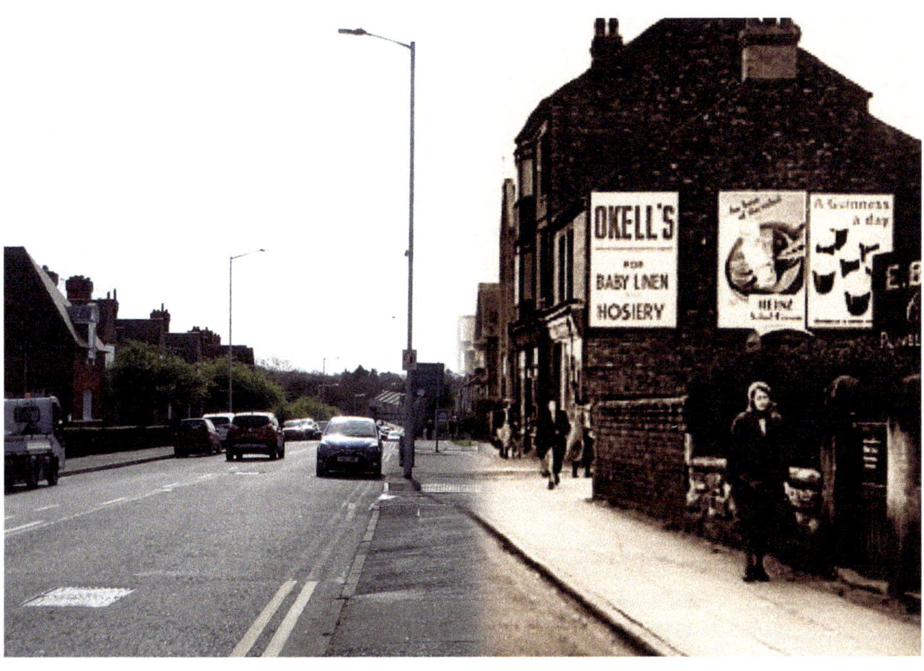

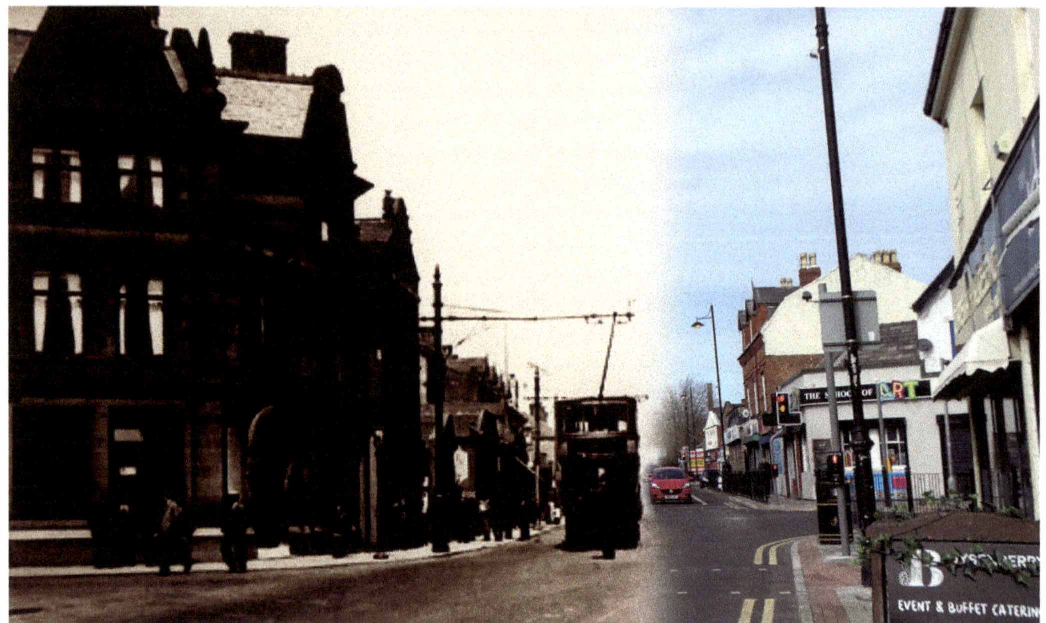

Electric Tram

The first electric tram began operating between Woodside and New Ferry in 1901. The service from Brandon Street commenced on 4 February as the track down to Woodside was not completed until 6 June that year. However, because of the low bridge in Chester Street, cars Nos 1–13 were single-deck vehicles. The vehicles were converted to double-deck cars, with reduced headroom on the top deck and introduced into service in 1910. Buses were placed on this route in 1930 and the tram service closed at the end of the following year. This part of the road included a toll bar, where drivers would have to pay a fee. This arrangement remained in force until 1883 and the area is often referred to as the 'Toll Bar'.

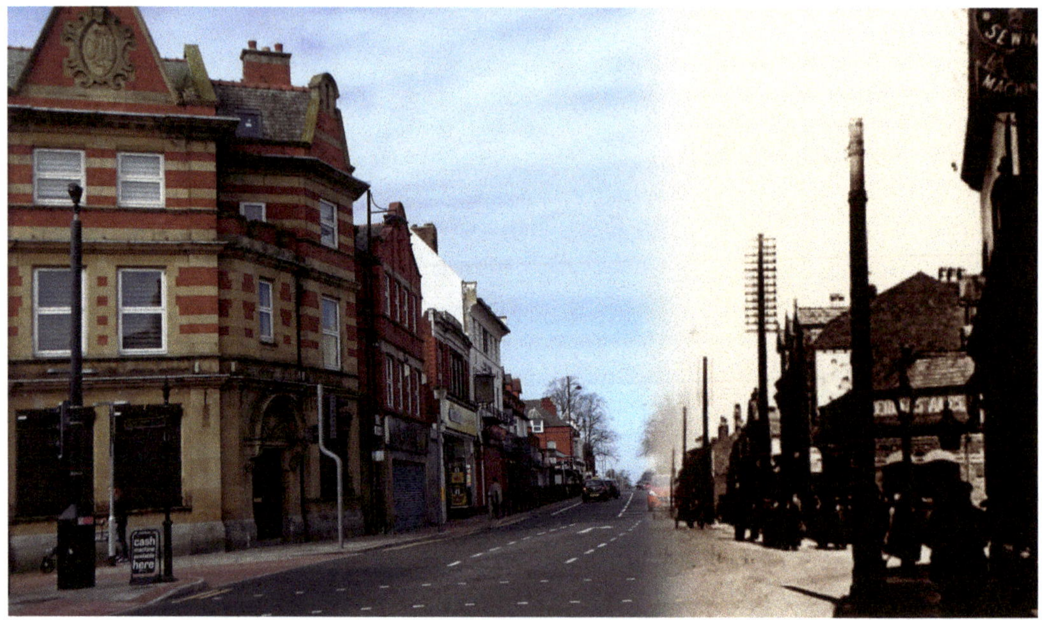

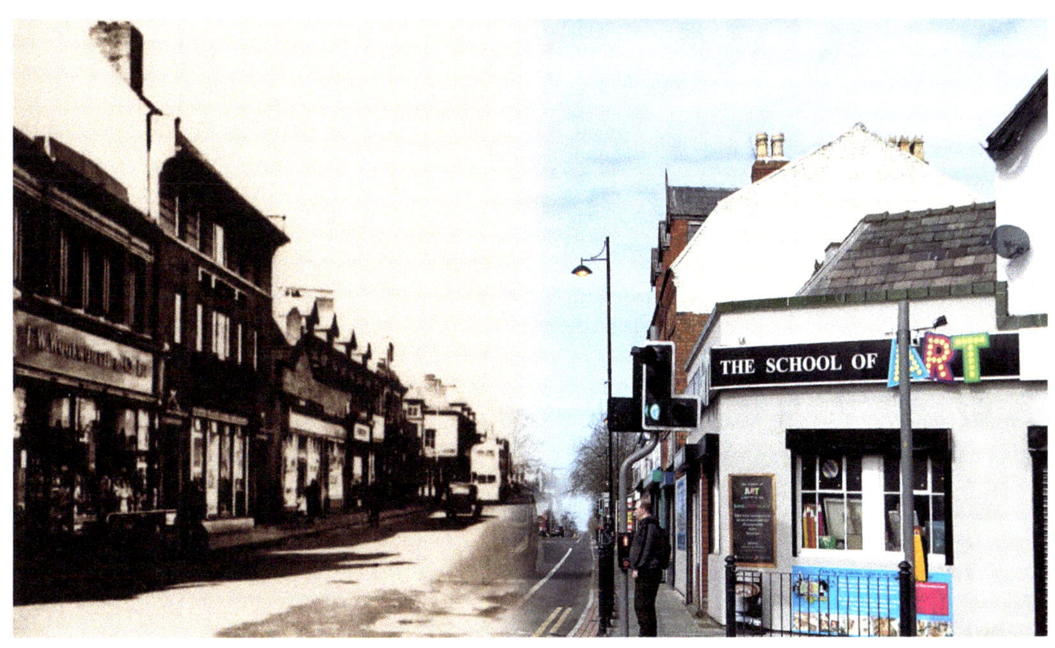

New Ferry, Town Centre

A ferry service gave its name to the locality and the first recorded mention of New Ferry was in 1774. In 1865 a ferry service was established between New Ferry and the southern docks at Liverpool, and from 1879 to Liverpool Pier Head. The lease of the ferry rights expired in 1927, although no service had operated from New Ferry for five years following a collision and damage to the pier. The town is on the A41, the main road between Birkenhead and London, and is adjacent to Port Sunlight Village.

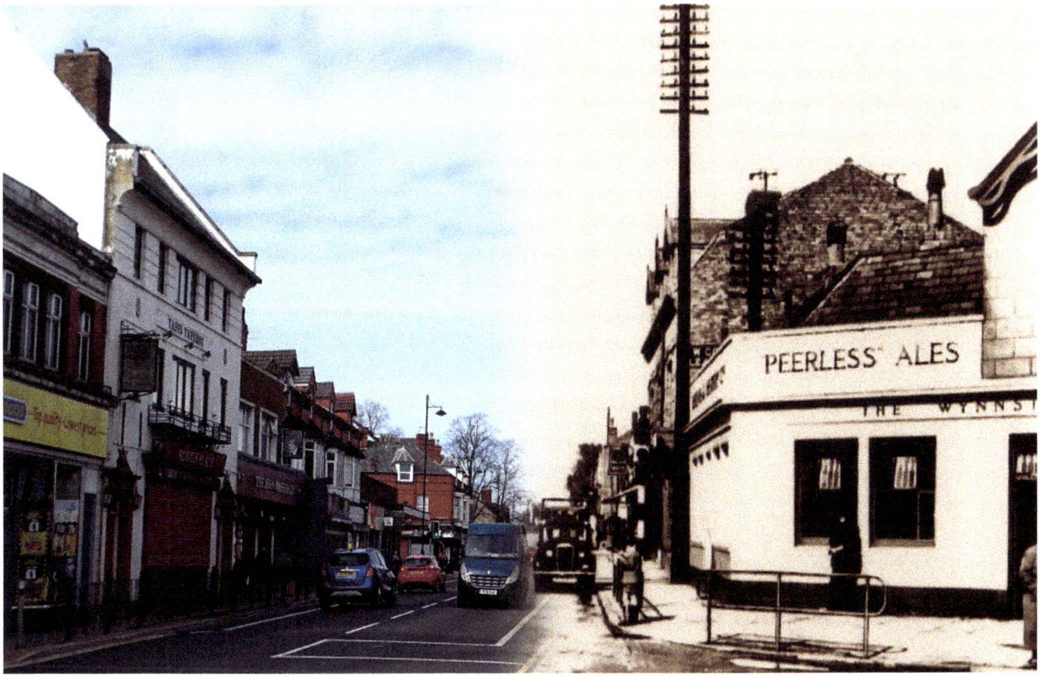

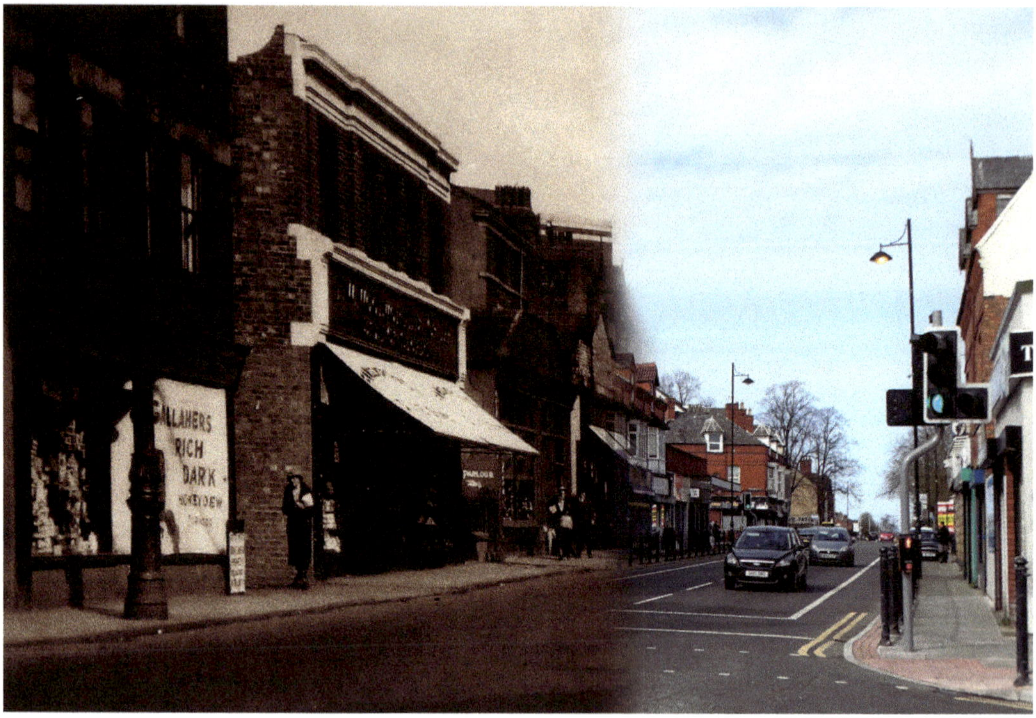

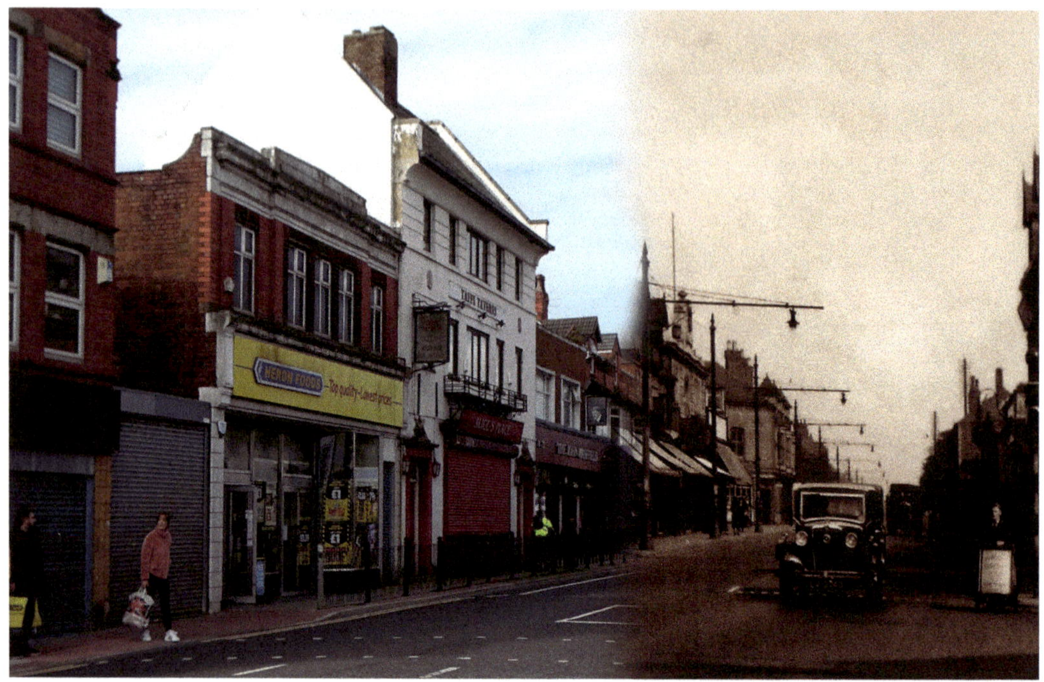

New Ferry Shopping Centre, New Chester Road

New Ferry was originally called 'The Pastures', and was common grazing land, of which a small piece now remains unenclosed. The open common land which at one time occupied large areas of Wirral has mostly been enclosed, mainly during the nineteenth century.

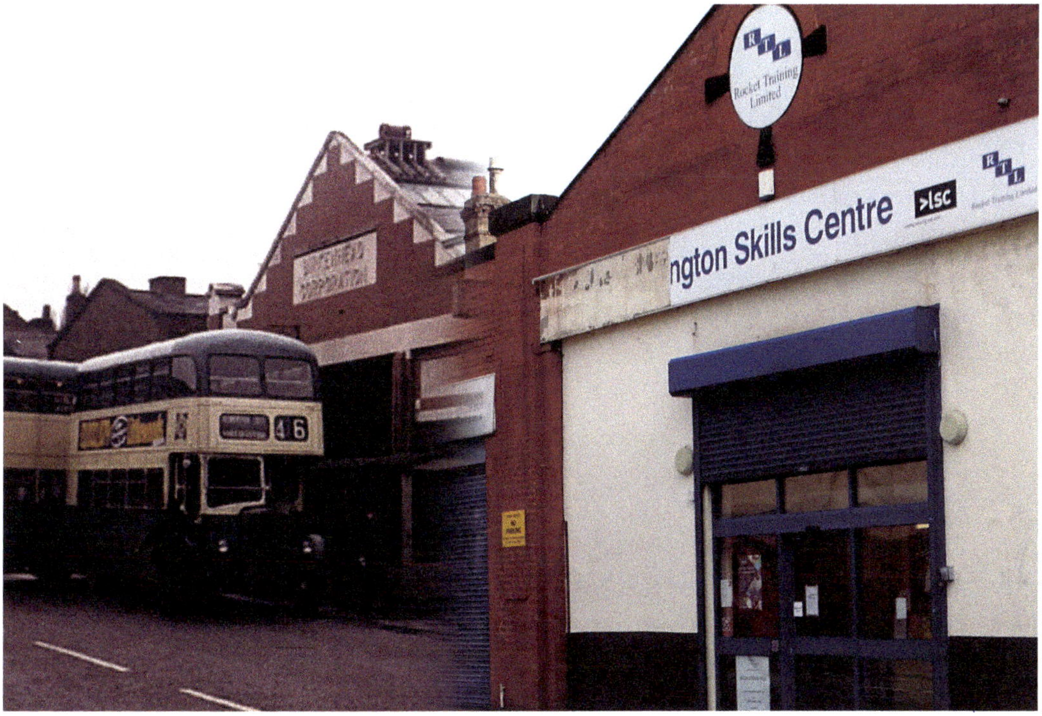

Birkenhead and Wallasey Corporation Buses, Birkenhead Corporation Motor Omnibus Garage, New Ferry

The number 10 bus operated to New Brighton via Birkenhead and Liscard. The depot was built in 1931, replacing an earlier building on the same site which had been used for the horse-drawn trams and it survived until 3 March 1973, when it was closed and a post office was built on the site.

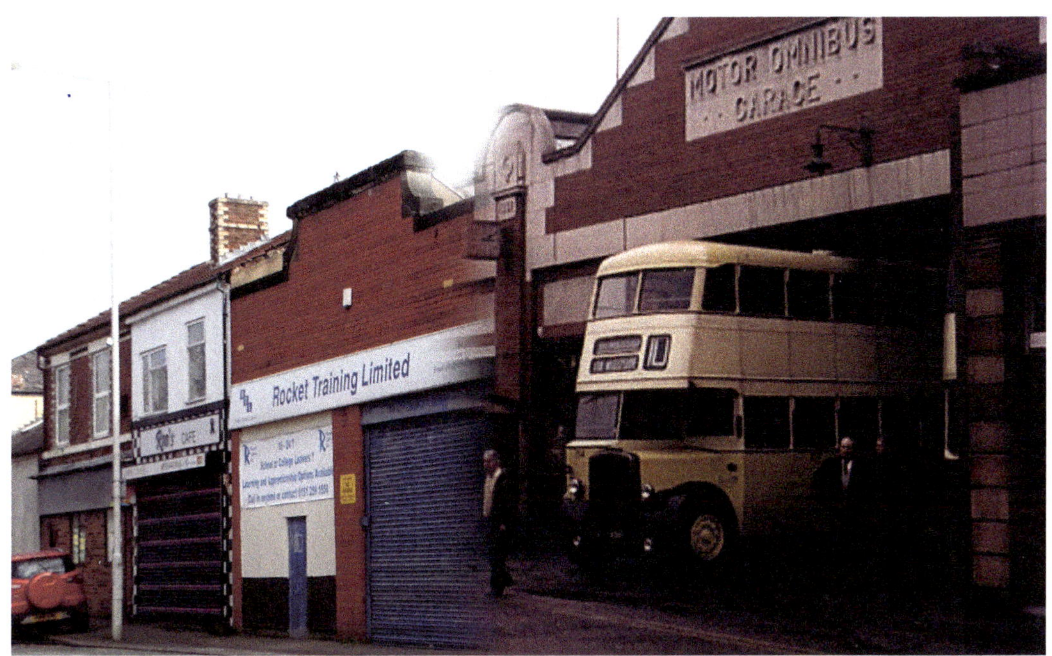

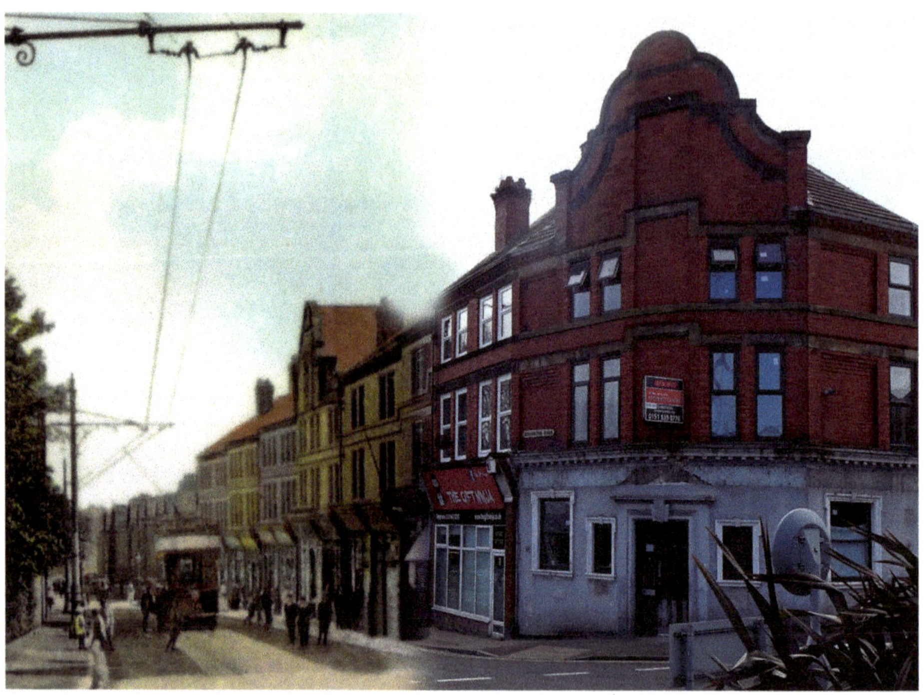

Bebington Road, Higher Tranmere

Tranmere was a township and chapelry in Bebington ancient parish and became a civil parish in 1866. The civil parish was abolished in 1898, when it became part of Birkenhead. It included the hamlets of Clifton Park, Devonshire Park, Lower Tranmere, Mersey Park and Victoria Park.

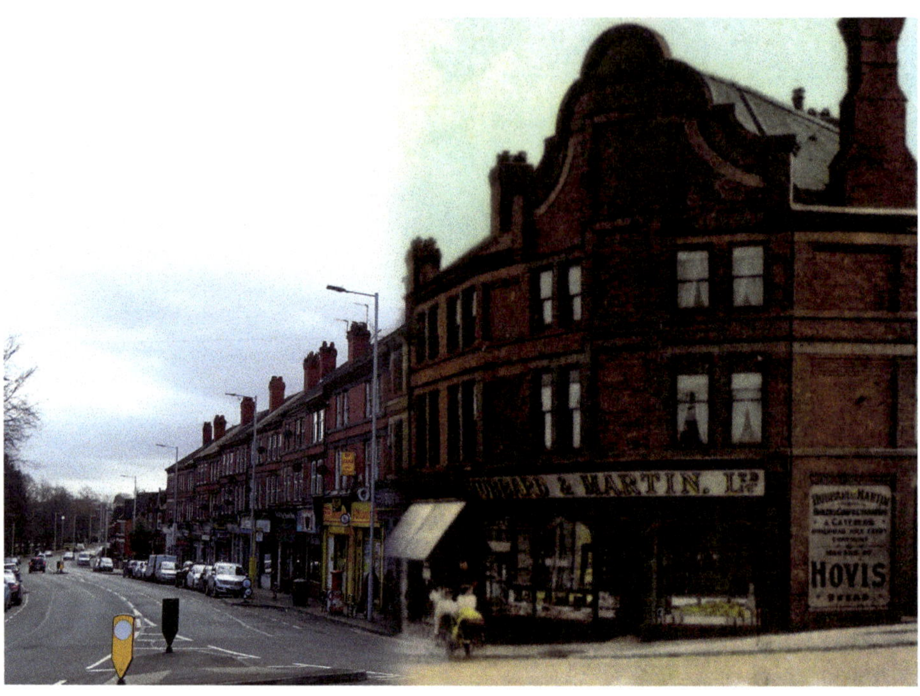

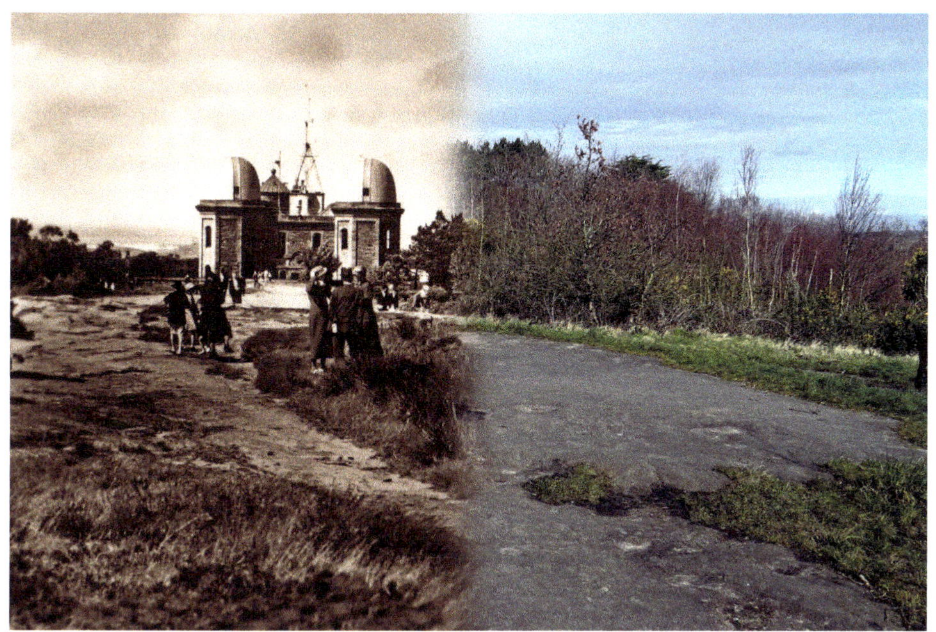

Bidston Hill

In 1883 and 1887 it was suggested that Bidston Hill should be acquired as an open space for public use. However, it was not until 1893 that the council supported the proposal and in 1894 the first section was purchased from Robert Vyner, partly with town money and also by public subscription. Further acquisitions were made until 140 acres were owned by the council. The Pine Woods were acquired as a memorial to Edmund Taylor, a Freeman of the Borough, in recognition of his help in the original purchase. An approach to the hill from Upton Road was opened by King George V in 1914 as King George's Way.

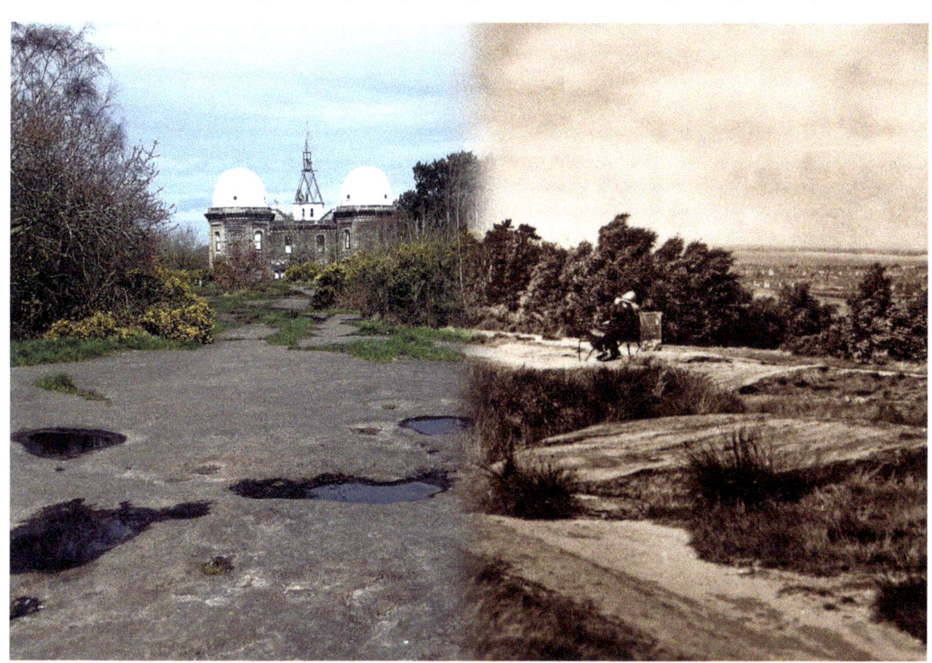

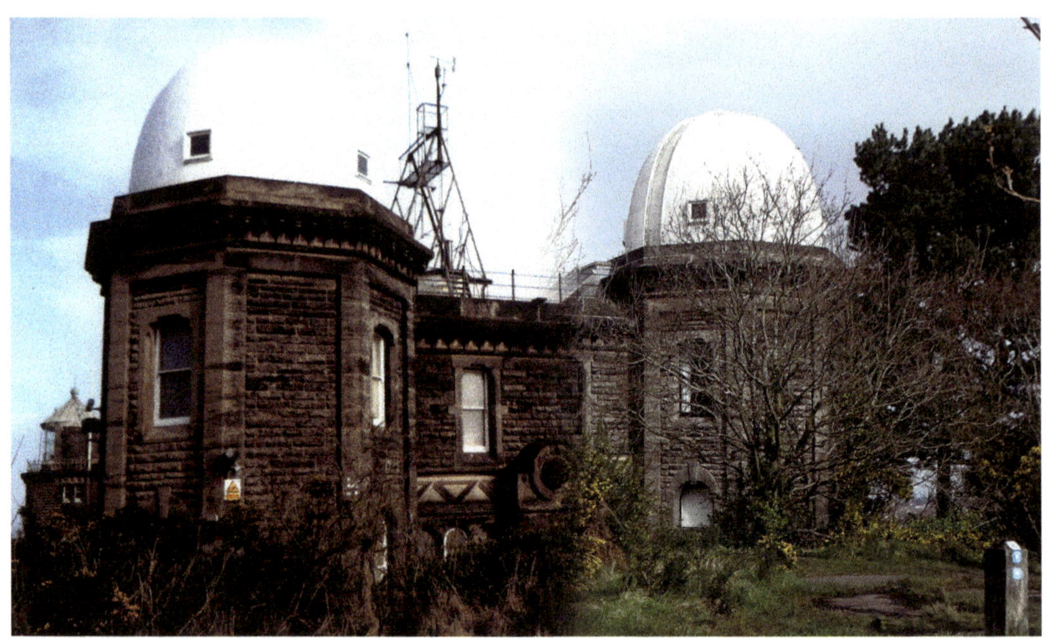

Bidston Observatory

The Bidston Observatory was the home of the Institute of Coastal Oceanography and Tides, which was founded in 1843. The observatory was transferred to the site in Bidston in 1864 where astronomical and meteorological observations were continued under the aegis of the newly formed Mersey Docks & Harbour Board. Tidal predictions were prepared at Bidston for more than half the major ports in the world and work was carried out on tidal streams, non-tidal currents, surface waves and other processes of tidal circulation and mixing. However, the Institute moved from the site at Bidston to Liverpool University in 2003 and the Grade II listed building was advertised for sale.

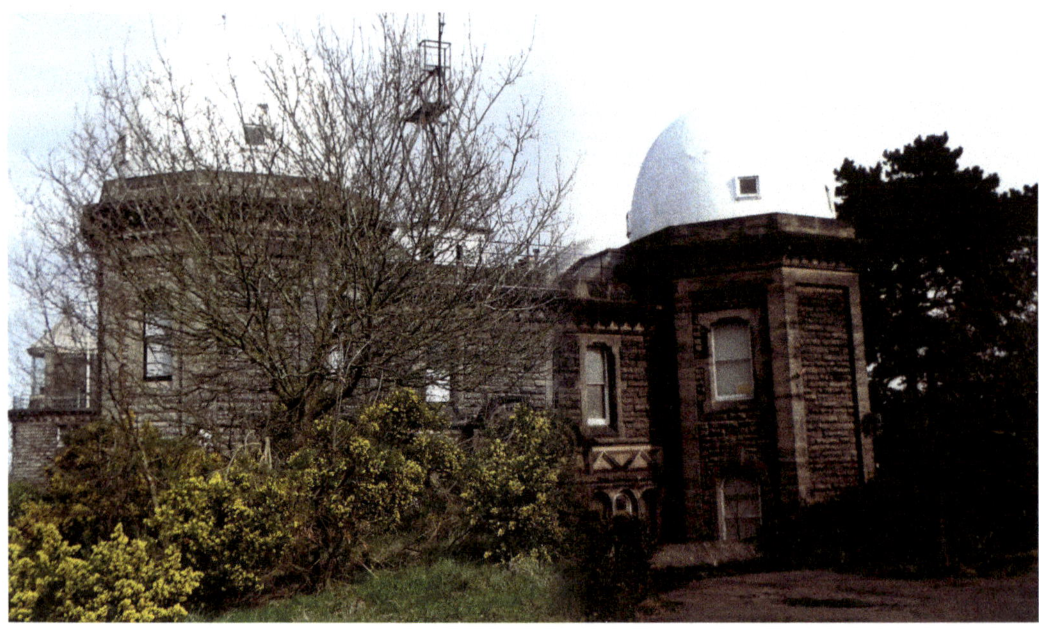

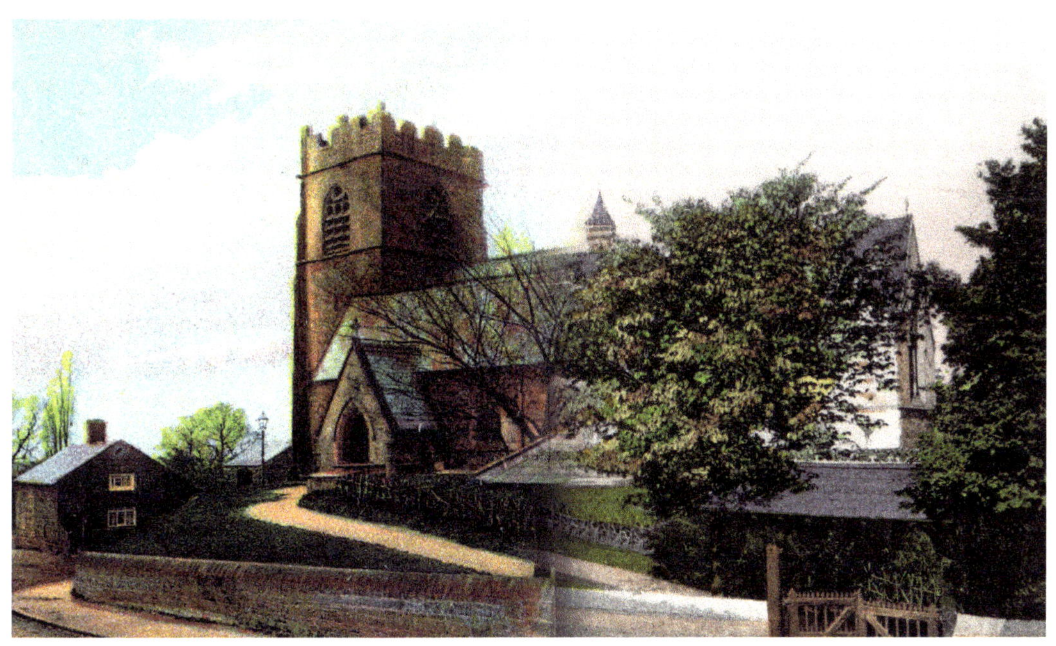

St Oswald's Church, Bidston, from School Lane

A church has stood on this ground since the twelfth century and the tower dates from around 1520. It was rebuilt in 1856 and a sanctuary was added in 1882. One of the bells has the inscription St Oswald, and it is thought that it came from St Oswald's Church in Chester.

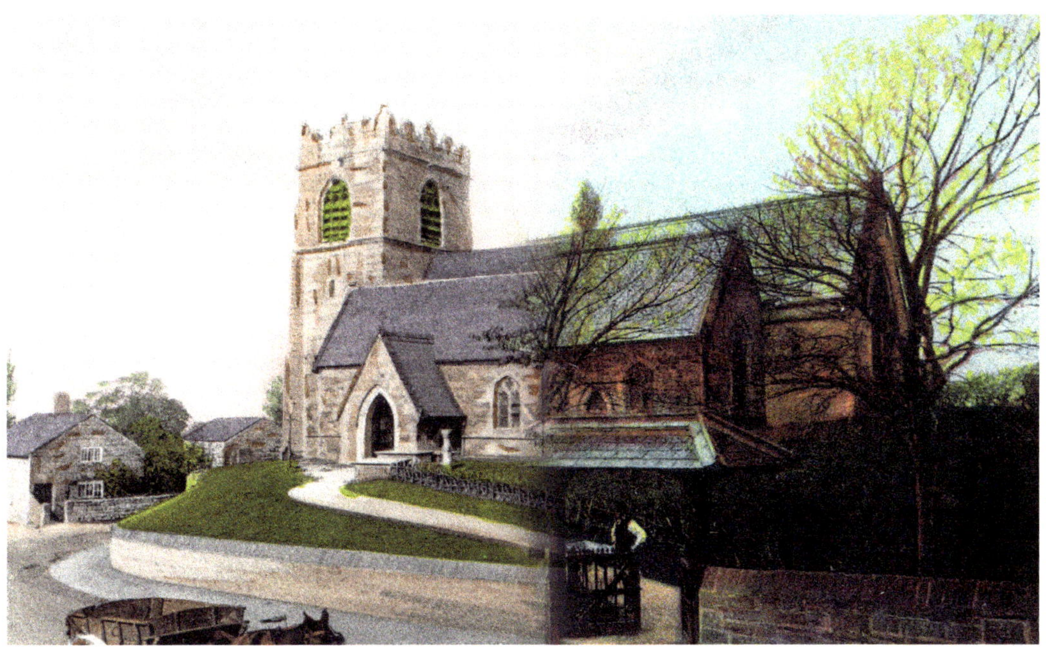

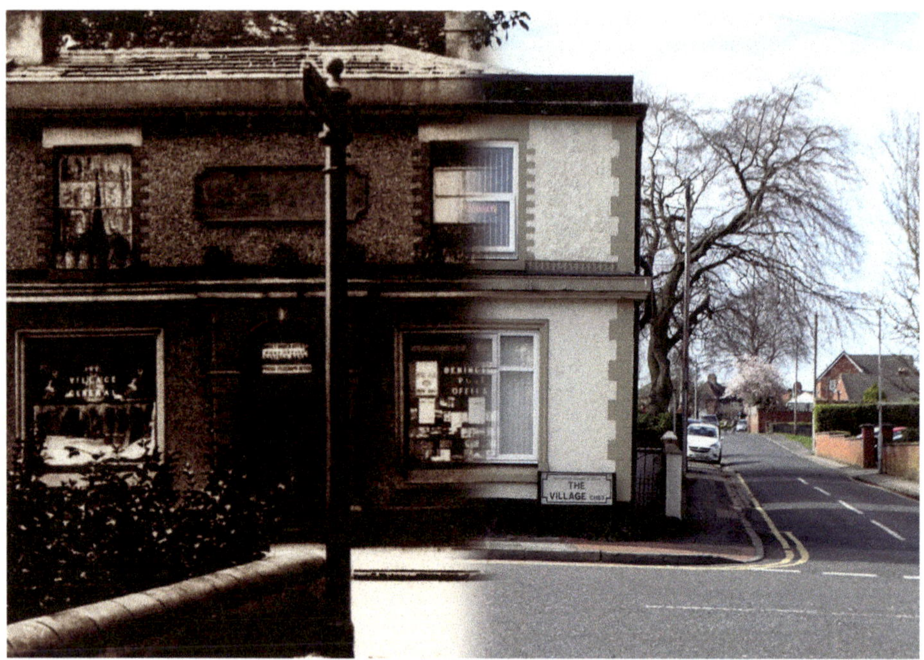

Old Post Office, Bebington, 1801

Although the building is now a private residence, the original public footpath sign remains. Bebington was a small country hamlet with a population of only 273, situated on the main road connecting Chester and Birkenhead, and then via ferry to Liverpool. It was reported that up to thirty horse-drawn coaches would pass through Bebington each day. By 1840 the Birkenhead and Chester Railway was operating, and in 1844 the New Chester Road was opened, which reduced the traffic through the village dramatically.

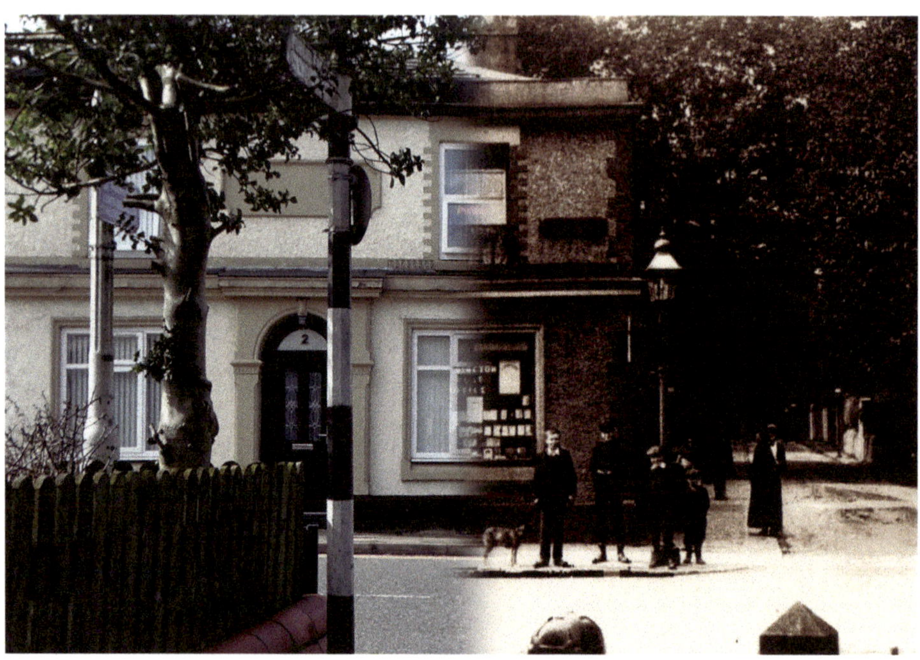

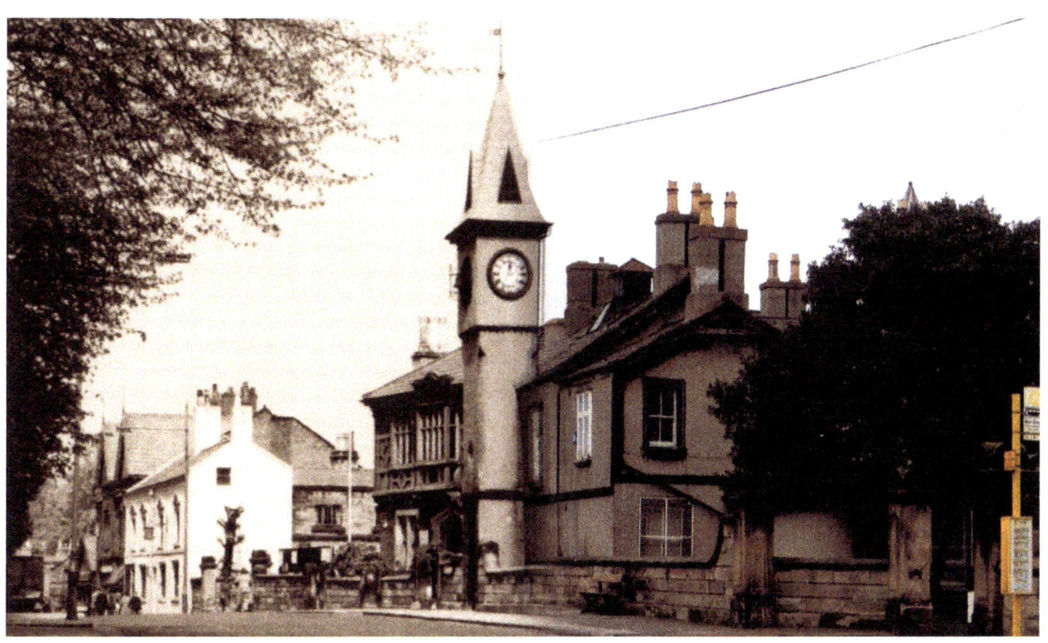

Joseph Mayer, the son of Samuel Mayer, tanner and currier, was born at Newcastle-under-Lyme on 23 February 1803. He moved to Liverpool in 1823 and set up as a jeweller and goldsmith. This enabled him to persue his hobby of collecting Greek coins, later glass and pottery, antiquities, gems and rings, enamels, miniatures, metalwork, drawings and engravings. He was a founder of the Historic Society of Lancashire and Cheshire and contributed papers to many publications. By 1860 he was benefactor to the village of Bebington and in 1866 he established a free library of 20,000 volumes at his expense. Mayer retired in 1873 and died at Bebington on 19 January 1886, at the age of eighty-two.

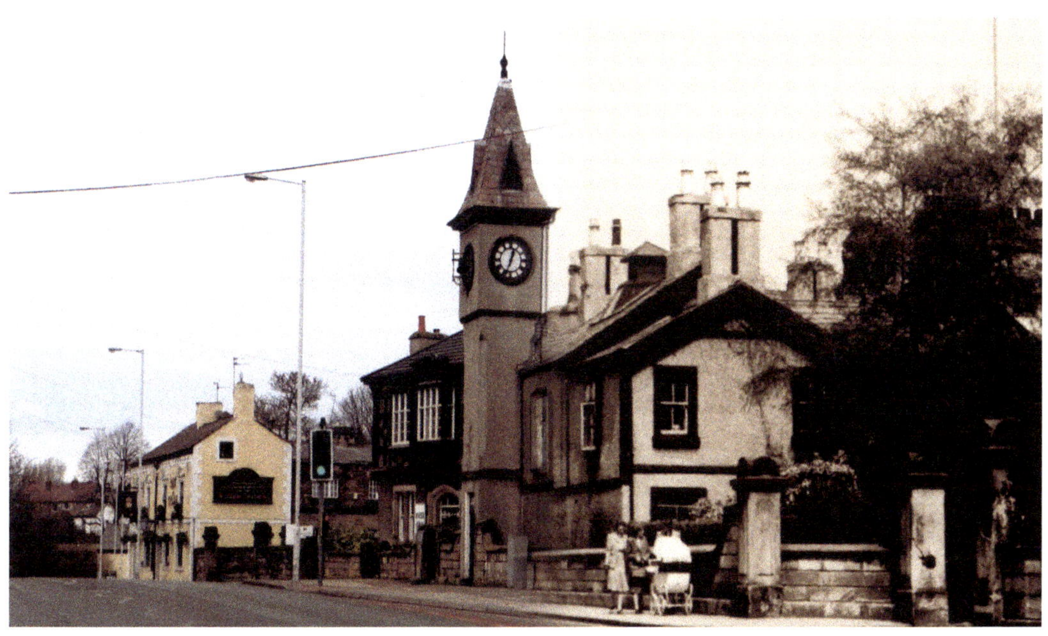

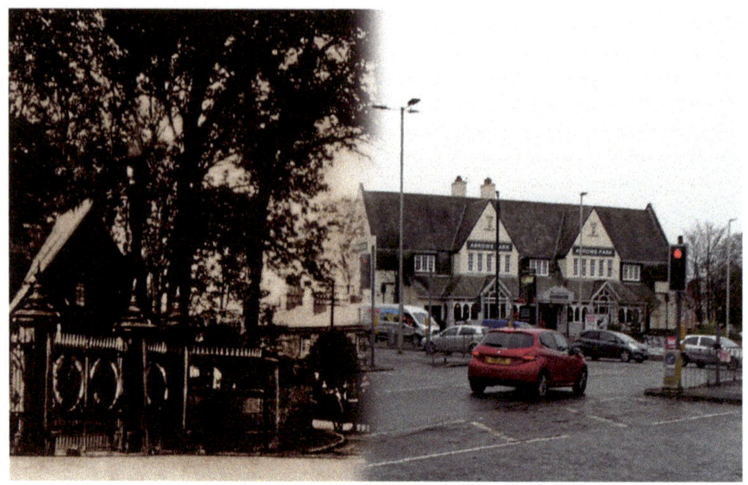

Arrowe Park

The Prince of Wales arrived at Birkenhead on 1 August 1929 to visit the World Jamboree of Boy Scouts at Arrowe Park. The Boy Scouts movement had originated in Birkenhead, in the YMCA headquarters in Whetstone Lane. The jamboree was the largest gathering of youth the world had seen and was a celebration of twenty-one years of the movement. The Arrowe Park Hotel was opened in 1937, and replaced the Horse and Jockey Inn. The Horse and Jockey at Woodchurch was opened around 1850. When the Arrowe Park Hotel opened in 1936 the licence was transferred to it from the Horse and Jockey. The public house was then demolished. The Arrowe Brook runs north along a valley to the west of the Thingwall and Arrowe Park ridge to Saughall Massey, near where it is joined by the Greasby Brook, rising near Thurstaston village and running in a northerly direction through the valley between Thurstaston Hill and Irby Hill. The combined streams run north and then north-east across the low land to join the Birket near Leasowe Lighthouse. Woodchurch village was little more than a hamlet, and in 1801 it had a population of only fifty-two, and by 1911 this had increased to 138 persons. It was not mentioned in the Doomsday Book, as it is believed to have been included in the adjoining township of Landican. Wudechurch is named in the charter of 1093 as being given to the Abbey of St Werburgh by Earl Hugh. Records do not show if the name is derived from a wooden church building, or a church in the woods.

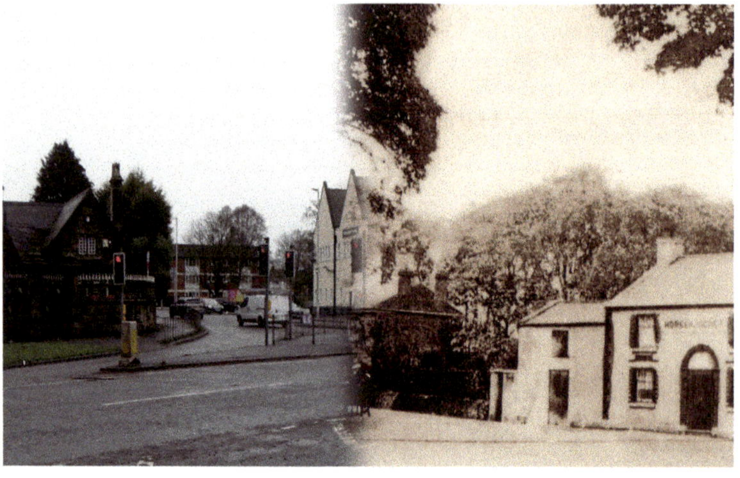

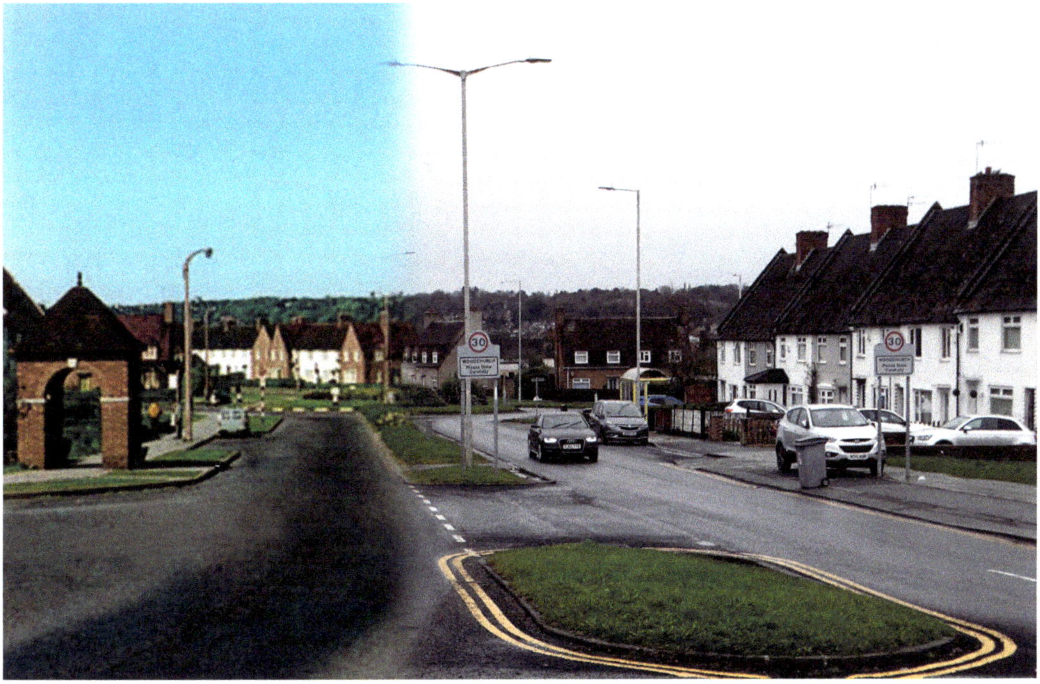

Woodchurch Estate, Arrowe Park

Over 2,000 dwellings were destroyed or damaged beyond repair during the Second World War, and at the end of hostilities 500 prefabs were built to provide temporary accommodation. The Mount Estate was opened, followed by the Woodchurch Estate in May 1949. Various plans were proposed and H. J. Rowse's was the one that was accepted. The estate was completed by the Borough Architect, T. A. Brittain, with shops, churches, schools and a community centre.

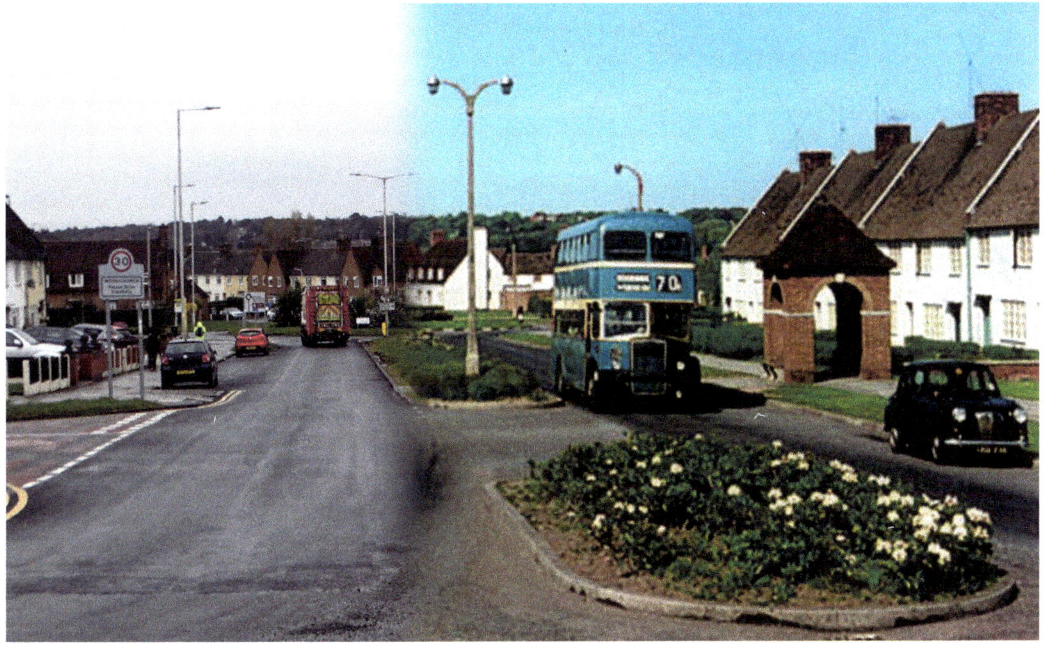

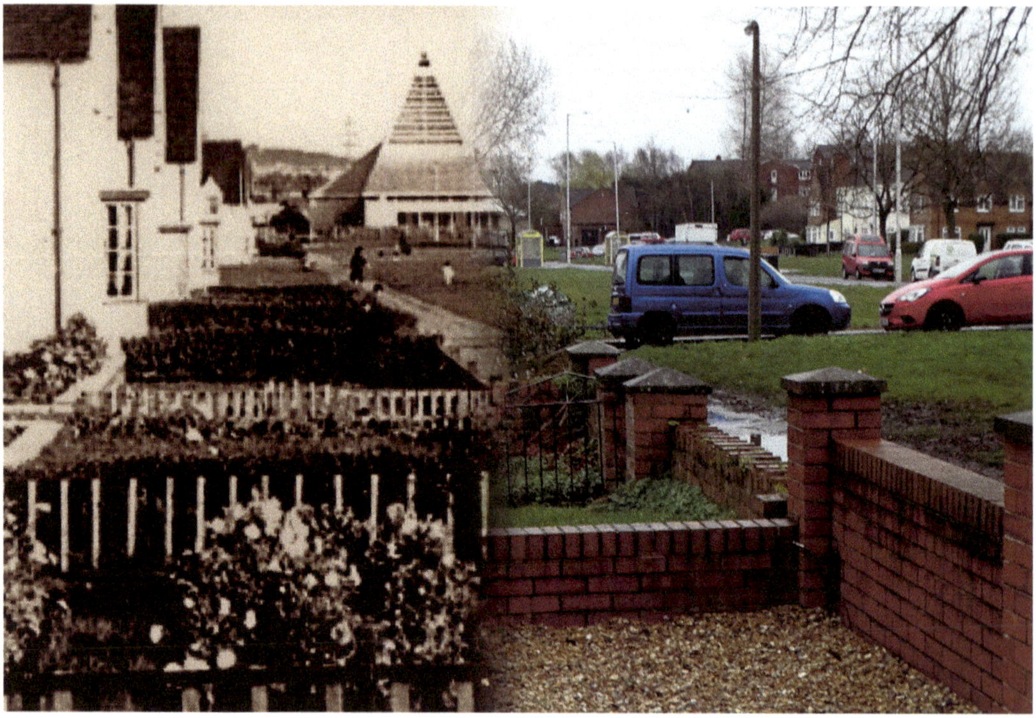

Houses and Church, Woodchurch Estate

Woodchurch Village was a small rural township until the mid-twentieth century when the large housing development transformed the area, providing modern homes and facilities to the people of Birkenhead.

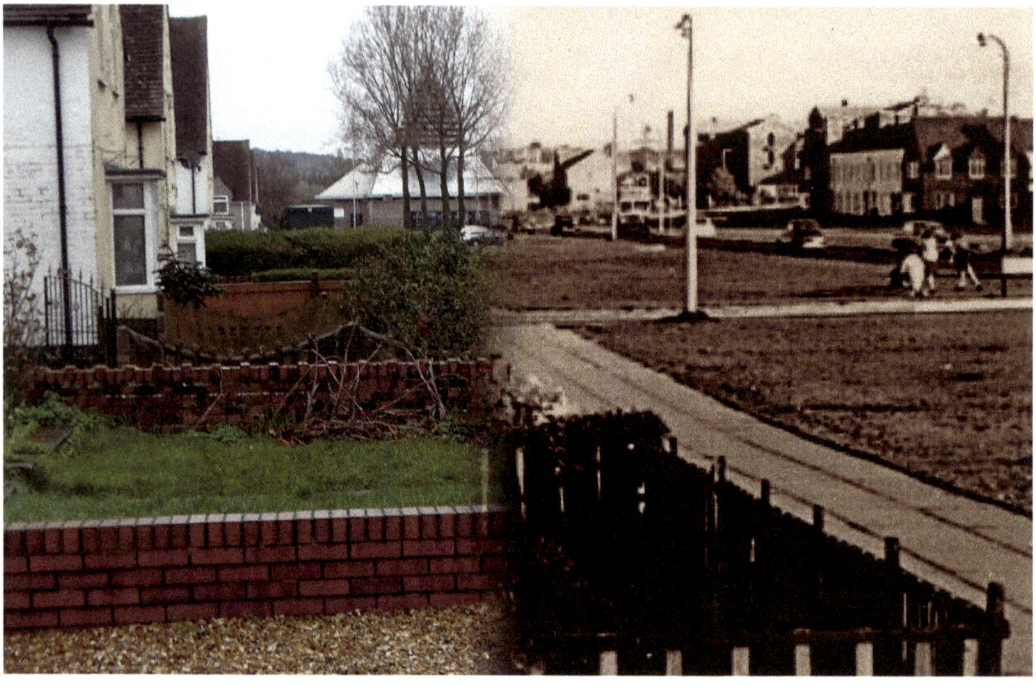

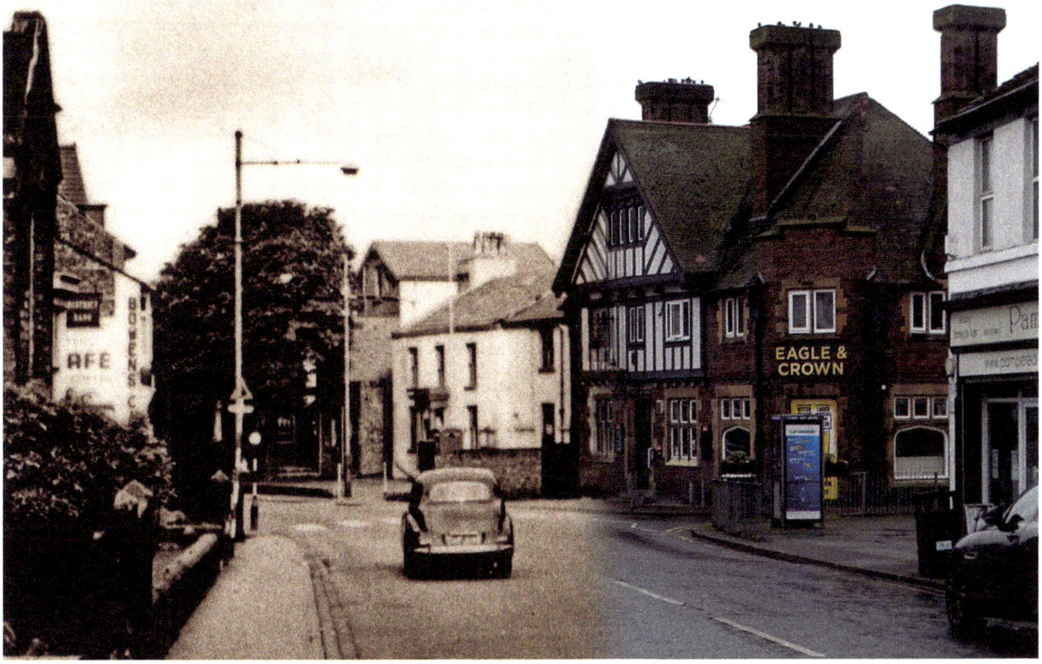

Upton Village

In the early nineteenth century a weekly market was held at Upton, where five roads led to the village. A fair was held twice a year, on the last Friday in April and on the Friday before Michaelmas. It was incorporated into the County Borough of Birkenhead in 1933.

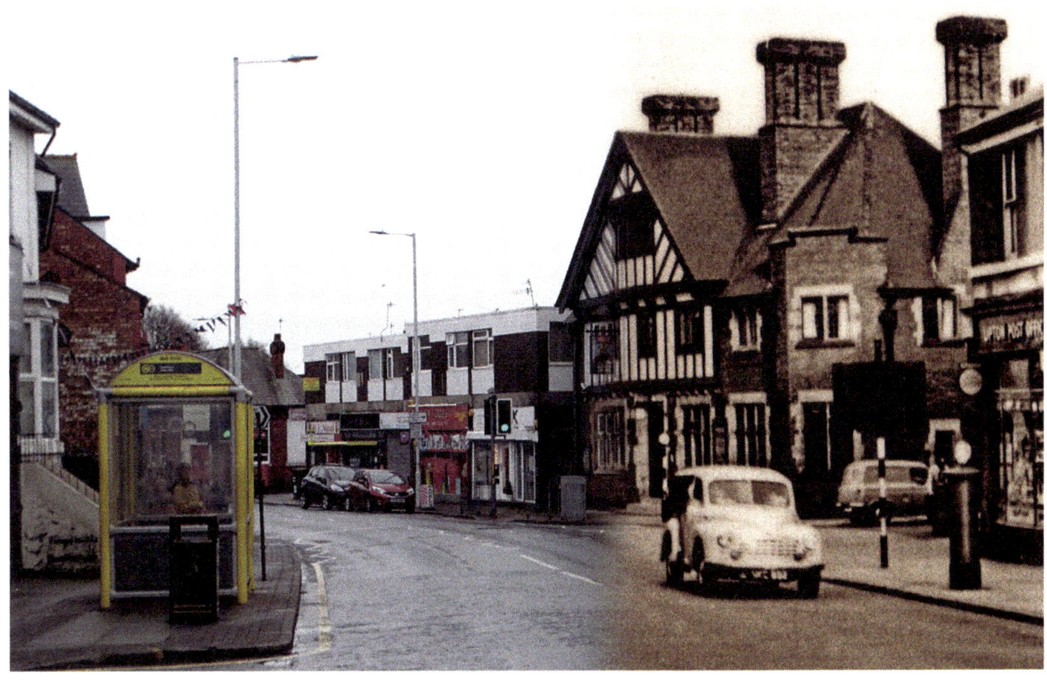

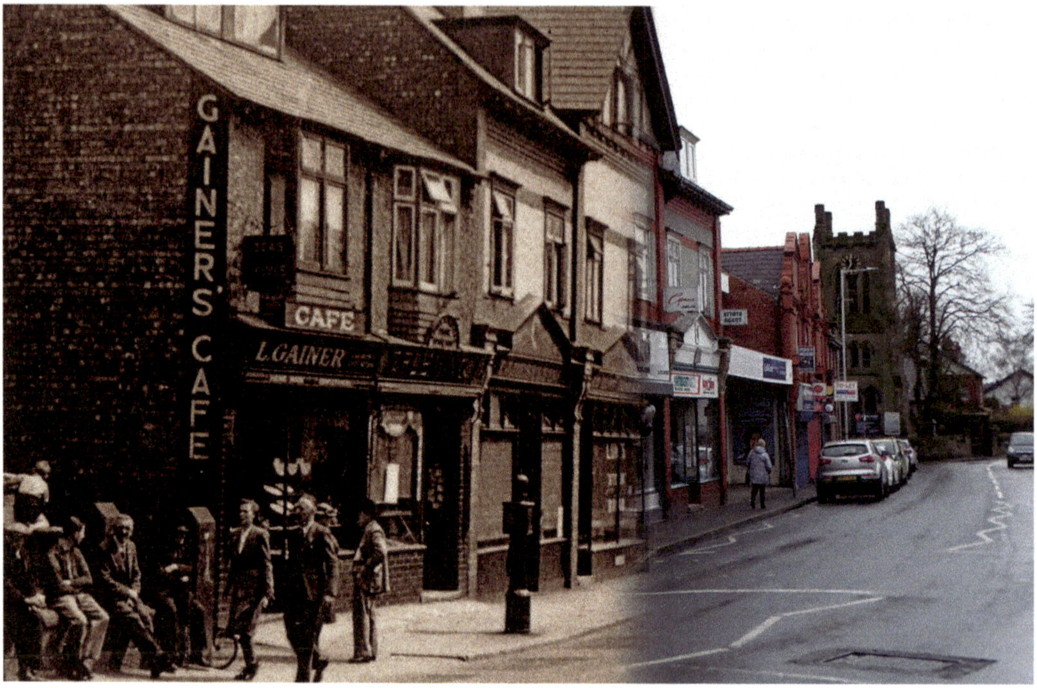

Upton Village

Looking towards St Mary's Church, the road to the library and the railway station, where trains operate to north Wales stations, Bidston, Birkenhead and Liverpool. Shone's Garage sold Shell petrol from pumps which were set back from the pavement. Gainers café was a popular meeting place providing a selection of tea, coffee and cakes.

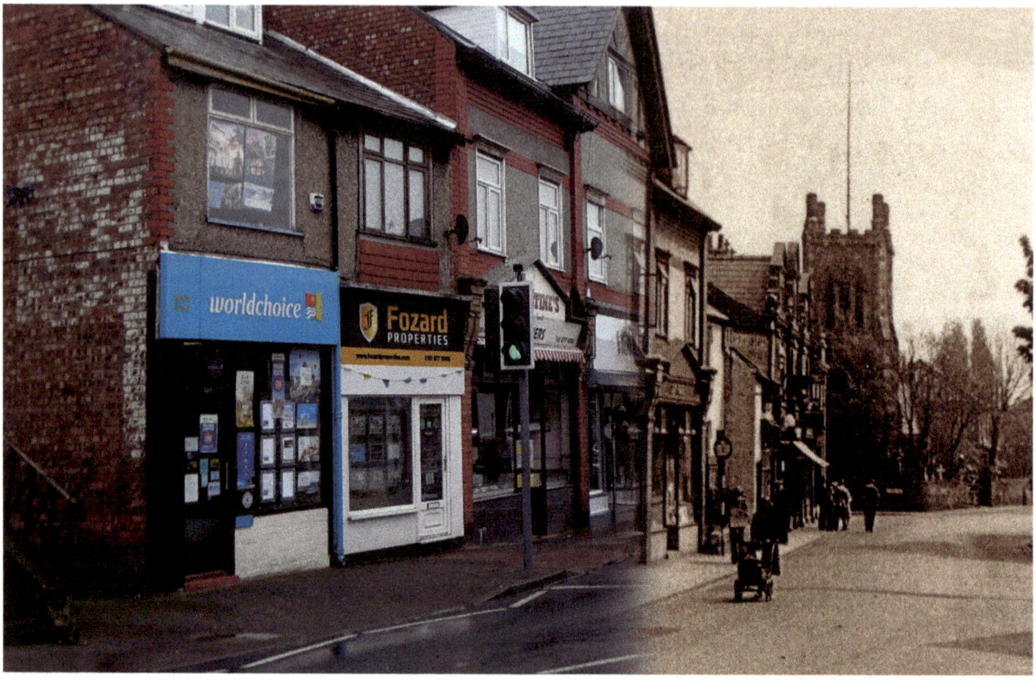

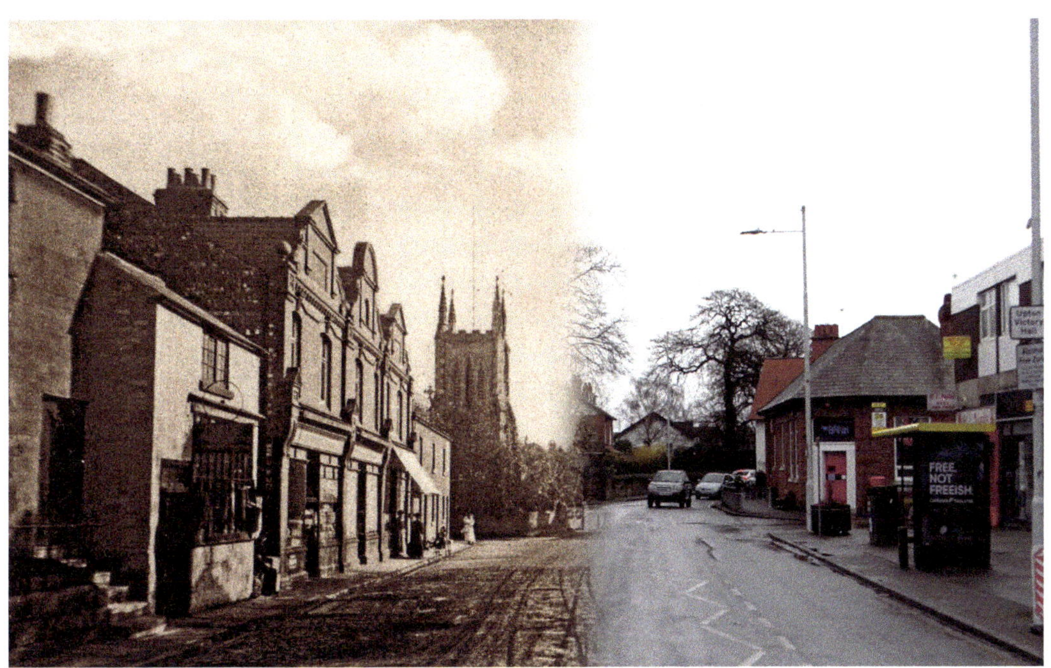

Upton Village

Upton village was originally settled as an Anglo-Saxon farming community and expanded rapidly in the mid-nineteenth century. The name Upton is from the Old English upp, meaning hill, and tun, meaning farm. It was listed as Optone in the Domesday Book of 1086, and was situated in the parish of Overchurch in the Wirral Hundred. It was known as Upton in Wyrhale in 1307, and later Upton by Birkenhead. William Inman, owner of the Inman line, donated money for the construction of St Mary's Church, which can be seen in the centre of this photograph.

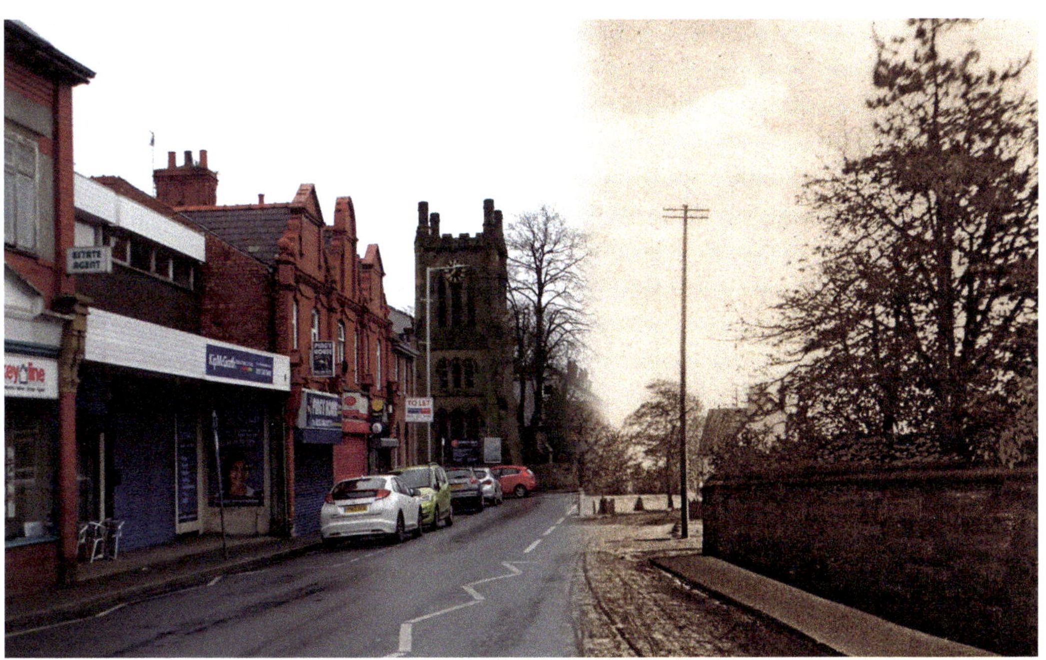

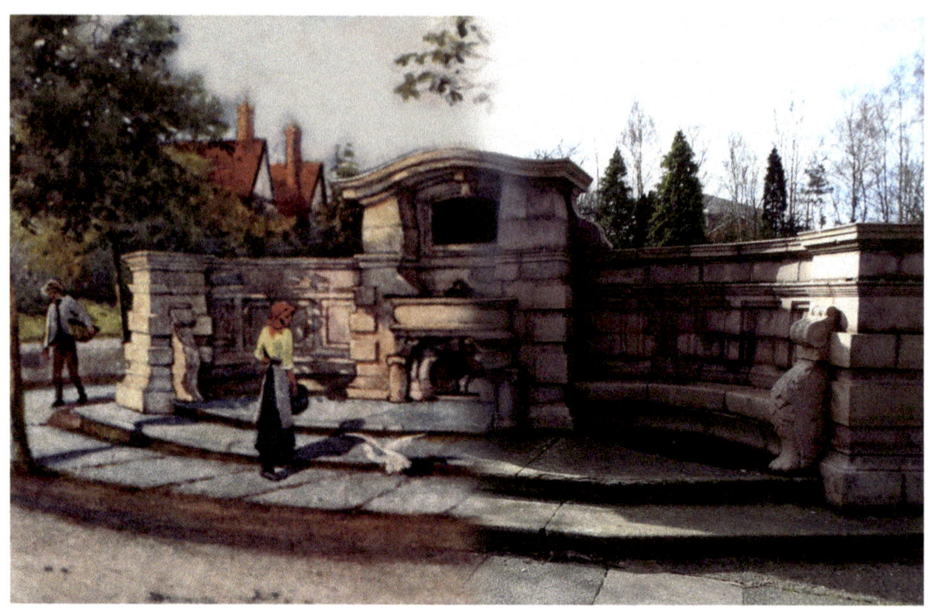

Village Fountain, Port Sunlight

Lever had completed 890 houses at Port Sunlight at the time of his death in 1925 and was responsible for the construction and provision of a number of important community buildings. Gladstone Hall, Hulme Hall, the Bridge Inn, the Gymnasium, Open Air Swimming Bath, the Girls' Club and Cottage Hospital and other community-based facilities were provided for the use of people living in the village. The company merged with the Dutch company Margarine Unie in 1930 to form Unilever, and Port Sunlight was placed under the management of Unilever Merseyside Ltd in 1960, becoming UML Ltd in 1968. The village was declared as a Conservation Area in 1978 and in 1980 the houses became available for the tenants to purchase.

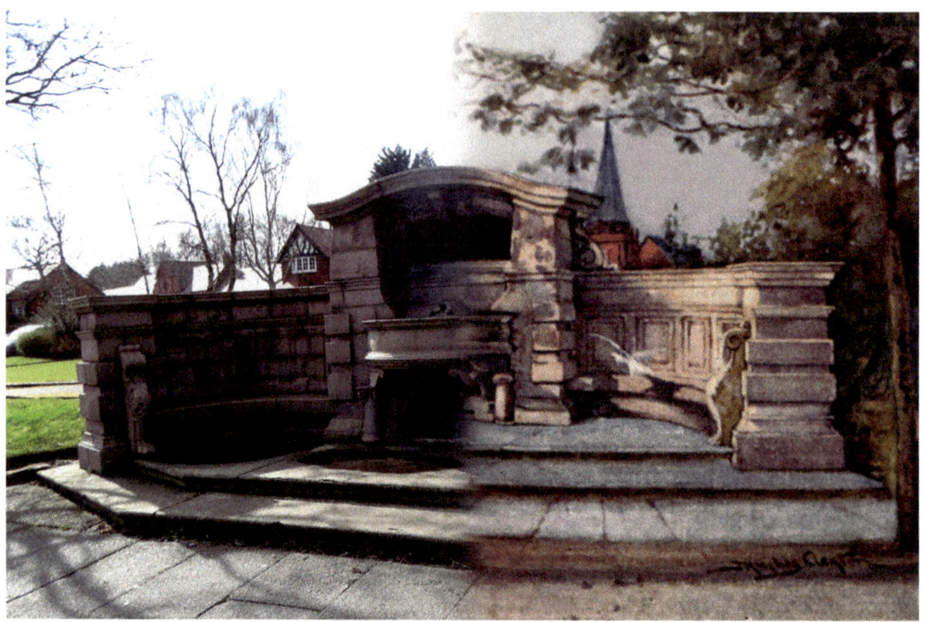

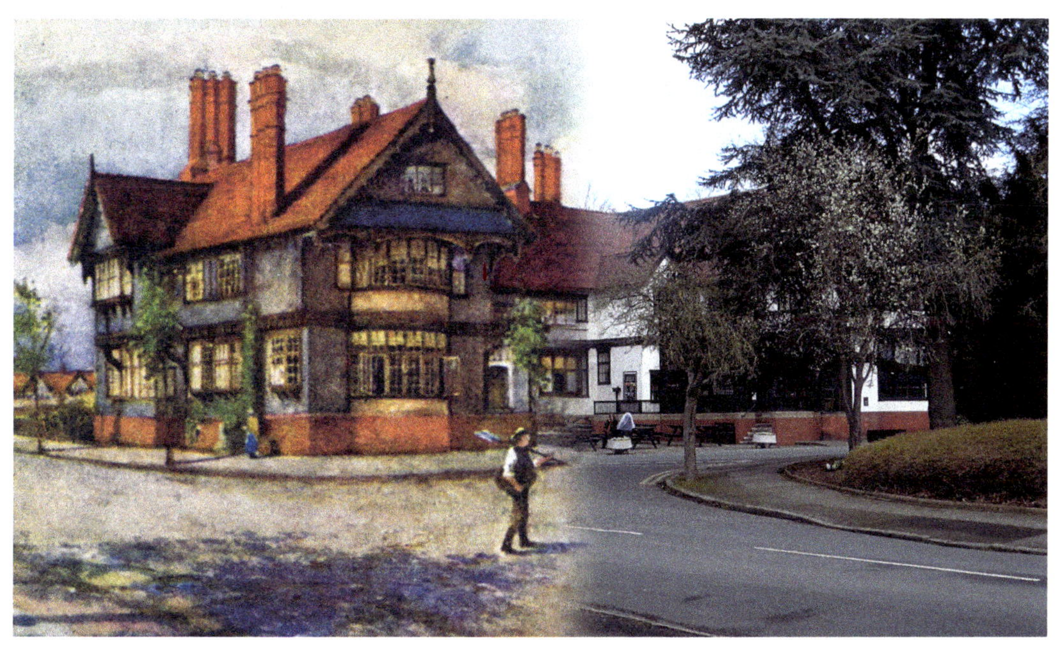

The Bridge Inn

The Bridge Inn, Port Sunlight, was designed by Edward Ould and George Grayson and is situated in Bolton Road, which is named after Lever's home town. The inn did not sell alcohol when it was opened and following a local referendum, the residents of the village voted 80 per cent in favour of a liquor licence being granted. The inn has been extended by the addition of a new wing, and the establishment now offers a total of eleven bedrooms. In the 1960s it was granted Grade II listed status.

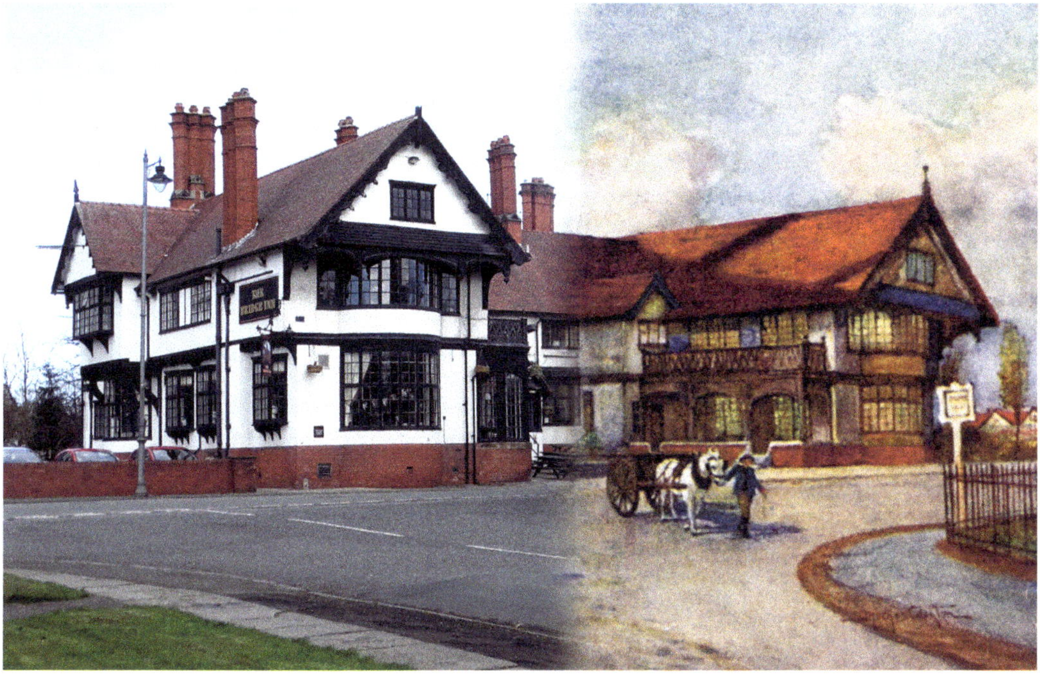

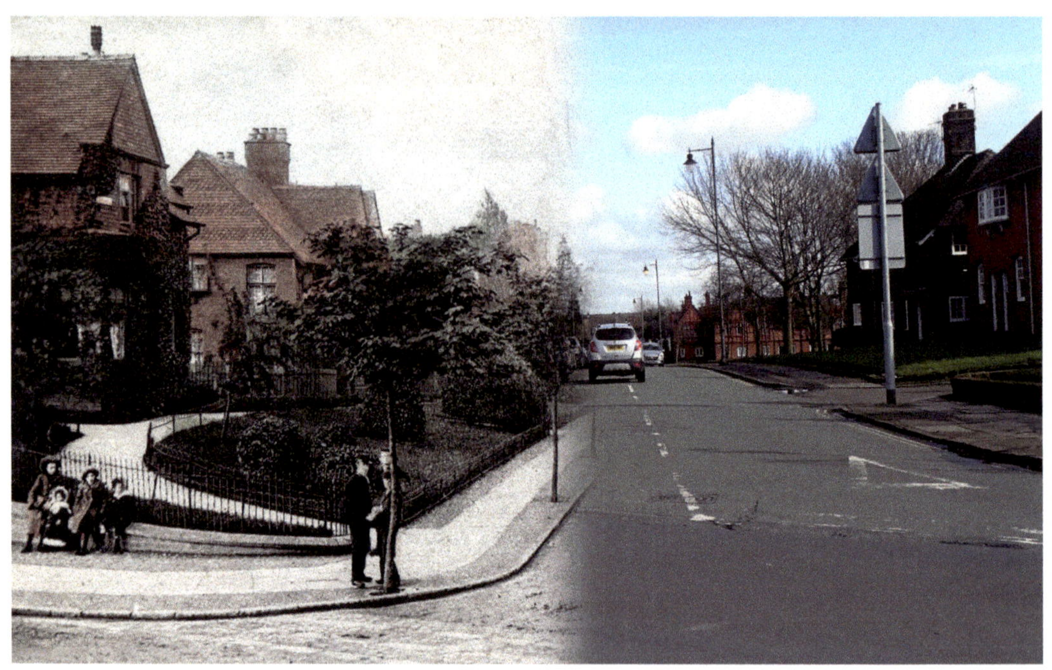

Bolton Road, Port Sunlight

No. 1 Bolton Road is a house by William Owen in two storeys with fronts of two and three bays. It is in brick with stone dressings and has a tiled roof. Nos 5 and 7 are a pair of houses by William Own in brick with tile-hanging in the gables and tiled roof. No. 15 is by Grayson and Ould in one storey with an attic and two bays on each front. Three houses, Nos 17–21, were later converted into apartments by William Owen.

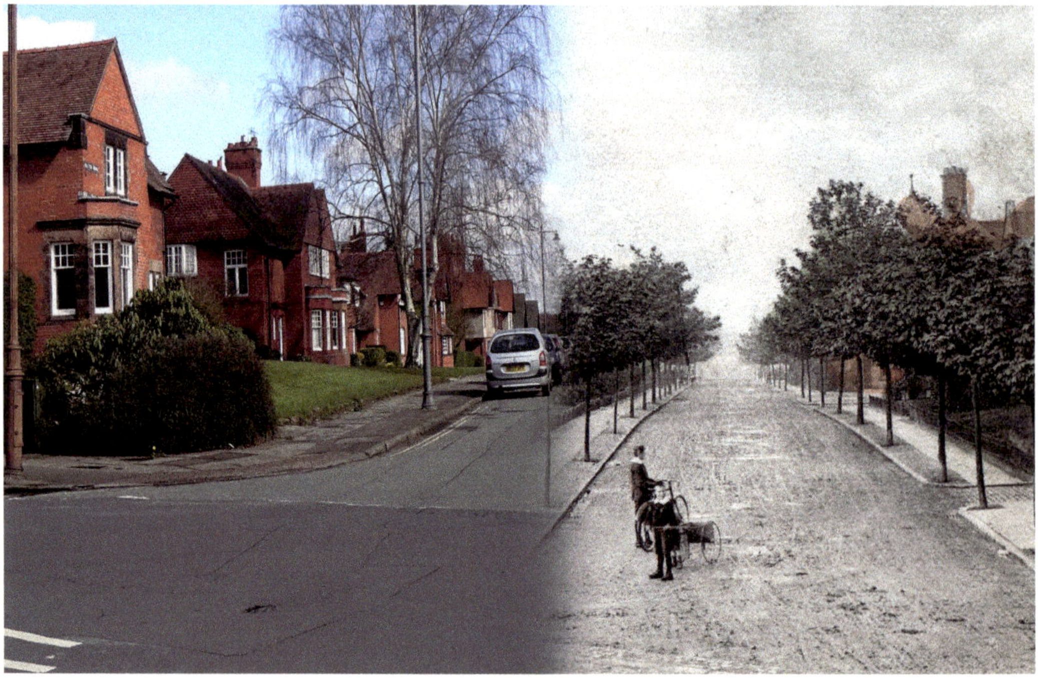

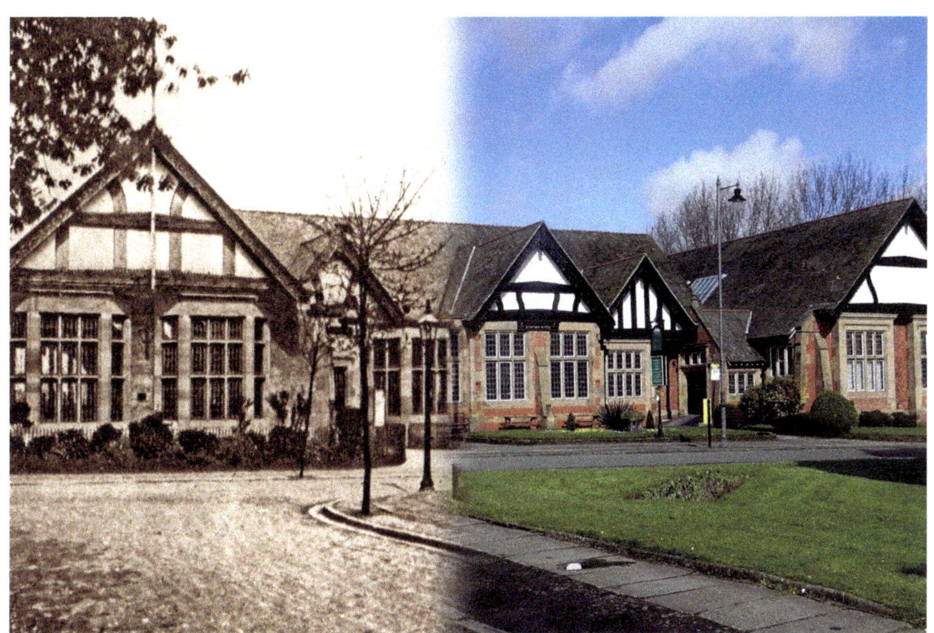

Hulme Hall

Hulme Hall, Port Sunlight, was designed by William Owen and his son and was built in 1901 as a women's dining hall. In 1911 it became an art gallery, housing some of the collection of William Lever, prior to the opening of the Lady Lever Art Gallery in 1922. The artworks were moved during the First World War and the building was used to house refugees from Belgium. The Beatles performed four times at the hall and it is the first place Ringo Starr performed as an official Beatle, following the departure of Pete Best from the group. It was registered as a Grade II listed building in 1965.

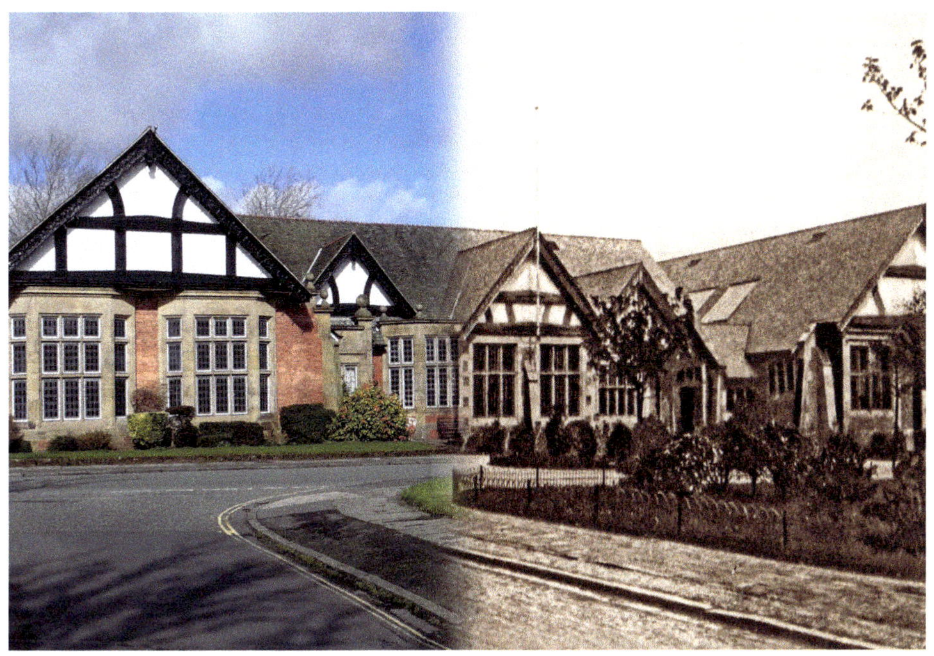

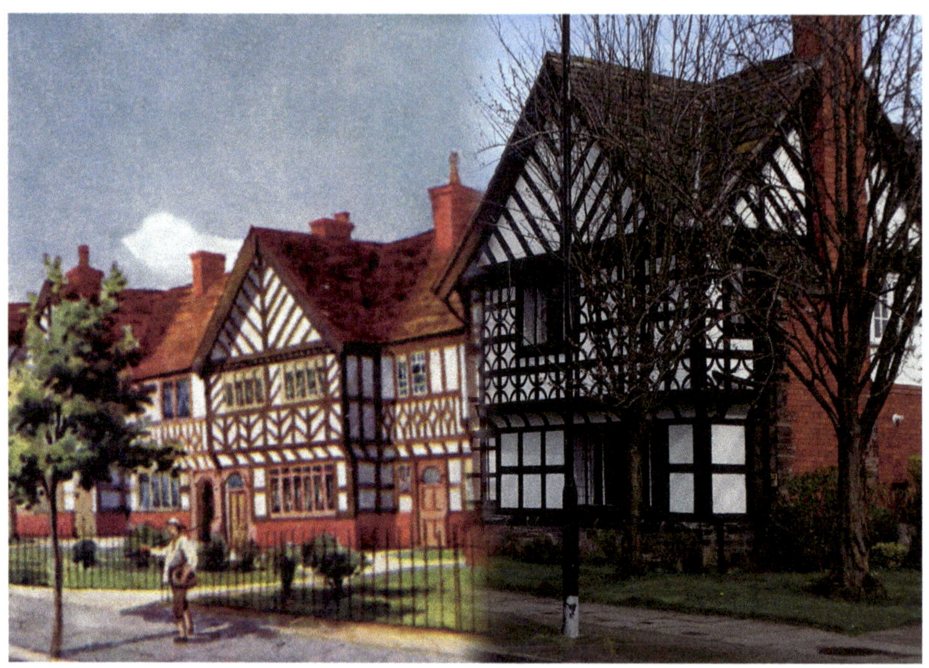

Greendale Road, Port Sunlight

The houses in Greendale Road were built in 1902, designed by Talbot and Wilson, and were constructed to resemble Kenyon Peel Hall in Little Hulton. Greendale Road runs parallel to the Merseyrail track and is the location of the Lever Free Library. Gladstone Hall was opened by William Gladstone in 1891 and is now known as the Gladstone Theatre, and Kenyon Old Hall Cottages was Grade II listed in 1965. The old village shop is now a tearoom, and the library and museum building has become the Village Heritage Centre.

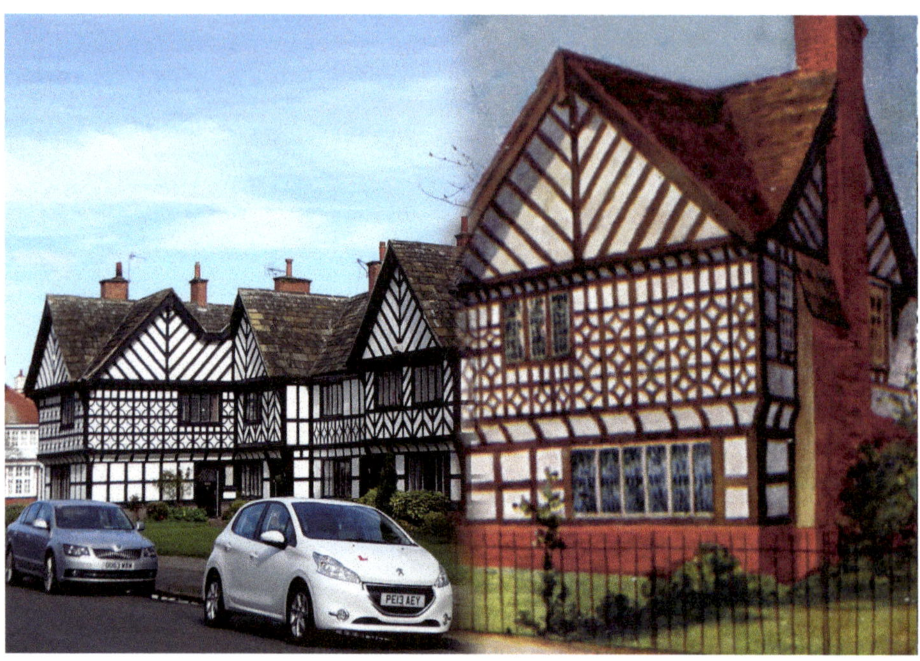

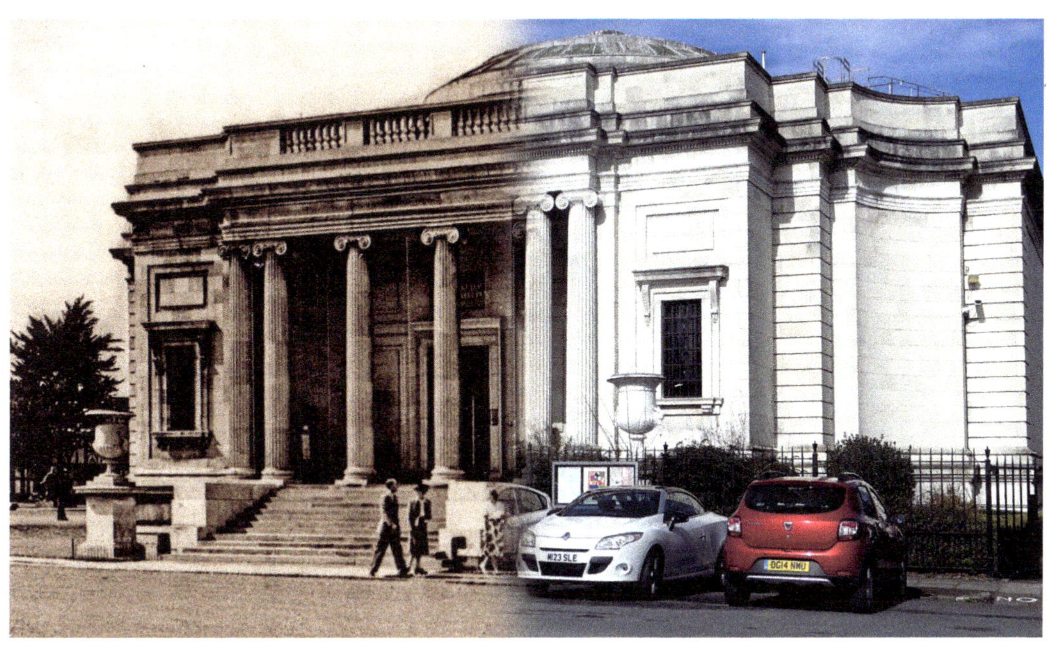

Lady Lever Art Gallery, Port Sunlight

The Lady Lever Art Gallery, Port Sunlight, was opened by Princess Beatrice. The Prince of Wales (later King Edward VIII) visited in 1931 and the Duke of York (later King George VI) opened a group of cottages which bear his name in 1934. It is a significant surviving example of late Victorian and Edwardian taste. The gallery houses major collections of fine and decorative art, and is strong in British nineteenth-century painting and sculpture. There are collections of English furniture, Wedgwood, especially jasperware and Chinese ceramics. In 2015 a touring exhibition visited museums in Japan and the South End galleries were restored as part of a £2.8 million project in 2016.

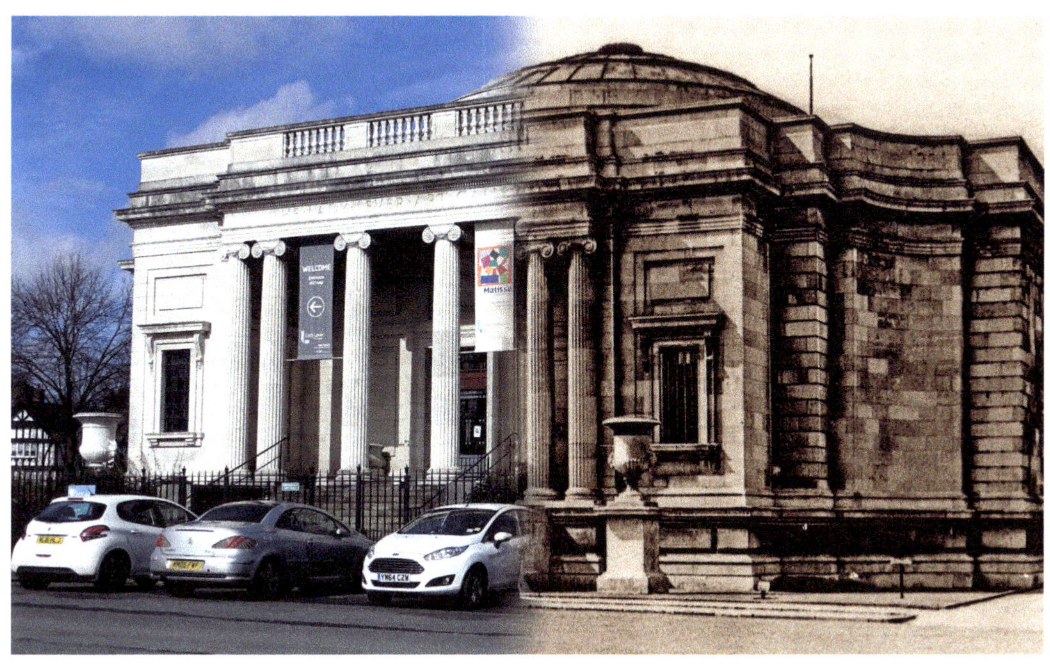

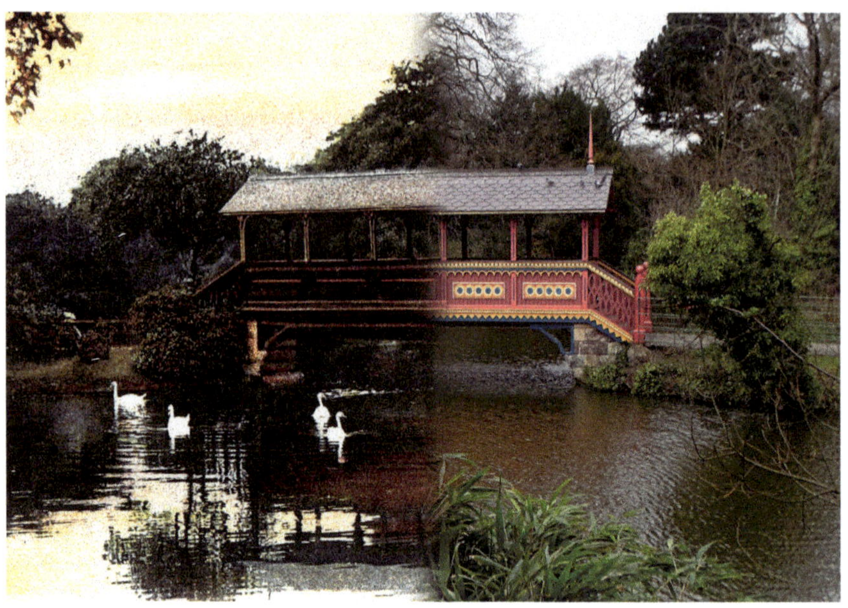

Swiss Bridge, Birkenhead Park

The Town Commissioners purchased 125 acres of land in 1843 and Joseph Paxton was commissioned to build a municipal park on the site. The park was opened to the public in 1847, on the day that Morpeth and Egerton Docks at Birkenhead were also opened. The Swiss Bridge is one of the main features of the park and was designed and built as a covered timber structure with a red-tiled roof. It is claimed that Central Park in New York was modelled on Birkenhead Park. The bridge, a 23-foot pedestrian span of stringer construction, was built in 1847 and is the only covered bridge of traditional wooden construction (similar to North American and European covered bridges) in the United Kingdom. It was modelled after similar wooden bridges in Switzerland. However, it was subject to vandalism for several years and was restored and painted in its original colours in 2008, with help and assistance from the National Lottery Heritage Fund.

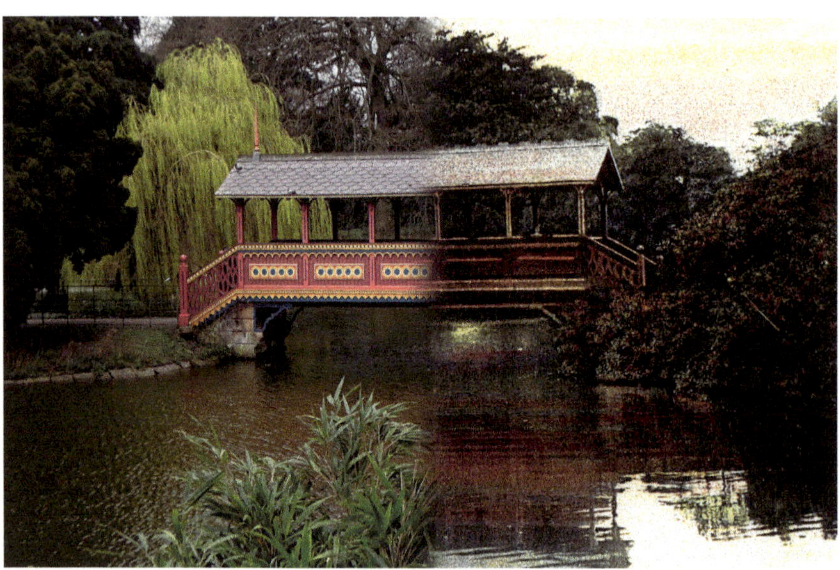

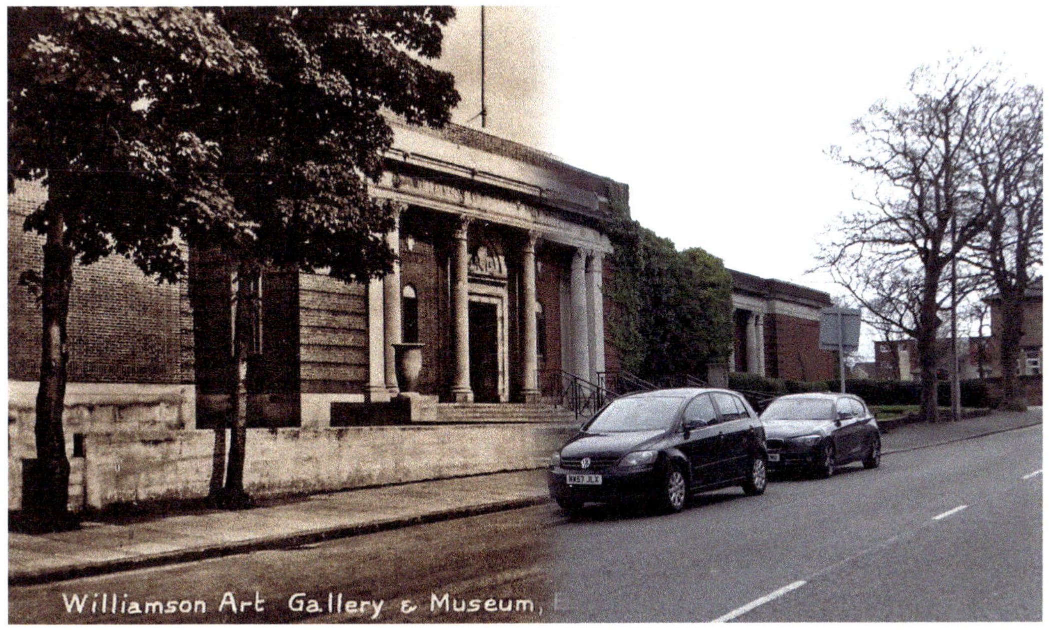

Williamson Art Gallery and Museum

The Williamson Art Gallery and Museum was opened in December 1928, funded by John Williamson, a director of the Cunard Line, and his son Patrick, who also contributed funds. The gallery was one of the first art galleries to be specifically equipped for presenting paintings and other art treasures. The English watercolours, of which some 560 paintings are on display, representing the work of 380 artists from 1750 until the present time, the Della Robbia pottery, produced in Birkenhead at the beginning of the twentieth century and pottery by Harold Rathbone and Robert Anning Bell are also displayed. Models of ships built by Cammell Laird are included, and the art gallery and museum now host concerts, films, local art exhibitions, lectures and other functions.

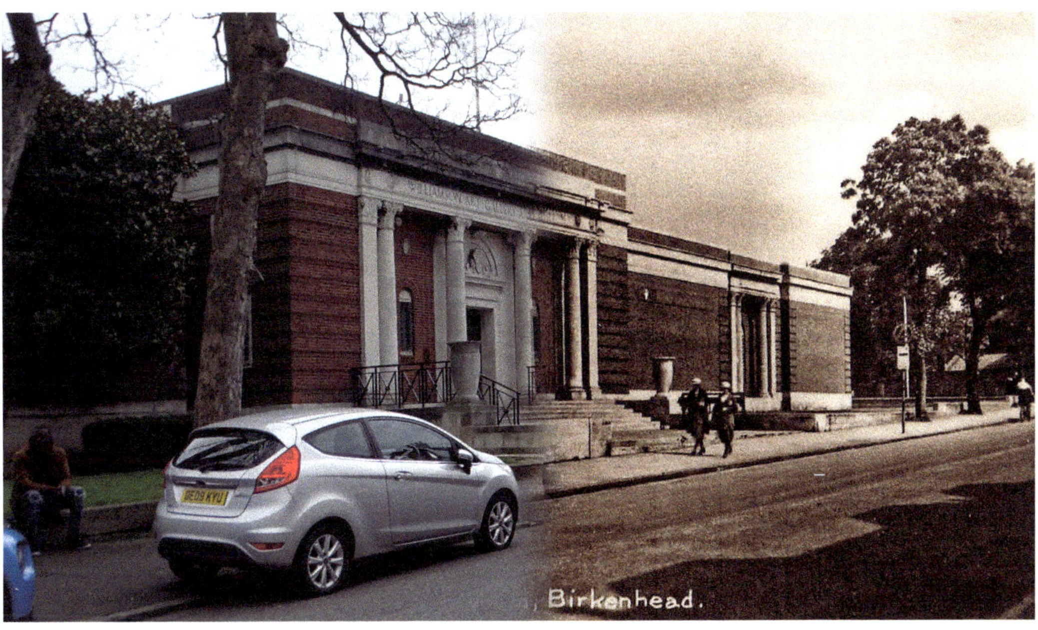

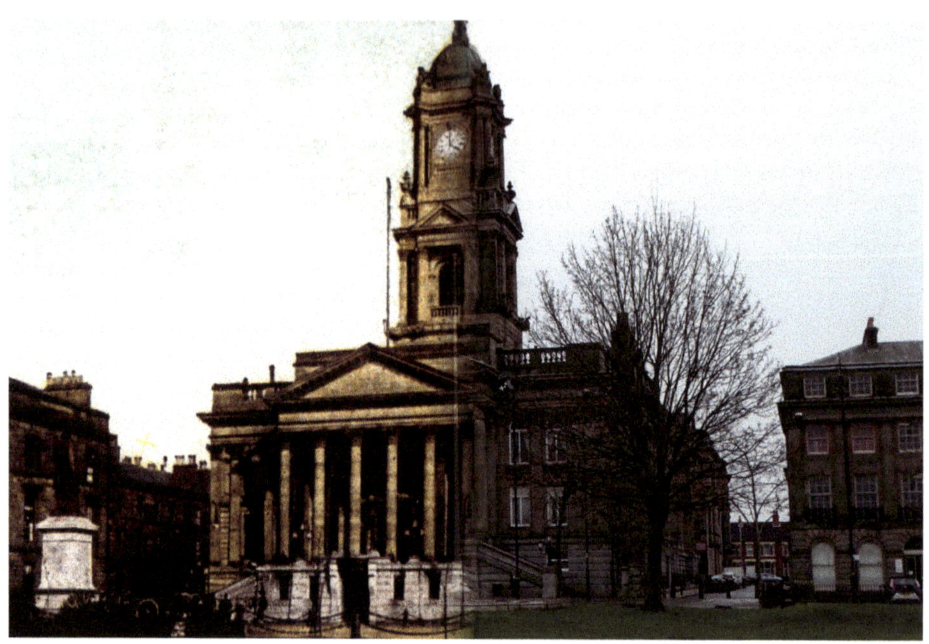

Birkenhead Town Hall

The foundation stone of the town hall was laid by the Mayor T. S. Deacon on 10 October 1883 and was opened in 1887. Hamilton Square Gardens in front of the town hall were purchased by the borough in 1903. The original spire of the town hall was damaged by fire on 10 July 1901, and was later replaced by a dome. The cenotaph in front of the town hall was unveiled on 5 July 1925 in front of a crowd of thousands of people. The town hall was designed by C. O. Ellison and consists of a central tower with clock faces, and surmounted by a copper dome with a finial. It is in stone with a granite basement and a Welsh slate roof.

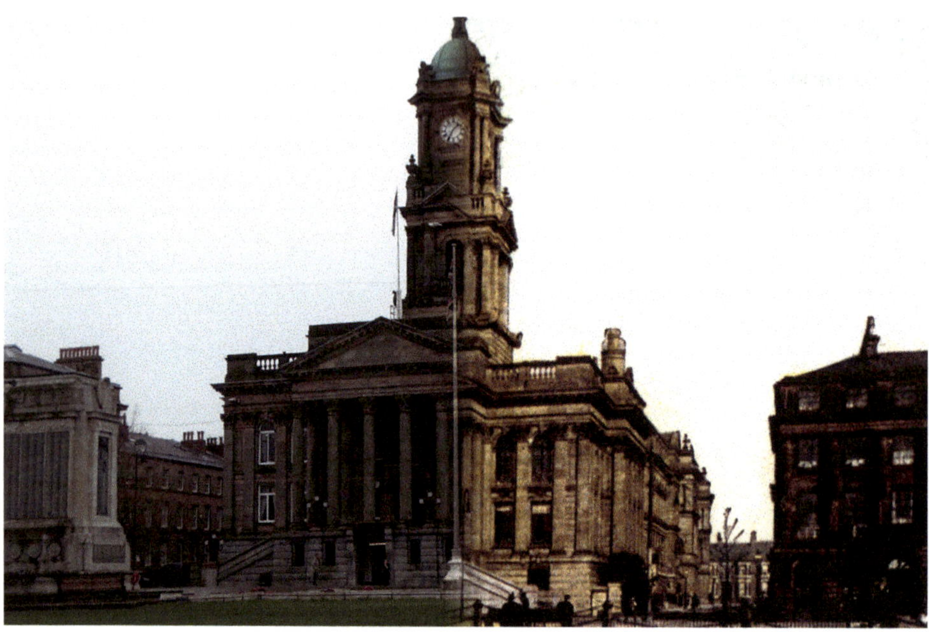

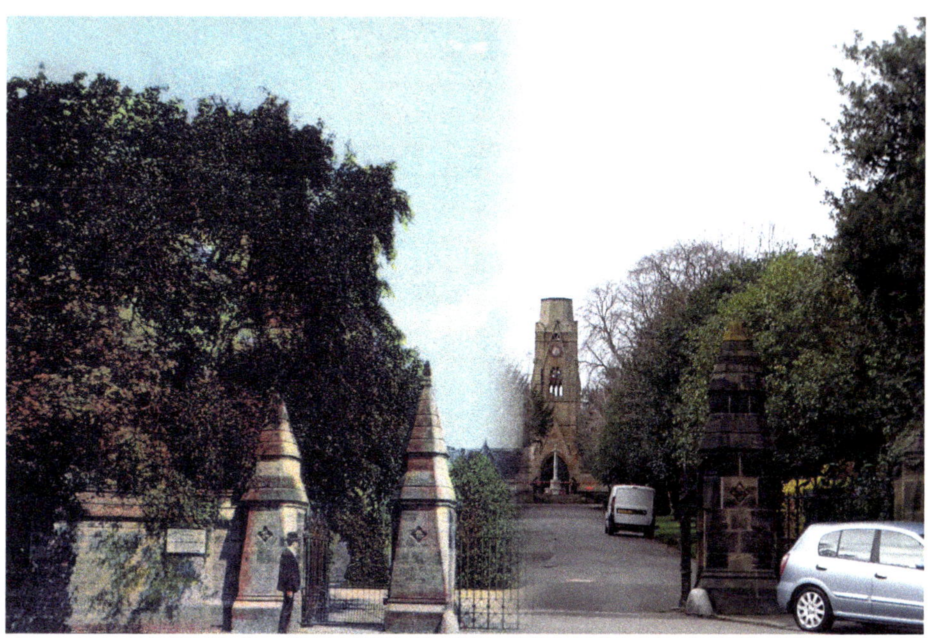

Flaybrick Cemetery

Flaybrick Cemetery was built by the Birkenhead Improvement Commissioners between 1862 and 1864 on Flaybrick Quarry. In the late nineteenth century Henry Kelsall Aspinall wrote, 'Bidston Hill, where foxes, hares and rabbits and all kind of game once abounded, is gradually becoming a place of residence for Liverpool merchants. Flaybrick Hill Cemetery was opened by the Birkenhead Commissioners as Birkenhead had grown into a town of some 110,000 people.' The chapels were designed by Lucy and Littler, and consisted of a symmetrical range, with chapels on the outside and central cloisters and a steeple. The steeple had a two-stage tower with archway, and has now been truncated.

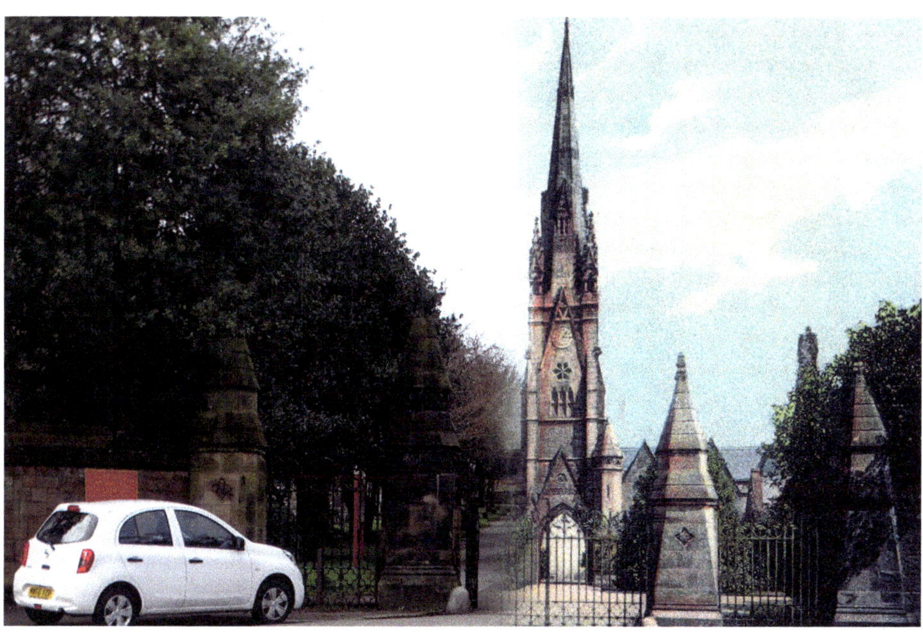

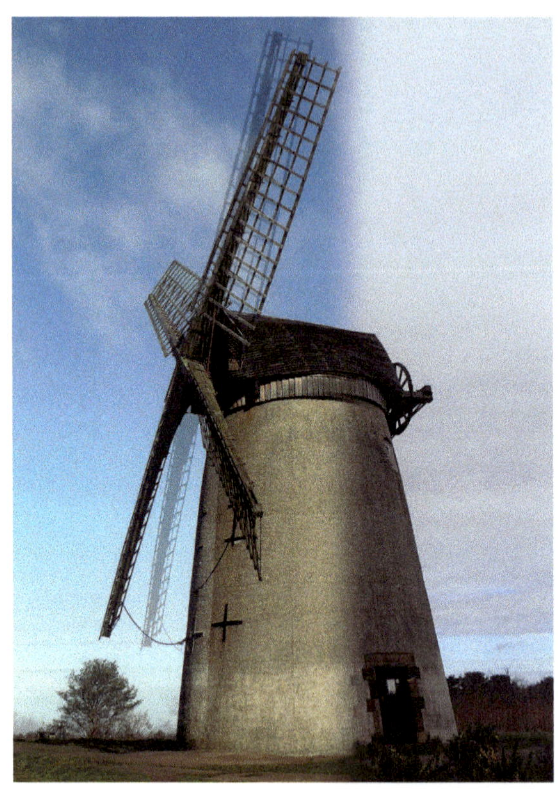

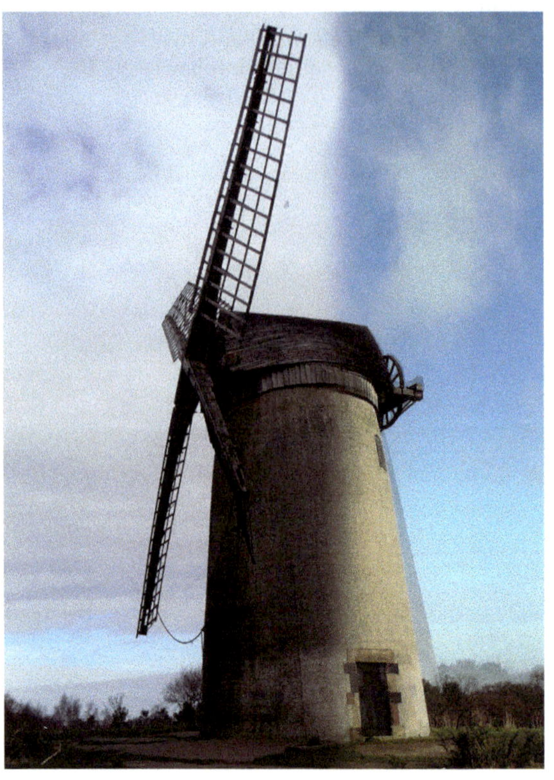

Windmill, Bidston Hill

One of the first major industries to develop in the Wirral was milling. At one time the farmers of Bridgend, Birkett Hall, Grange, Claughton and the Toad Hole farms carried their corn up the rough roads to Bidston or Tranmere mills. There the millers cleaned the wheat by sieving it and then set the sails of their mills to the wind to start the grinding stones. There had been a windmill on Bidston Hill since 1600, while the Tranmere Mill was built at the end of the eighteenth century. The Tranmere Mill was pulled down around 1870 and the Bidston Mill was closed five years later.

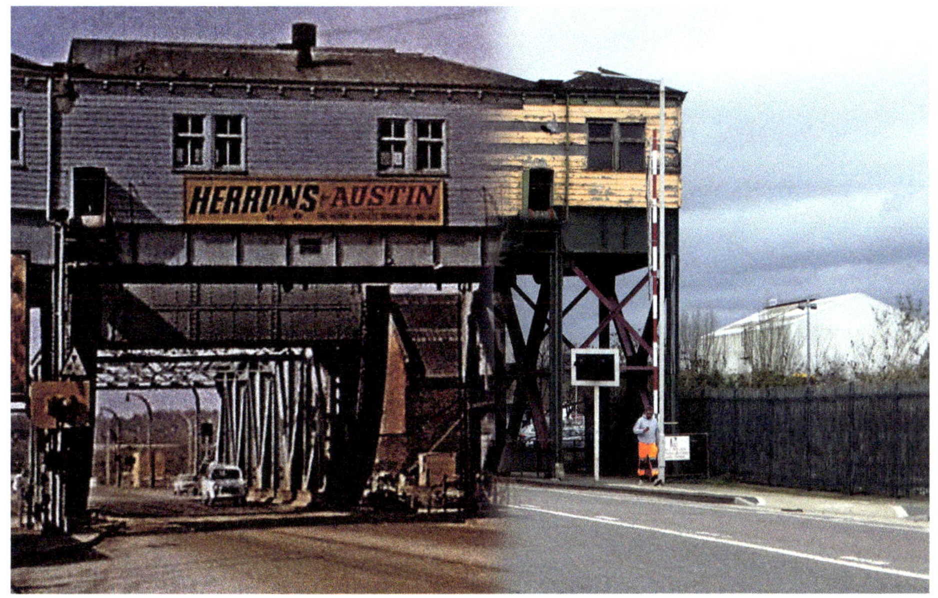

Duke Street Bridge

The engineers Telford, Robert Stephenson and Nimmo put forward an ambitious scheme for a ship canal through Wallasey Pool in 1828. Dock Commissioners could not agree to the details of the plan, and this was followed by financial difficulties until parliamentary powers were sought. An Act of Parliament of 1848 repealed the appointment of Dock Commissioners and established trustees instead. The Mersey Docks and Harbour Board Act of 1857 consolidated all the docks into one estate and the control and management vested in one public trust. Morpeth and Alfred docks were completed, followed by the Great Float, Wallasey Dock, Vittoria Dock and the West Float. The final stage in the expansion of the Birkenhead Dock Estate came in 1933 with the opening of the Bidston Dock at the extreme end of the West Float.

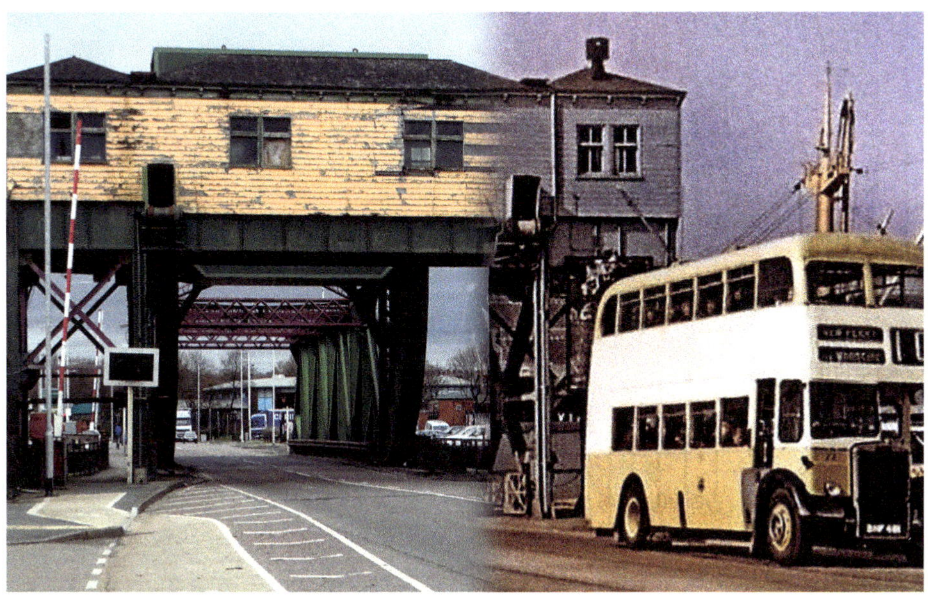

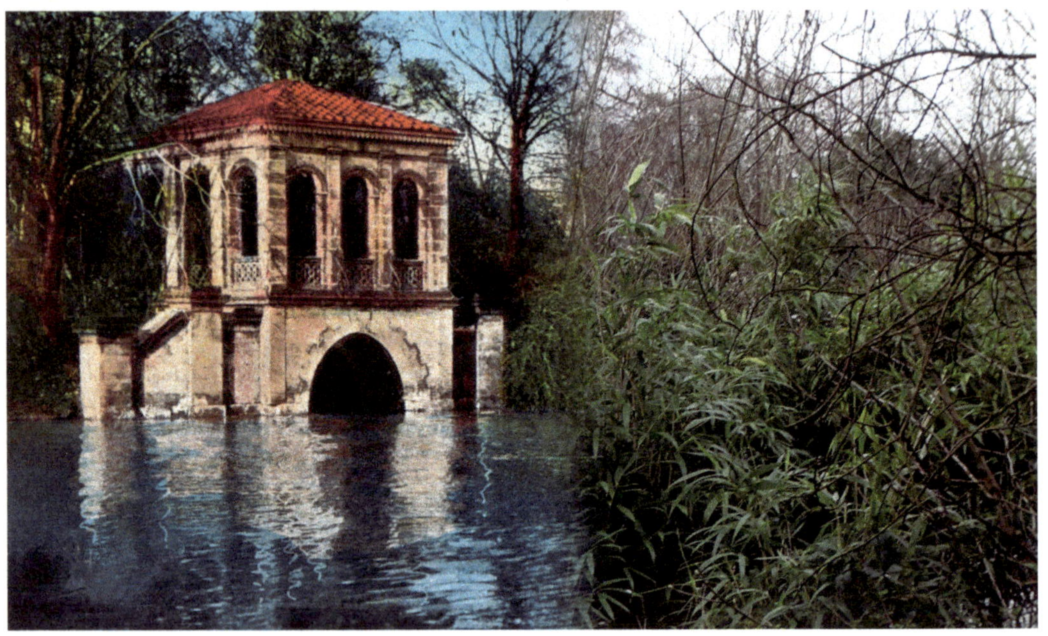

Boathouse, Birkenhead Park

The Roman Boathouse stands by the lake in the park. The upper storey was originally intended to be a bandstand. It is built in stone and consists of a square pavilion with a segmental arch to the boathouse, above which is an arcaded and pilastered storey with a pantile roof. In 1990, the Mobil Oil Co. sponsored the restoration of the Boathouse and Maggy Howarth was commissioned to design a pebble mosaic for the floor. The mosaic bears the inscription 'The Boathouse 1847'. In 2002 the park received an £11.5 million grant from the Heritage Lottery Fund, and the Boathouse was refurbished. A new tiled roof was fitted to the building and concrete platforms were built for the anglers who fish in the lake.

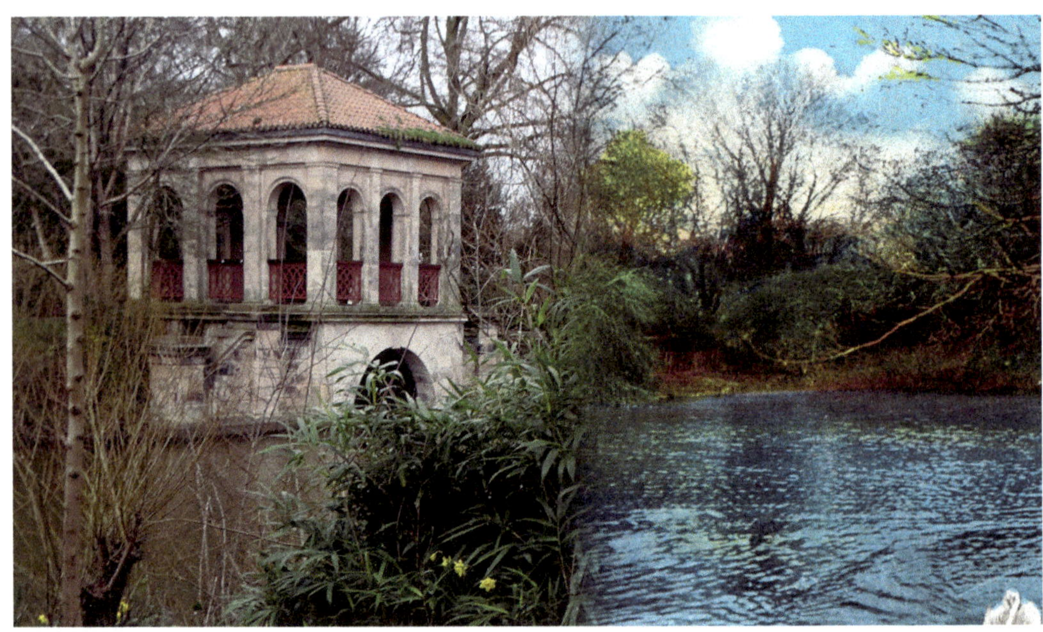